Blue Hills AND Shoofly Pie

Blue Hills

AND

Shoofly Pie

IN PENNSYLVANIA DUTCHLAND

BY

Ann Hark

DRAWINGS BY OLIVER GRIMLEY

J. B. LIPPINCOTT COMPANY

PHILADELPHIA AND NEW YORK

"The Last of the Old-Time Potters" was published in its original form as "Pennsylvania Pottery" in the April 1943 issue of HOUSE & GARDEN; copyright, The Condé Nast Publications, Inc., 1943.

"Old Bethlehem Days" was published in its original form as "O Little Town" in the December 1946 issue of GOURMET.

"It's Done with Mirrors," "The Mystery Deepens," "Sidetracked," "At Last a Clue," "The Plot Thickens," and "Dead End" were published in their original form as "Erdspiegel Mystery" in the October 1941 issue of THE AMERICAN-GERMAN REVIEW.

Sixteen recipes from PENNSYLVANIA GERMAN COOKERY, by Ann Hark and Preston A. Barba copyright 1950 by Schlechter's.

Library of Congress Catalog card number 52-9537

To
My Chauffeur
and
Patsy
who still in memory ride beside
me through Pennsylvania Dutchland

IN MEMORIAM

Contents

[7]

Foreword

THIS BOOK was begun a long time ago. Another book about my favorite group of people, the Pennsylvania Dutch, had already been written and I'd breathed a sigh of more or less satisfied accomplishment when it was finished. From my own particular angle, I'd thought, the field had been covered pretty thoroughly—there just wasn't anything more to be written on the subject! But I was wrong. At that time I was still living in Mt. Gretna, Lebanon County, and new incidents and experiences among my Pennsylvania Dutch neighbors and friends kept cropping up continually. It wasn't long before I had enough material, and more, for a second book. And so I started writing it.

But at that point Fate stepped in and took a hand. Various things began happening—including illness and sudden death, a World War, physical disability, and general upheaval. I sold my cottage in the woods and moved to the city. I'd developed a mysterious eye ailment and could work only for the very briefest periods. For a long time I put aside all thought of doing any real writing. Every so often, though, I'd pick up my notes for the new book and go over them longingly. Occasionally I'd even try to take up where I'd left off. But immediately my eyes would protest and I'd have to stop entirely for a week, or a month, or a couple of months, as the case might be. I was almost ready to give up.

But the book refused to be denied. Despite the fact that I was now firmly anchored in the city, my heart still lay in the country among the friendly folk of Pennsylvania Dutchland whom I'd left behind. Somehow, eyes or no eyes, I *had* to write about them!

And so at last, with infinite pains and infinite discouragement, I gradually worked out a system of procedure. Slowly, laboriously, the book began to take shape.

It's finished now, at last—the record of a happy year among my own people, in my own home, in my own beloved Pennsylvania hills. Some of those who walk through its pages are no longer here, but I've written of them as they were at the time the book was first conceived. A great deal of love, a great deal of patience, a great deal of dogged stubbornness have gone into its making. It's been a heart-breaking task—but a rewarding one. For I've lived again the many happy hours and many heart-warming experiences I've had among my favorite people in my favorite blue-clad hills.

If the book brings to those who read it half the pleasure that I've had in writing it, I shall feel that it has been worth while.

A. H.

So blue my hills, so misty blue,
So tender sweet the skies above,
So old my hills, so ever new,
So rich with life this land I love.

Here on its warm breast let me lie,
By hex-starred barns and ancient mills,
Where distant heaven bends close by—
Here in my everlasting hills!

A. H.

Blue Hills AND Shoofly Pie

July

HOME, SWEET HOME

IT WAS two years ago this July that I became a landowner.

Of course, I realize there are some who mightn't call it that. A plot of ground the size of mine isn't exactly land in the more expansive sense of the word. And some people just can't think of real estate except in terms of miles and acres. I've met a lot of them.

"So you have a little place in the country!" they begin brightly. "How many acres are there?" And right there I lose interest in the conversation. I never was much good at figures.

Anyway, what does it matter? Have you ever known a bloated land baron who could tell you fondly every stick and stone on his estate? Or a proprietor of vast and ample acreage who could name each clump of fern and piece of moss and kind of flowers on his domain? Well, *I* can. I've chaperoned every stalk and stem and leaf and bud that sprouts on my particular piece of realty. I know intimately each stump and rock, each moldy length of log, each stubborn weed that grows there. I even have a friendly acquaintance with the mole that burrows little tunnels underneath my moss bed, and the flying squirrel that scampers on my roof at night, sounding like half a dozen elephants at least—not to mention the bright-eyed fieldmouse that I frighten nearly into fits each time I pay a visit to my garbage can.

Besides, it isn't how much land you own, but where it is and who your neighbors are that really count. And personally, I think I'm pretty lucky. For the special bit of Mother Earth I proudly claim as mine reposes on a hillside in the heart of God's own country—or if you want to be more definite about it, Pennsylvania Dutchland. Land of rolling fields and fertile farms and soft, blue-shadowed mountains in the distance. Of big, red barns with sloping ramps and staunch stone ends and sheltering overhangs to keep the sun and wind and rain away from livestock. Barns with old iron weathervanes of rooster, cow or running horse atop the roof, and swallow holes of varied pattern underneath the eaves, and painted symbols—anywhere from one to seven or more of them—along the sides.

It was those symbols, incidentally—gay in red and black and green and blue, with stars and flowers, hearts and teardrops, and a score of other quaint designs—that first had caught my fancy some years back. Blithely I'd started out to learn their whys and wherefores, and not so blithely I'd admitted my defeat about two years and several thousand road miles later. *Hexerei*—religion—decoration—who can tell? I'd had those theories, and a lot of others, given me. But when it came to actual proof—well, that was something else again.

According to some experts whom I talked to, the main purpose of the symbols was to ward off lightning. Others told me they were meant to turn away the spells of witches and insure fertility to cattle. Seven symbols on one barn, they said, protected it and everything inside it from the acts of God and witches both. Some seemed to think the markings were related to the symbolism of the Rosicrucian Order. And one special gentleman believed the figures represented suns and moons and stars, and thus were modern relics of sun worship.

Anyway, the whole thing left me somewhat puzzled. But with dogged purpose I kept asking questions—and I reaped another harvest of weird explanations. One brash soul insisted that the marks were linked up with the Scandinavian cult of Ygdrasil; another thought they had a special sex significance; a third suggested that they were descended from Etruscan art. The symbols that I'd always thought were stars weren't stars at all, I learned from other quarters; they were tulips. No, not tulips either; they were lilies, someone else declared—and lilies of a pure religious origin, besides. Spoke up another: No, not lilies, passion flowers—that was what they really were.

And so it went. Devices meant to bring good luck; bad spirits' footsteps painted by the farmer to warn other spirits off; insignia to catch the tourist's eye and call attention to the quilts and rugs and cows and horses that he sold; sheer decoration, with no hidden meaning whatsoever—such were just a few of the solutions I encountered.

So today I'm just as ignorant of origins and meanings as I was in the beginning—but happy even in my ignorance. For after all, no matter if they're marks of superstition or religion or pure love of color, those intriguing symbols are to me the very essence of this land I love to call my own. This rich and blooming countryside where friendly faces peer at me from under broad-brimmed hats and modest bonnets tied beneath the chin; where teeming fields of wheat and corn and ripe tobacco tell a tale of industry and toil that never end; where hospitality speaks loud from table tops concealed beneath amazing loads of *Schnitz un Knepp* and oyster soup, of *Fassnachts*, sauerkraut and shoofly pie, of chow-chow, *Schmierkase*, coleslaw, *Pannhaas*, *Buweschenkel*, homemade bread, and other foods too tempting and too numerous to mention.

My countryside by right of fond association. And now, at last, by closer and more deeply rooted right of ownership, my *home* as well.

PICNICS AND WHAT THEY LEAD TO

MY FAVORITE July crop is picnics.

Personally, I have no use for those benighted beings who, at the first mention of the word, raise eyebrows snootily and tell you that as far as *they're* concerned you'd better count them out—they'll stay at home and eat their meals in peace and comfort, thank you! Now, I belong to a different school of thought. My firm contention is that picnics *can* be comfortable. And my Chauffeur agrees with me. (Of course, he isn't *really* my chauffeur. It's a purely honorary title that I've given him—a somewhat joking reference to his status as self-constituted pilot on our little jaunts about the countryside.) For he's that priceless pearl of masculinity who actually enjoys consuming food out in the open spaces, with a fire smoking merrily on one side and wide stretches of unhampered landscape on the other.

As it happens, I was brought up in a family where the male contingent sniffed and snorted audibly at the very thought of packing food into a basket and sallying out of doors. ("Why can't we stay at home and eat sensibly off a table?" "I don't *like* ants in my sandwiches!") So it was rather a shock to me when I discovered that my driver shares not only my convictions but my whole technique as well.

It's really very simple. All you do is make things just as easy for yourself as possible. No cooking in advance. No broiling of chicken over a hot stove. No spreading of endless sandwiches. No baking of cakes and pies in a hot and stuffy kitchen. No, indeed—not for us! We take our cooking out of doors, and like it.

The first step, as it happens, usually turns out to be the hardest. Due to some peculiar masculine vagary, the unearthing of the picnic basket offers quite an obstacle to my Chauffeur. I keep it in the storeroom underneath the porch—less formally referred to as the Doghouse. Here, if you believe the gentleman's dark mutterings, I conceal a vast array of articles that should have been discarded years ago. What's more, I add to them with such abandon that a man just *can't* keep track of anything from one week to the next!

At this point I'm apt to remark, mildly, that the picnic basket is a large and lidded affair, with paper plates, two thermos bottles, cups and napkins, salt and pepper shakers, and a couple of stove rags inside. It *should* be perfectly easy to find! Whereupon he grunts and vanishes, to bang his head against the Doghouse rafters, while I get out my oldest frying pan, one of the grills from the oven, some butter, and whatever fruit is on hand, tactfully ignoring the protesting thumps and bumps that issue from below. By the times he emerges, dusty but triumphant, I've hastily squeezed some limes or oranges and filled the thermos bottles, or perhaps laid out some ginger ale or root beer. Or, if we want coffee, I've added the percolator and "makings" to our contemplated equipment. Then, while the gentleman with the long arms gathers up the pad from the porch cot, a yacht chair, and a bucket of ice—plus, of course, the basket—I collect a couple of magazines, my sun hat, some dog biscuits and a bottle of water for Patsy, my little black and white fox terrier, and we're off. Simple, isn't it?

The second step is even more so: We stop at the village store. Here we do our real fueling. A loaf of bread, whatever meat we've chosen, half a dozen of our favorite cakes, a relish of some sort— these are our staples. If we're having cantaloupe, we may get reckless and add a carton of vanilla ice-cream to the ice bucket. Or perhaps a bar of chocolate, or some candy, for dessert. And, if we're feeling really fancy, we may even go so far as to buy some "spreadin's" for the bread. But the main idea is to do as the spirit dictates at the moment, without a lot of brainwork in advance. A picnic ought to be fun—not heavy labor. Such, at least, is our quaint theory.

And it's had a good workout lately. My Chauffeur's vacation came this month, and with it a spell of hot weather. Not unbearably hot—just hot enough to make it fun to spend a couple of hours at the beach each morning, "dunking" in the lake and sprawling out on chairs to soak up Vitamin D. Now, my Chauffeur is the victim of a strange and rare fixation. Personally, I'm in favor of it—there ought to be more men afflicted with it. He doesn't like to see a woman work. So every day when our modest luncheon has been over, he's announced with male determination that my chores are finished for the day—we're going on a picnic, or maybe to the Inn for dinner, and no objections on my part, please! (Perhaps I should mention at this point that I'm really not a bad cook!)

Anyway, the picnic basket has been working overtime—and so has my Chauffeur. For he's nothing if not consistent. While I've sat in slothful ease and idleness on the yacht chair (didn't I tell you picnics could be comfortable?) he's been acting as fire-builder, cook, and general handy-man-about-the-place. And the results have been something to remember. Ham and eggs fried over an outdoor fire, with the sun sinking behind the mountaintop and the evening coolness stealing softly down and the first fireflies lighting their little lamps—could anything taste better? Nothing —you can take my word for it! Nothing, that is, except perhaps two large and juicy steaks broiled over the same sort of fire—or half a dozen lamb chops ditto—or a mixed grill of sausage, liver, steak, and chops done to a sizzling turn, each piece a little more mouth-watering than the one before. We've had them all.

Of course, I realize that our little system mightn't be so good for everyone. A large family, for instance. But there are only three of us, including Patsy, and we all believe in following that impulse. Sometimes it leads us into real adventure—like stumbling on a deserted castle, as we did not long ago—and sometimes into nothing more exciting than gathering mushrooms. But at that, mushrooms can be exciting, too—provided they're the kind of mushrooms *I'm* thinking of. Greenish Russulas—that's what they're called. They grow all through the woods at this time of the year, and their very name throws me into such gustatory rapture that occasionally someone rises up and demands concrete evidence of the basis for my ecstasies. My visiting fireman once did.

"How about letting me taste some?" he demanded with the air of one reserving judgment but fearing the worst. So we started out to look for them.

Fortunately, it had rained the day before—the kind of drenching rain that inspires mushrooms to their highest efforts—and we came home with a nice mess of them. Fresh, white parasols with short, thick stems and fluted caps all moldy green on top. I cleaned them, cut them in small pieces, added chopped onion, green pepper, and hard-boiled egg, sautéd them in butter—and set them before my Chauffeur. Gingerly he took the first mouthful. A look of doubting wonder crossed his face. He took a second mouthful —and peace descended like a halo on his brow. Silently he cleaned his plate. Then, in a tone of would-be nonchalance: "Not bad!"

he said. "Not bad at all! I didn't know mushrooms could taste like that!" And neither do a lot of other poor, benighted city dwellers.

But to get back to that deserted castle we discovered recently. We were driving slowly through the fragrant countryside in that delightful state of leisurely content induced by a full stomach and a mind at peace with all the world, when suddenly my driver turned the car's nose toward a pair of square stone pillars on the right. An inviting roadway curved ahead of us, between two rows of drooping pines whose lower branches trailed along the ground. We followed it a little way and found it turning to the right again, between a second pair of pillars, past a lotus pond, and toward an intermittent gleam of water spouting upward in the last rays of the dying sun.

With shameless curiosity, expecting to be stopped and thrown out any minute, we drove on. As we approached, the sun struck fire from the glass panes of a greenhouse, and the outlines of a sprawling sandstone mansion loomed up dark and shadowy against the evening sky. Before the house a fountain tinkled softly in a grassy circle edged by rambler roses, and on the lawn still other flowers—cosmos, lilies, rose-of-Sharon bushes, phlox, and golden glow—bloomed in profusion. There were tubs of date palms stationed near the front steps leading to the porch, and on the porch itself tall pots of ferns and cactus stood as if on guard before the tight-shut doors and windows of the building.

We stopped and my Chauffeur turned off the engine. For a moment we sat listening quietly. Except for the soft plashing of the fountain, only silence greeted us. No human sound, no human figure anywhere. There was something eerie about the place, as if it were bewitched. Perhaps, who knows, behind those silent, brooding walls there lay a sleeping princess and her sleeping household, waiting only for a gallant prince to come a-riding and break the evil spell that held them in its sway.

"Look—there's a gate!" Unconsciously I kept my voice down almost to a whisper. Despite the beauty that surrounded us, the atmosphere of this peculiar spot seemed strangely sombre and forlorn. The terraced garden stretching off at one side, and the boxwood bushes, taller than a man, that formed a sort of dusky labyrinth beyond, the stately trees that swayed and whispered overhead—beech, locust, sycamore, oak, maple, chinkapin—all seemed to my imagination peopled by dark shadows. Where were the owners of this place we'd stumbled on, and why was it deserted?

I shivered slightly as I stepped out from the car and headed toward an opening in a stone wall at the right. My driver followed silently. The gate was unlocked, we discovered. We went through it, glimpsing as we passed the house a large conservatory and a vista of huge rooms with high, carved lintels over the doors, and windows whose top portions were of brilliant-hued stained glass. Behind the house we found three dome-shaped cellars tunneled underneath the grass—refrigerators of a bygone day, no doubt—with three small whitewashed tenant houses in the distance, surrounded by bright flowergardens in full bloom. Beyond them, stretching out as far as eye could reach, lay mile on mile of darkly lowering woodland.

We circled the entire house, inspecting each detail with puzzled interest. Quite evidently it was empty, and yet everything about the place spoke unmistakably of careful tending. The mystery seemed to deepen with each step we took, and I was fairly dripping curiosity as finally we came back to our starting point, no wiser than we'd been when we arrived. With some reluctance we were getting in the car again, when suddenly, around the corner of a near-by hedge, the figure of a man appeared. Involuntarily we breathed more freely. So our haunted castle wasn't really haunted, after all—real human beings lived here, too, it seemed!

The new arrival looked at us inquiringly, and my Chauffeur

proceeded to explain our presence. With ready friendliness the man informed us in his turn that he was hired as caretaker of the place. The owner, he went on, had died some years ago, and while the various heirs did battle over who'd succeed to what, the vast estate (three thousand acres it amounted to, he said) was kept intact. The fountain ran all year around, he told us proudly, and the lawns were groomed, the flowers tended, and the reservoir that furnished electricity was kept at normal level all the time.

As we conversed a gradual change seemed taking place about us. Somehow, I thought, the dreariness on every side was lifting slightly. With this normal human contact, things were settling back into more commonplace perspective, and the eerie feeling that had weighed us down was slowly disappearing. By the time we said good-bye at last and started down the winding lane that led back to the highway, only the sheer beauty of the spot we'd chanced on still remained with us—a beauty that our new friend had informed us we were free to share at any time.

I think we'll take him up on that companionable offer. After all, what more impressive setting for a picnic could anybody ever hope to find?

THRASHING DAY

ELEANOR had come to spend a week with me.

Like me, she has a weakness for the Pennsylvania Dutch, and it was partly my proprietary pride in showing off this countryside of mine and all my friendly P.D. neighbors that made me ask her in the first place. As bait, I promised that I'd take her to the Amish country, where her mania for painting hills and fields and neat, white houses huddled in the lee of big, red barns—as well as any Amish people lurking in the offing—could find a natural outlet.

But I was a little optimistic, as it happened. Finding an Amish family willing to take in two perfect strangers, even for a single

night, was just a little harder than I'd thought. In fact, we had no
luck at all in the beginning. But finally, thanks mainly to a bright
idea of my Chauffeur's, we tracked down a completely perfect
place.

We'd started early in the morning, heading straight for the
Amish country. There we'd stopped at every farmhouse flaunting
the House Amish badge of sky-blue shutters, hand-run implements, and no electric wires, but it wasn't till my driver took a
hand that things began to happen. By that time we had driven
over miles and miles of countryside, and Eleanor and I were on
the point of giving up, when suddenly he had his bright idea.

"I know the very person who can help us!" he announced
abruptly. "She's got the population all around here at her finger
tips. I'll bet she can direct us to the sort of place we want!"

And sure enough, the lady knew a family on the other side of
the Welsh Mountain who might take us in. And so, with her
to introduce and vouch for us as harmless and respectable, we were
accepted by the Goods as paying guests. The Goods are Mennonites, not Amish, it turned out. Their ancient limestone house
looks out across a sweep of tidy fields that march straight to the
base of Octoraro Mountain, and the huge, red barns and neat
brick dwellings scattered here and there on every side are owned
by Amish families. The Goods themselves, we found, are five in
number. There's Mom Rachel, to begin with, tall and forthright,
with a round and kindly face beneath a spotless "house cap"—
quite apparently the motivating spirit of the whole *Freindschaft*
(family). Next comes Katie, small but very competent, with
glasses and a quick, straightforward smile, who drives each morning to the stocking mill ten miles or so away where she's employed
as "topper." The second daughter, Mary, strong and well-built,
with a pair of fine, dark eyes and white teeth flashing in a sun-
tanned face, stays home to help Mom Rachel on the farm, while
David—twenty-five or so, a slight but wiry young fellow—and his

husky younger brother, Jacob, look after the more manly chores about the place. Their father, they informed us, died last autumn, and they all still dress in black on Saturdays and Sundays as a token of respect.

But on the day when Eleanor and I went bumping up the hillside in the Rat (my fond abbreviation for the Rattletrap), the Goods had laid aside their mourning garb for ordinary work clothes. It was "thrashing day," apparently, for just outside the big, white barn a thresher with its buzzing engine filled the air with noise and dust. We rattled to a stop beside a lawn whose velvet greenness set off pleasantly the whitewashed incandescence of the house ahead. A whining growl from Sandy, the Goods' watch-dog chained beside the road, saluted us, and Patsy leaped out from her seat between us to investigate. We followed suit —and stopped right in our tracks. For there before us stretched a sweep of woods and fields and hills whose breathless beauty held us silent in sheer rapture for a moment. In the foreground lay a wheatfield, only lately shorn of its ripe harvest. Just beyond it shimmered row on row of tasseled cornstalks, and still farther in the distance, half a mile or so apart, three well-kept Amish farmsteads nestled comfortably. Another cornfield reached out on the right, touching a brilliant garden where the glow of flowers and ripe vegetables combined to form a quaint and homely pattern. And, as final touch to make the picture perfect, on the far horizon loomed the soft, blue border of the everlasting hills.

The motor's hum went with us as we started finally along the concrete walk that led us to the kitchen door. Mom Rachel's face, a trifle flushed from her activities above the stove, appeared in greeting. Her voice, though cordial, was a bit preoccupied, we thought.

"Just make yourselves at home!" she told us in her deep, well-rounded tones. "I'm getting supper for the men—it won't go long now till they're done!"

Behind her Mary's smile showed for a moment also. But it seemed that she, too, had her hands full with the supper preparations, so we took the hint and turned away. While Eleanor unslung her box of paints and settled unobtrusively to work, I made myself as scarce as possible behind the chugging motor, thrilled at this golden chance to study for the first time in my life the complicated process known as "thrashing."

It took eleven men, I gathered—sturdy neighbor-farmers and their sons, who turned out every year to lend a willing hand at this familiar task. A bearded Amishman in bright green shirt and "barn door britches" acted as the genius of the engine, with a lame young man replacing him occasionally upon the lofty perch beneath the engine's hood. Inside the barn a third man, standing on a platform, poked the endless shocks of wheat into the thresher's mouth, while from below two helpers forked up other shocks, and still another man, with a handkerchief tied loosely over nose and mouth to keep away the swirling dust, collected and tossed up the pieces that had fallen on the ground.

At last the deep throb of the engine faded to a gentle hum, the belts connecting with the thresher were unfastened, and the moving slide was carefully hooked back. The men tucked in their loosened shirttails, mopped their streaming brows, and stood at ease. The "thrashing" evidently was completed—next in order came the evening meal.

Much to our disappointment, Eleanor and I were served our supper in the living-room. We'd hoped to be invited to the dining-room next door, where all the workers were already seated at a loaded table. As we ate we listened curiously, but except for the occasional clang of fork or spoon on china, only silence filtered to us through the door between. Apparently stout country appetites and weary bodies left no time for anything as unimportant as mere conversation. It was plain that the men were concentrating single-mindedly on food, the women on the job of serving them. And when at last the eaters rose and went outdoors, without a pause for any sort of social interlude, they climbed inside their waiting cars and drove away. The thresher and the engine, guided by the Amishman, brought up the rear.

With seventeen substantial suppers safely served and stowed away, it seemed to us as though a little rest might be in order. But we didn't know the Goods! Quite evidently no such thought had entered any of their heads. In wordless habit, both the boys departed for the barnyard, while Katie and Mom Rachel, with the help of Eleanor, prepared to clear away the traces of the meal. Quite shamelessly I left them to their task when Mary asked me if I wouldn't like to go along with her and a young Amish friend to gather huckleberries in the mountain.

A good two hours later we came back with brimming pails, to find the trio of dishwashers sitting on the porch. Dusk was just falling, and the gleam of fireflies showed intermittently against the darkling hills. From a deserted limekiln down beyond the cornfield came the silver tinkle of a sheep bell, sounding wistful and nostalgic on the evening air.

Mom Rachel, won completely by the water color Eleanor had started, greeted us with lavish praises of the artist's skill. "It wonders me," she marveled, "how she draws it off so quick! I just can't hardly wait to see it done!" And Eleanor, to please her, promised that she'd finish it before we left.

When finally we rose and started for the second floor, the stars were thick and friendly in a sky so close above our heads it seemed as though we easily could touch them. In the distance a dog barked, shattering for a moment the tremendous hush that lay about us, and it seemed to me that on this tranquil hilltop all the peace and quiet of the world had come to rest.

In noisy contrast, I was wakened by the clatter of a washmachine next morning. I rose to find a scene of industry already in full progress down below. True to her promise, Eleanor was putting the last touches on her water color as she sat, a bit uncomfortably, upon a rock that crowned a little rise behind the barn. Katie long since had started for the factory, while in the barnyard David and his brother were already busy at their various chores, with Mary laboring in the washshed and her mother bent once more above the kitchen stove.

As I emerged from the front door the sound of sundry squeals and yappings fell upon my startled ears, and I was greeted with the fact that Sandy, in complete reversal of her masculine-appearing name, had had a batch of puppies—seven of them—underneath the porch! "They *make* so bad!" Mom Rachel was complaining. "*Ach*, it spites me awful that she got in under there! I don't know right just how the boys are going to get her out!"

But get her out they did somehow, and when that evening Eleanor and I returned from jaunts to other fields, we found that peace had once more settled on the landscape. All the chores were finished and our hostesses, for once relaxing, settled down to have a little visit with us on the porch.

"You ought of been here last week!" Katie told us proudly, as she pointed to the big tobacco shed beside the house. "We had a 'raising'!" And she went on to describe the great event in some detail. It seems that eighty persons had assisted—a grand total that of course included numerous wives and daughters of the men who did the actual work. The Goods had served them all a hearty meal at noon, besides a cold lunch in the middle of the morning. Just a meagre snack, I gathered—several hundred sandwiches, a peck or so of pretzels, half a dozen pounds of cheese, and heaven knows how many quarts of lemonade and tea. The workers had arrived soon after daylight, Katie said, and by the time that ten o'clock rolled round the framework of the building was already up. They'd finished it that afternoon, she added, and the main ranks of the helpers had then left for home, leaving a mere thirty-five or so to share the evening meal.

Our talk turned to the subject of the Amish, and I asked about the various neighbors roundabout. House Amish, most of them, I learned—still practising their church's ancient custom of "avoiding," still refusing all electric power as unnecessary and a mark of worldliness, still riding round in dashless buggies and "top wagons," and still using hooks and eyes in place of buttons on their coats and vests.

With childlike relish, Mary told us briefly what the practice of "avoiding" meant. It seems that when an Amishman is censured by his church, all other Amishmen must shun him conscientiously. The culprit's family, even, shares in the avoidance, and no intercourse whatever may be had with him until he's seen the error of his ways. At mealtime he's an outcast from the family table and compelled to eat in solitary grandeur. But—and Mary's dark eyes twinkled as she told us this—it's said that some folks use a separate table for the sinner, but conceal its separateness beneath a common cloth!

We were still talking when Mom Rachel rose without excuse and went indoors. A moment later Katie followed her, and shortly afterward the summons to the evening meal was given. With pleased surprise we saw that places had been laid for us beside the family's at the kitchen table. We'd passed muster, evidently, and were now accepted friends.

The meal that followed I'll not soon forget. Here's what we had: potatoes freshly dug up from the garden, firm but creamy, with a flavor that I never knew those homely tubers could achieve —young, tender, juicy corn, just picked and floating in a luscious bath of milk and butter—an enormous platterful of ham, as soft and pinkly tender as a sunset cloud—round, homemade loaves of bread just baked that very morning—huckleberries from our mountain sortie of the night before—and, crowning touch of all, large, heaping portions of vanilla ice-cream made especially for us!

With a Herculean effort we got up at last to leave. The sun was sinking slowly as we piled our various chattels in the Rat—chattels increased by several new additions since we'd first set foot among the hospitable Goods. A pair of flowering plants in brightly painted tins for Eleanor, some clumps of ferns I'd gathered in the mountain, several purple "gladiolas" from Mom Rachel's garden for us both, and a round, fat load of her delicious bread. We asked her for the recipe, of course, and with the usual ready bounty of the Pennsylvania Dutch she gave it to us. Here it is:

HOMEMADE BREAD

5 medium-size potatoes, mashed	5 cups lukewarm water
½ cup sugar	1 cake yeast
pinch of salt	2 tablespoons lard
flour to thicken	

Dissolve yeast in water, mix with potatoes, sugar, salt, and flour, and place in a gallon jar. When it has risen to top of jar, knead with the lard and a little more salt, put in pans and allow to rise till double its bulk. Makes 5 loaves.

We said good-bye reluctantly and started off. I'd turned the Rat and headed down the lane when Katie's voice rose suddenly above the clatter of the engine.

"*Ach*, I forgot to tell youse!" she called after us. "Next Sunday-week there's going to be a 'singing' not so far from here. The Amish Mennonites are giving it—they have it every year. We thought perhaps you'd like to come along?"

I looked at Eleanor. She shook her head. She'd have to leave next week, she said, and sighed regretfully.

"*I'll* come!" I promised.

Just let anybody try to stop me! I put a ring around the date of "Sunday-week" on my desk calendar—I wouldn't miss that "singing" for the world!

SING UNTO THE LORD

IT RAINED the night before the "singing"—a steady, heavy down-pour—and the morning promised little in the way of sun. My heart sank as I saw the lowering clouds that hovered overhead. I simply couldn't bear the thought that it might have to be post-poned! But luckily by noon the sky had cleared, and though the air was hot and sultry and not calculated to call forth unneeded effort, still, it wasn't raining and I knew the big event would actu-ally take place.

We started off right after luncheon, my Chauffeur and I. I'd written Katie that we'd meet her and her family, at the place she'd specified, at two o'clock, the hour scheduled for the "sing-ing" to begin. But radiator trouble on the way delayed us, and we got there slightly later than we'd planned. We had no diffi-culty in finding the place, however. As we turned off from the main road, on our left we saw a sun-baked meadow dotted thickly with conveyances of every kind. Hitched to a gray rail fence there was a line of topless, dashless buggies such as the House Amish use, while farther on, ranged neatly on the slope that led up to a grove of trees above, stood row on row of shining autos. For this, of course, was a Church Amish singing, and the members of that younger, more progressive order ride in cars, just like the Dunkers and the Mennonites and others of the less severe Plain People.

Until quite recently this fact was one of very few I'd known about the Amish Mennonites. Indeed I hadn't even known that was their proper title till I'd interviewed a gentleman belonging to the group the week before. From him I'd gathered various bits of fascinating data—such as, for example, that his church had left the older and more strait-laced branch of Amish Men-nonites in 1877. Unlike these stricter cousins, he informed me, they used churches for their worship rather than their barns and houses—hence the common title of "Church Amish." They wore buttons on their clothing, too, he said, but frowned on gold and precious stones, and like the other Plain sects they refused to go to war, take oaths, or have recourse to law for settling grievances. He added that they held communion and feet-washing twice a year, baptized by pouring, not immersion, and excluded infants from the last-named rite.

With this as partial background, I was more than ever interested in what was going on ahead of us as we bumped carefully along the stony lane that led into the field. The singing evidently had begun, for as we started up the hillside there came wafting toward us on the summer breeze the sound of rhythmic voices raised in fervent melody. In eager haste I got out as my driver stopped the car along the outer fringes of the parking space. It seemed too bad he couldn't join me, but the ailing radiator must be overhauled, and so, regretfully, he turned and headed for the nearest town. I waved him out of sight, then plodded purposefully upward underneath a blazing sun.

As I ascended, gradually the sound of singing grew in volume, and unconsciously my footsteps quickened. I was panting slightly as I reached the grateful shade that bathed the small grove like a cooling fountain. Curiously, I stopped and looked about. Before me lay a scene not soon to be forgotten. In a natural amphitheater beneath the maples, with a wall of huge, gray boulders as a backdrop, several thousand persons had assembled for this quaint and picturesque event. They sat on backless wooden benches—merely wide boards placed on sturdy trestles, with occasional rocks and slender saplings forming little islands in the sea of seats. The ground sloped gently downward toward a platform at the front where three men in their shirt sleeves stood before an amplifier that conveyed their voices clearly into every nook and corner of the open-air retreat.

My eyes took in the picture slowly. Everywhere I looked, it

seemed, was color—color in profusion. Never in my life before, I thought, had so much of it dawned upon my vision at a single glance. On every side the brilliant hues of neat House Amish dresses stood out unmistakably in those bright shades of blue and green and red and purple that they love so well. There were some "Peachey" Amish, too, among them—members of that smaller branch whose leader gave the sect its curious-sounding name—as well as Dunkers, Mennonites, and River Brethren, with of course a few "gay" people like myself as guests.

I started to set up the folding chair with which I'd come equipped, when suddenly a palmleaf fan waved briskly at me from the center of the crowd. It was Mom Rachel wielding it, I saw, her round and rosy face wreathed in a smile of cordial welcome as she motioned to a vacant place beside her on the bench. A moment later Katie made her way in my direction, and without a qualm I left my chair propped up against a tree and followed as she led me through the close-packed singers to the section where her mother and her sister Mary sat. I settled down between them, and they handed me a hymnbook opened to the proper place. Beneath the cover of the music that now swelled in vibrant harmony on every side I looked about me once again.

A sea of white-capped heads surrounded me, with just a few black bonnets serving as a sort of background for the rest. The snowy headgear, uniform in color only, showed all sorts of variations when it came to cut and fabric, and the differences, I knew, were filled with meaning for the educated eye. House Amish caps, for instance—full and generous—were of finest nainsook, tied beneath the chin with strings of like material into broad, flat bows. The Peachey Amish, though their caps were made of nainsook also, wore the strings a trifle narrower and fastened in a smooth, straight loop *without* a bow. The smaller coverings of the Mennonites and Dunkers, difficult for almost anyone to tell apart, were fashioned out of net or organdie, with ribbon strings of black or white according to the owner's individual taste.

Among the spotless caps of the House Amish, here and there I saw a small, bare head encircled by a velvet ribbon if its owner were a little girl, square-cropped and banged above a shirt of Amish blue or green or purple if a little boy. The men's heads, too, were bare of hats and cropped exactly like their sons', with full chin beards announcing to the world that they were married men. The older members of the other Plain sects were adorned with chin beards also, and their hats had slightly wider brims than usual, but the younger men wore clothes and haircuts just like those of any other church.

The singing rose and fell around me in great waves of surging harmony—"I Want to Love Him More"—"Glory for Me"— "Christ Receiveth Sinful Men." With every hymn the voices seemed to grow more free and joyful, as the shrill sopranos of the women clung in swelling fervor to the high notes and the men's deep tones boomed forth in echoing refrains. These people knew their hymns and loved to sing them—there could be no doubt of that.

At frequent intervals it was announced that Brother So-and-So would say a few words, and the gentleman in question would push forward to the platform and proceed to speak. Two minutes was the time allotted each, and for the most part they kept well within the designated period. A ruddy-bearded man in gray Plain suit, with short-tailed coat that buttoned to the neck and low, straight collar, took the rostrum shortly after I arrived. He was a River Brethren minister, Mom Rachel whispered, and the ease with which he spoke denoted frequent practice in addressing audiences like this. A Presbyterian clergyman came next—a guest, apparently —who dwelt with earnest briefness on the fact that there are no denominations to be found in Heaven. Then the owner of the grove, an old man with a white chin beard and spectacles perched

far down on his nose, shirtsleeved and rubber-armleted, contributed a few remarks that ended with the proud announcement
that the audience included visitors from half a dozen different
states.

Occasionally informal orders from the platform punctuated
the proceedings. A group of boys, adventurously minded, had
swarmed restlessly across the boulders at the back. In no uncertain phrases they were told to come and sit on benches or to go
straight home! A little later word was given out that someone's
child was crying in a parked car with a certain license number.
Would the parent kindly go at once and see what it was all
about, the spokesman asked. But no one seemed to mind these
small digressions, and the service moved comfortably upon its
ordered way.

About the middle of the singing one of the three leaders rose
to make a brief announcement. A certain brother known and
liked by all, he said, was in their midst today, and as a special
mark of favor would be given fifteen minutes, rather than the
usual two, in which to have his say. A little stir of pleasure swept
the listeners as the gentleman alluded to arose. A twinkle in his
eye bespoke a sense of humor, and he lost no time in getting to
the point. There were nine rules for singing that he wished to
outline, he informed them, and he hoped they'd listen carefully
and take them all to heart. The first was very simple: Everyone
should know the number of the hymn that they were going to
sing and pay attention to the leader's voice. Next, all should start
to sing *immediately*, with no late stragglers coming in to spoil
the whole effect. Third, no results worth mentioning could be
had unless the singers followed their director's lead. Of course,
that lead might leave a lot to be desired in the way of timing,
he admitted with a smile, but faulty timing done by all together
was far better than good timing done by each apart!

The fourth rule, he went on, was most important: Sing the

meaning of the words—and sing it so that others were aware of what was being sung. Fifth, there were songs with jingle but no mental nourishment, so stick to psalms and hymns and other melodies with spiritual intent. Sixth, when you sing, he warned, be sure to follow carefully the rules of music—or if you don't know anything about the rules, then simply sing by rote. And seventh, when you choose selections, choose the ones adapted to the time and place. Don't sing "The Day Is Past and Gone" at morning services, for instance. Eighth, introduce a new song now and then—don't sing the same old tunes at every meeting. But remember, too, that one new song is quite enough for any gathering—and above all, let the first and last hymns be familiar so that everyone can sing. And, ninth and finally, be sure to sing your music to God's glory, or don't sing at all. No matter how impressive the rendition, he insisted, it's mere vanity unless the singer is sincere in offering prayer and praise.

The brother's manner, earnest but informal, seemed to please the crowd. They nodded in approval as he went on to apply the rules he'd just laid down.

"You children of eleven years and under!" he commanded suddenly. "I want you to come down here! Hurry, now—come on!"

In half-excited, half-reluctant little groups the youngsters started to obey. A few hung back, but active urging from their parents overcame their bashfulness, and finally they took their places with the rest. They made a picturesquely varied group, I thought, with white-capped heads next door to bare ones, some with square-cropped hair and some with hair cut short and close, with velvet bands and braided "bops" and dangling pigtails all in evidence—plus one male head that boldly wore an ordinary visored cap.

The singing-master's eye lit on the wearer of this last bit of apparel, and he frowned in disapproval.

"Take your cap off, boy!" he ordered briskly. Then, by way

of putting the young culprit at his ease: "I guess you just forgot
it, didn't you?"

With this small matter straightened out, the gentleman got
down to business. "Now, everybody sing!" he ordered, and struck
up a lively tune. The youthful choir raised their voices in obedience, following the movements of their leader's outstretched arms.
With pleased enjoyment audible in every note, they sang enthu-
siastically:

> *"It's all right now,*
> *It's all right now;*
> *My sins are all forgiven,*
> *I'm on my way to Heaven.*
> *Hallelujah!*
> *It's all right now!"*

Clear and sweet, the treble voices wavered on the drowsy summer air, and from the treetops overhead the shrilling of the
locusts answered. As if in echo, restless babies here and there
throughout the audience raised their voices in protesting whim-
pers. But the choir master, quite unruffled, calmly shouted the
intruders down. His singing class, responsive and alert, performed
with gusto, and when finally they were dismissed, swarmed quickly
back to their respective places, all aglow with virtuous accomplishment.

The singing now was in its final stages, it appeared. Additional
hymns were sung, and then a gray-haired brother with a shovel
beard and black suspenders made some final brief remarks. At
last the strains of "God Be with Us Till We Meet Again" rang
out—and suddenly the space beneath the trees became a rich
kaleidoscope of shifting color. Linking hands, a group of girls
—House Amish by their dresses—ran off laughing down the hillside. In the center, knots of older people milled about exchanging
news. Close by, a young House Amish father with a rather sparse

and tentative-appearing beard, stood holding in his arms a tiny boy. Except for size and facial smoothness, little Junior was a perfect replica of Pop, with black felt hat pulled low upon a cropped, tow-colored head, a miniature green shirt beneath an open vest, and microscopic trousers reaching to the shoetops held in place by broad, homemade suspenders just exactly like those his father wore. Not far away, a young House Amish mother sat upon a folding stool and nursed her baby as the crowd passed by, while little girls in pinafores and bright-toned frocks ran in and out among the vacant benches.

With Katie, Mary, and Mom Rachel, I moved slowly toward the open field. Our progress was delayed by frequent stops to speak to various friends along the way. But finally we reached the Goods' machine, where David and another youth were waiting patiently. I looked around for my Chauffeur, but he was nowhere to be seen.

Mom Rachel rose to the occasion. "Come along with us once!" she suggested kindly. "In the lane there's such a line of cars, perhaps he can't get through. He may be waiting for you in the road, still!"

I thanked her gratefully, and crowded in the auto with the Goods and several friends that they were taking home for dinner. We moved along at snail's pace in the long procession of machines, enveloped in a cloud of dust churned up by those ahead of us. At last we reached the shady lane, to bump along its rutty length and come out finally upon the open road. And sure enough, there was my driver, waiting for a chance to come and pick me up.

"Youse both can come along for supper with us!" Katie offered hospitably, and the others seconded her invitation. But the long drive home still lay ahead of us, and though the radiator of our car had been repaired, it wasn't all it should be even yet, my charioteer explained. And so we said good-bye and climbed back in our ailing equipage.

"Too bad!" the gentleman observed with feeling. "And I certainly did hate to miss the singing! Was it really good?"

I nodded silently. To my surprise, I found I hadn't any words that seemed to fit. A scene like that I'd witnessed needed time and distance to be properly digested.

"Yes—really good!" I said inadequately. And, with that gift of his for sensing what was in my thoughts, my driver let it go at that.

August

SPEAKING OF BIRTHDAYS

$\mathcal{M}$Y BIRTHDAY comes in August—a fact that usually I make a noble effort to ignore. But not this year. Not after what the gentleman who hauls away my refuse said to me the other morning!

I was on the front porch, as it happened, when my knight of the garbage pail came toiling up the hillside on his daily quest. Now, this slightly smelly individual, like most of my other year-round neighbors in the country, is a Pennsylvania Dutchman and a friend of mine. So, as he passed my steps, I greeted him politely: "Good morning!"

He stopped, and for a moment stood there gaping at me. Then, with genial sociability, he said: "You look chust like a dollbaby! How old are you?"

I must admit I was a trifle startled. But I laughed indulgently. "Well, really now," I pointed out with maidenly reserve, "I don't ask *you* your age, do I? Do you think you ought to ask me mine?"

My odoriferous boy friend chuckled. As plainly as the day his manner said: "You can't fool me!" He spat—accurately. "You ain't so old!" he said, and passed on, leaving me all of a girlish twitter.

What if his eyesight *isn't* all it should be? And suppose I do at times have more than a suspicion that he's not quite bright? After all, if I "ain't so old" to the garbage man—! The thought has definite possibilities.

And speaking of birthdays, I'm reminded that a very special friend of mine will have one, too, this month—a birthday celebrated from a narrow bed in a quiet hospital room. Gerber Schafer has celebrated a good many birthdays from that bed, and from other beds in other hospitals, too. There he lies, day after day, month after month, year after year—rigid, motionless, completely still. How, I've often wondered, must it feel to lie like that? How must it feel to be Gerber Schafer?

I'll never forget the day of my first visit to that now-familiar hospital high on a Reading hill. I'd come to town on a speaking engagement, and when the luncheon was over someone had said to me brightly: "Oh, you *must* meet Gerber Schafer! Everybody who *is* anybody has to meet Gerber!" And they took me to that small, twilit room with its flowers, and its cheerful pictures on the wall, and its high, white bed like a throne dominating all the rest, and I met him. It was only a brief visit, that first one, but it was the beginning of a friendship that has lasted ever since. Each time after that, whenever I've found myself near Reading, I've stopped off to see Gerber Schafer. And one day he was moved to tell me his story.

He showed me a picture first. It was the picture of an eager, fresh-faced lad in uniform, with a sergeant's chevrons on his arm. That was in 1918. Gerber Schafer was twenty-three then, just discharged from the Army, with the honorable record of a year's service behind him. He'd made a good soldier, I know. For Gerber comes of sturdy Pennsylvania German stock, and the Pennsylvania Dutch have always been good soldiers. Back in Revolutionary days an ancestor of his had crossed the Delaware with Washington. And in a later war, in camps and flying fields of half a dozen states, Gerber, too, had done his part. He'd never gotten across, it's true, but even so, first as aviation mechanic, then later as an aerial gunner, a soldier's life, he'd found, had had its thrills. Once, on a test flight, he'd missed death by seconds when his plane rolled over and cracked up. But he and his companion had been pronounced unhurt. And when the war was over, as cheerfully as he'd left his job to enlist, Gerber had gone back to it once more.

Somehow, though, he told me now, that old job of his had seemed too hard for him. So he'd taken a lighter one—and had to quit. Then for a year or so he'd tried his luck as salesman. And one morning, suddenly, when he woke up he found himself unable to get out of bed. That crackup back in Army days was catching up with him at last.

The years that followed were one long and bitter nightmare—a nightmare of endless experiments and suffering, of new doctors and strange hospitals and fruitless operations. And at last, in 1932, Gerber Schafer found a permanent home in St. Joseph's Hospital at Reading. By that time, though, he'd found something else—something that today, despite the constant pain which racks his wasted body, despite the fact that only his eyes and lips still answer to the dictates of his will, enables him to go on.

It began one morning some years ago. It was his birthday, August twenty-first, he told me, and he was still living at his home in Laureldale. At his sister's urgent request, Gerber had listened in that morning to a certain radio program. To his amazement he had heard a man's voice asking that his hearers send a word of cheer to an ex-soldier named Gerber Schafer. Almost at once a flood of cards and gifts and letters had come pouring in, and Gerber's family, instigators of the plot in the first place, were wise enough to insist that he must answer them himself.

"It was the best thing they ever did for me!" Gerber confided to me cheerfully. "You know, if you let machinery stand still, it rusts. Well, that was what was happening to my mind. My body had already rusted fast—the thing I needed was an interest to keep my mind from rusting, too. And those letters were what did it!"

Actually, though, they were just the starting point. With quiet sincerity Gerber told me the rest. One night, he said, as he lay wide awake a voice within him seemed to speak. "What's the matter with you?" it asked. "Here you lie just thinking of yourself—day in, day out, all the time. Why aren't you trying to help others?" And Gerber's life since then has been an answer to that question.

He started by selling magazines for charity—by telephone, of course, the only way he had. He gathered money, clothing, food, and coal by the same method. Day and night his 'phone was always busy—selling Christmas cards and tickets, raising money for the American Legion post he'd helped to organize, enlisting gifts from influential men. And when at last in 1932 he was admitted to the Reading hospital, he set himself to raising funds for that institution as well.

But chief among his interests are the shut-ins—men and women like himself who spend their lives within the confines of four walls. Today he corresponds with hundreds of them, in this country and around the world, and four volunteer secretaries are kept busy answering his mail. For Gerber Schafer's name has come to stand for something big and fine in the community, and Reading folks are proud to be associated with him. When famous men or women come to town, there's always someone to suggest a call, and the one who pays a visit to that bedside comes away a little humbler and a little happier because of Gerber Schafer.

Yes, life for Gerber is a rich and rare adventure—an adventure which, despite the suffering that attends it, he clings to with tenacious zest. Only one thing worries him, he says: "Will I live long enough to do the things I'm planning for mankind?" Perhaps that's why there hangs beside his bed this motto: "Opportunity shall pass through this world but once. Any good, therefore, that I can show to any human being, let me do it now. Let me not defer or neglect it, for I shall not pass this way again."

Yes, I'm quite sure that every birthday Gerber has will be a happy one. For despite the handicaps that life has dealt him, he's one of the few persons I know who have found the secret of real living. His body may lie stiff and helpless, chained to a bed and wrenched by never-ending pain, but the indomitable soul of Gerber Schafer still goes marching on.

VANILLA PIE

For weeks past now the weather's been abominably hot. Even the nights have barely managed to cool off enough to make the daytime bearable. The woods and fields on every side have had a tired, frayed-around-the-edges look—and so has Patsy. Flat on the living-room floor, her soft, white body limp, her black ears drooping, my little dog has lain and panted by the hour. And I, remembering with undying self-reproach my well-meant efforts of the past, have done exactly nothing to relieve her.

For my last attempt was far from a success. On a certain stifling day I shan't forget, I placed on Patsy's head a piece of ice, and kept it there despite her protests. The result was a combination of pneumonia and distemper, and a small dog's patient, silent suffering that nearly broke my heart. Hereafter I'll let Nature take her course, with no officiousness on my part.

Unfortunately for Patsy, dogs are positively not permitted in the lake. And the lake has been the only cool spot in the neighborhood for many a long and weary day. The fact has percolated, evidently, to the ears of practically everybody south of Canada, and the beach, looking like a miniature Coney Island and sounding even more so, has been a-swarm with people. Young and old, fat and lean, copper-brown and lily-white, every man, woman, and child who owns a bathing-suit, and some who apparently picked up a colored handkerchief by mistake and wore that instead, have been splashing gaily and vociferously. Till late at night the heavy, sultry air has echoed with their shrieks, augmented by the strains of an untiring juke box wafted over the lake and up on my porch with all the gentle ululations of a steam calliope. Whoever invented that delightful phrase, "the peace and quiet of the woods," certainly wasn't thinking of *my* cozy retreat on these mid-August days!

But now at last there's been a respite from the heat. A cool breeze stirs the tired trees, the air is clearer. Sunshine and shadows are more sharply defined. The water of the lake looks smoother, deeper, darker, and soft violet clouds, low-hung on the horizon, show in bold relief against a golden sky. The evening air is filled to overflowing with the rasp of katydids. There's a red leaf on the sweet-gum tree before the house, and already, to sensitized nostrils, the scent of dying grass is noticeable—of goldenrod and Joe Pye weed and other growing things dried by the sun. Fall, I've realized suddenly, is just around the corner.

Inspired partly by the blessed coolness, and partly by a letter I unearthed the other day from my small Amish friend, Lavina

Beiler, my Chauffeur suggested after dinner that we pay a visit to the Beiler family. Lavina's letter went like this:

Hello Ann Hark,

I wonder where youns stick these few month. Why we don't here anything of you don't see anything of you or nothing. I have homesick for youns I wish you would come done here some time. We are looking for you every week-end.

Well Ann I got my birthday card was awful glad for it. Thank you ever so much for it and for Annie's birthday present. We thought it was an awful pretty towel set. When my birthday was we had ice-cream. Uumm it was good. Ha Ha.

I wonder if it is cold up there to. It is pretty cool down here these few weeks. Last week it hailed a little. Are yard was all white it looked like little cherries bouncing down. I wonder if it hailed up there. Since it hailed it is pretty cool down here but the crops grow if it is a little cool. We planted our corn and potatoes the potatoes are up but the corn isn't up yet. The wheat field is nice and green and the grass field is nice and green I wish youns would come down here sometime and see how pretty it looks. We also whitewashed but it isn't so white as it was because it rained some of it off.

I wonder if you write books and magazines yet. We don't we work on the farm. Mother has a nice garden but her beans were frozen a little. We had a little Jack Frost down here then the beans got frozen.

Well Jack how are you don't you feel good or don't you want to come down here any more. I guess youns are tired of us. Ha Ha Ha. You and Ann come down here some time youns can come quicker than us because youns have a machine and we don't. Write me or come down some time now come or write. Sooner come than write. Hello Patsy. How are you. Good-bye.

LAVINA BEILER

So, to ease Lavina's "homesick," we started off. With Patsy in her usual state of somnolent contentment on the seat between us, we rolled through the quiet evening countryside, between rich

fields of golden wheat stacks, past tidy, well-groomed houses, each
with its flowergarden riotous in bloom. And at last we reached the
Amish country. Bright blue shutters and blue windowblinds—
glimpses of manly square-cropped heads and white-capped feminine ones—an open buggy topped by broad-brimmed hat and wide
black bonnet jogging rhythmically side by side—a picture of
simplicity as quaint and charming as an Old World scene.

We turned into the Beiler lane just as the first bright fireflies
appeared, and I solemnly made a wish. *Lichti* (small lights) is
what the Pennsylvania Dutch call fireflies, Lavina once had told
me, and of course the first one of the season is the signal for
the voicing of one's heart's desire. As if in answer to my thought
of her, I saw Lavina standing at the far end of the lane ahead,
watching the road by which we came as if expecting us. Her long,
full dress was Amish blue in color and her smoothly parted hair
was bound with a black velvet ribbon. Beside her stood Selina,
dressed in Amish purple, with little Susie of the rosy cheeks and
shyly downcast lashes wearing that delightful shade of green
which follows next in Amish favor.

We drove around the corner of the barnyard just as Pop, accompanied by his two small sons, came out to greet us. In the
open doorway of the house we saw Mom's more substantial form,
barefooted and for once without the spotless "house cap" that
all Amish women wear. And suddenly it struck us that today
was Saturday—we'd come right in the middle of the family
bathing hour!

Our *faux pas* was politely overlooked, however, and it wasn't
long before the lady of the house, once more completely clothed
and smiling heartily, came out to add her welcome to the rest.
Although the air was warm and gentle, we were ushered firmly in
the house, where lamps were lit—lamps fed by gasoline, since
Amish of the House variety don't use electric lights—and seated
in the large, cool sitting-room that opens from the kitchen.

Since Saturday, of course, is "beau night," both of the two older boys were out. And long ago Seth Fisher, Annie's boy friend, had arrived in his shining, topless buggy to carry her off with him to some near-by neighbor's home. The rest of us, ensconced in rocking chairs, launched forth upon the usual talk of crops and other timely topics, while Patsy entertained the younger members of the family with her repertoire of tricks. Her trusting friendliness and perfect manners won the Beilers' hearts a long time back and she's a privileged character by now, permitted even in that special inner sanctum of a Pennsylvania Dutch abode—the scrubbed and spotless kitchen.

For upwards of an hour Patsy staged her little show before an audience of five small Beilers thoroughly enchanted by such wondrous feats. Delighted at so much attention, she sat up and begged, danced on her hind legs, washed her face, shook hands, rolled over, closed the door, and otherwise showed off obediently.

We got up finally to go—and found ourselves beset by warm objections. Leave without eating something first? The very thought struck horror to Mom Beiler's hospitable heart. No *Hausfraa* worthy of the name could possibly be guilty of such rank discourtesy! So, with our hostess in the lead, we trooped out to the kitchen. There on the oilcloth-covered table we discovered a small feast awaiting us. At each place stood a dish of mixed sliced fruit, with two tall layer cakes arranged exactly in the center, plus a bowl of pretzels and—my eyes popped out incredulously— a vanilla pie!

I gasped. Vanilla pie! For months my mouth had watered for that special species of ambrosia which I'd tasted once, and only once, before. A year or so ago I'd come across a sample of it in a market stall at Lancaster, and out of curiosity had bought it on the spot. It bore the general earmarks of my special favorite among piecrust-bottom pastries—shoofly pie. But where the middle portion of a shoofly pie, between its crumb-besprinkled surface and the flaky crust, is a dark, rich brown in color, vanilla pie is somewhat paler, with a flavor even more mouth-wateringly divine. One taste of its ecstatic goodness and I knew that life would never be complete for me until I'd learned the why and how of its concoction. But, alas, I never did locate the Dunker woman who had sold me that first tantalizing sample. Frequent and importunate descriptions of the pie I yearned for had brought no answering light of intelligence to the face of anyone I questioned. And finally, with a tear and a sigh, I'd laid away in lavender the memory of that smoothly crumby, caramel-flavored paragon of pastries. It looked as though I were doomed to go through life vanilla pieless.

But now at last—! I licked my lips in greedy rapture. Here it was—right here before me on the table! With a genteel shriek of joy I fell upon it. Would Mom Beiler let me have the recipe, I humbly asked?

"Why, sure!" With generous promptness she agreed. "Just cut yourself a slice once, while I go and get it for you!"

So, while I reveled in the beatific savor of the crumb pie that I'd sought so long and found at last, she wrote out in a round and childish hand the way it's made. It goes like this:

Filling: Boil together

1 cup sugar	2 cups water
1 cup light molasses	1 teaspoon flour

Set aside, and add 1 teaspoon vanilla.

Crumbs: With the fingers work well together the following:

½ cup lard	1 cup sugar
2 cups flour	1 teaspoon baking soda
1 teaspoon cream of tartar	

Place filling in 4 unbaked pie shells, sprinkle the crumbs over the top of each pie, and bake in a medium oven.

IF AT FIRST YOU DON'T SUCCEED—

WELL, I tried making it.

My mouth was watering as I lit the oven and got out my favorite rolling pin, unlimbered sundry pots and pans and measuring cups, and blithely started struggling with my first vanilla pie.

And "struggling," it turned out, is just the right word to describe what happened. For the finished product wasn't an unqualified success. In fact, to be completely honest, it was a total loss. But I can hardly blame it on Mom Beiler's recipe. If I'd just had sense enough to follow her directions blindly, with no added touches of my own, the whole thing would have turned out as it should, no doubt. At any rate, it would have turned out as per recipe. The fact that Mrs. Beiler evidently swears allegiance to the school of thought which leans toward plenty of moisture at the bottom of the pastry could have been intelligently dealt with later on.

Because, as every Pennsylvania Dutch *Hausfraa* can tell you, this whole shoofly business—whether just the usual dark brunette variety or my beloved blond vanilla version—isn't quite as simple as it sounds. The reason seems to be that two conflicting systems of opinion are in vogue. You've got to figure out beforehand which you're going to follow—and that's exactly what I didn't do.

You see, one little group of serious thinkers is convinced the pie should come out from the oven with a damp, dark, gummy zone above the crust. The other school scorns such a wet and sloppy mess, insisting that the texture should be firm throughout, thus making for a neater job of "dunking" when the coffee stage is reached. And, just by way of further complication, there's an extra group that uses crumbs and moisture in alternate layers. So—you've got to make a choice.

It seems that Mrs. Beiler makes hers on the damp and gummy side. Because when finally I laid her recipe before me and prepared for work, I found it called for only one teaspoon of flour as against a pint of water and a cup of light molasses. Well, it didn't seem quite right to me, somehow. That's mighty little thickening for a large amount of liquid. Probably, I thought, you had to boil it first. And so—I boiled it. Boiled and boiled and boiled it. And at last, a bit discouraged by the fact that it still failed to look at all like cake, I poured it in the piecrust, sprinkled crumbs on top, and popped it in the oven with my fingers crossed.

Well, the result was something that I'd just as soon forget. There wasn't any wet and sticky layer at the bottom—that was *something*, anyway. But the entire mixture—filling, crust, and crumbs together—turned out just about a quarter of an inch in thickness, and as hard and stiff and chewy as molasses taffy. I took one look at it, and then, with laudable restraint, I left the whole sad mess just where it lay and went out for a walk.

When I came back I felt a trifle better. If at first you don't succeed, I told myself, the thing to do is start all over again! And so I did. This time I used a little common sense in mixing the ingredients. That first *débâcle* had been hard and stiff and chewy, which meant, of course, that it had boiled too long. So I decided that I'd boil it only fifteen minutes this time. Still, one teaspoonful of flour to three cups of liquid *isn't* very much—and Mrs. Beiler's pie, I suddenly remembered, *had* been pretty runny at the bottom. Perhaps more flour would correct that feature. So—I added three more teaspoonfuls and waited hopefully for the result.

It proved as satisfactory as I possibly could wish. My pie came out quite thick and moist, with just the right amount of dampness at the bottom and a caky softness in the middle, topped by rich, delicious crumbs that melted in the mouth. So that's the version of vanilla pie which I shall stick to stubbornly hereafter!

WALDECK WEEK-END

IT WAS at least a year ago that I first heard of Waldeck Farm and its presiding geniuses, the Gable sisters. All sorts of highly-colored tales had been relayed to me about the wondrous food to be partaken of in that establishment—food always freshly gathered from surrounding acres and prepared by hands that loftily refused to note such things as shortages or other city limitations. Tales, too, about the simple kindliness that made all visitors feel welcome, and brought them back time after time for further samples of real Pennsylvania German hospitality and pleasant living. But until quite recently those tales were merely hearsay, and I must admit I'd taken them with several grains of salt.

I know much better now, however. For I've proved the truth of all those glowing stories. Mabel will bear me witness that the fame of Waldeck Farm was not a bit exaggerated!

It was early afternoon when she and I rolled up to the garden entrance of the Gable dwelling. We could almost feel the aura of heart-warming hospitality that seemed to reach out from its sturdy sandstone walls a full two centuries old. We sensed it still more plainly as we walked along the pathway leading to the porch. Upon our left a flowergarden flaming in late summer beauty greeted us, the blazing red and gold and purple of its marigolds and zinnias, its dahlias and petunias and chrysanthemums, marked off by a neat wire fence entwined with climbing vines. On either side, a bed of coleus glowed in slightly less flamboyant color, and a slender pear tree whose ripe harvest spilled in golden plenty on the ground reached into a misty gray-blue sky. Two pointed arbor-vitae trees guarded the steps of the veranda, and a row of cushioned rockers, empty now of guests, looked out upon a well-kept lawn where towering pines and maples cast their pleasant shadows.

We stepped up on the porch just as the screen door opened

and a gray-haired woman with a dignified but friendly smile came out to meet us. This was Miss Emma, evidently—youngest of the Gable trio and chief hostess of this fabulous ménage. Behind her, smiling in warm welcome also, was Miss Lottie, eldest of the sisters, with snow-white hair and spectacles and an air of calm command that spoke of many years spent as a teacher. We looked about expectantly for the third sister, but except for certain nostril-tickling odors wafting from the kitchen, there was no indication of Miss Mollie's presence anywhere.

We stood in casual conversation for a moment in the living-room—a large and cheerful room with wide, deep windowsills filled full to overflowing with the pink and lavender and rich, deep purple of innumerable pots of African violets. The sun that streamed in brightly lit to cozy warmth a gay rag carpet on the floor, a gaudy crocheted afghan draped across a cushioned couch, and an amazing row of vari-colored paperweights lined up inside a bookcase near the door. But we were given little chance to take in the details. With other and more pressing matters evidently on her mind, Miss Emma led the way upstairs and, after showing us our rooms, descended quickly toward the general precincts of the kitchen.

We made short work of our unpacking, marveling as we did so at the handmade lace that edged our pillowslips and bureau covers, and the neatly crocheted rugs that formed soft little islands in the sea of brightly striped rag carpet on the floor. On every side, it seemed, no matter where we looked, some bit of handiwork bore witness to the industry that seemed to be the watchword of this busy household.

As soon as possible we went downstairs again, where Mabel slothfully decided to enjoy the view afforded from a rocker on the porch. A bit more curious, I made straight for the enormous barn that bulked up solidly beyond the flowerbeds—a region, I discovered, managed by a gentleman named Henner. For thirty years this genial Pennsylvania Dutchman had been part and parcel of the Gable acres, he informed me—as chauffeur, caretaker, livestock groom, and tiller of the soil all rolled in one. With modest pride, plus some amusement at my eager questions as I viewed the teeming barnyard, Henner started to recite for me the list of animals he chaperoned. Two horses, half a dozen cows, a score or more of ducks, a dozen pigs, five cats, a dog, and several hundred chickens—such, it seemed, made up the livestock section of the Gable farm. The land itself, he said, consisted of a hundred and twenty acres, of which eighty-nine were cultivated. Corn, tobacco, oats, and wheat were the main harvest, with the crops rotated carefully according to the best traditions of the Pennsylvania Dutch.

I asked how old the barn was, and his weather-beaten face lit up with real affection.

"It was built in 1803!" he told me proudly. "You can see the logs dovetailed together at the corners if you just climb up them steps and take a look!"

Obediently I did as he suggested. He watched me from below, his deep-set eyes a-twinkle, as I fumbled in the semi-darkness of the loft and finally announced that I could see the joining of the great, square beams that made the inner walls. "They've lasted pretty good!" he said with satisfaction, and turned away to take up once again the evening chores whose leisurely routine I'd interrupted.

I left him juggling skillfully the various milk cans cooling in their trough of water in the near-by pumphouse. The shadows of late afternoon were falling, and the odors emanating from the kitchen as I neared the house once more held unmistakable appeal. Miss Emma had informed us there'd be other guests for dinner, and a car was turning off the highway even now, to bowl along the Gable lane and bring up just outside a small tobacco shed that crowned the slope behind the barn.

"I'm starving!" Mabel whispered as I joined her on the porch, and with a hungry sniff at the ambrosial atmosphere surrounding us, I nodded in agreement. We hadn't long to wait, however, for as soon as the new party had alighted and been introduced, the welcome summons to the dining-room was given and we all trooped out. A separate table had been set for Mabel and myself, with five additional places at another, larger board across the room. Miss Emma and Miss Lottie, hovering hospitably back and forth, brought steaming plates and platters from the kitchen and began to set them in bewildering array upon the cloth before us. I looked at Mabel and she looked at me. No comment was forthcoming. With a wordless sigh of rapture we fell to.

A platter of pink home-cured ham was passed us by Miss Emma. Candied sweet potatoes, richly yellow in their bath of butter and brown sugar, followed; next, a dish of breaded onions, crunchy but still succulent, asparagus, fresh carrots liberally bedewed with butter, broccoli, a casserole of lima beans combined with bacon, fluffy mashed potatoes, and—most ravishing of all—a plate of golden, crisp corn fritters with a flavor rich and melting beyond words to tell! As if this weren't enough, there was a salad also— not to mention beverages, of course—and for dessert large, flaky-crusted cuts of coconut custard pie!

It came as somewhat of a shock on top of this plethoric menu when Miss Emma, with an air of half-apology, remarked: "The reason we're not giving you the full of everything tonight is that tomorrow you'll be getting a real chicken dinner!" Once again I looked at Mabel and she looked at me. How "full," we wondered silently, could any dinner be?

We'd ploughed our way ecstatically through the main part of the meal and started on the creamy smoothness of the pie when, unobtrusively, the lady to whose culinary skill we were indebted for this sumptuous repast appeared upon the scene. A trifle flushed from her activities as cook, but with a smile of conscious satisfac-

tion on her sweet, round face, Miss Mollie sat and listened to our
fervid comments on the beatific food we'd just consumed. The
salad, she informed us modestly, was made according to an ancient
recipe her Grandmom had bequeathed her. Probably, she thought,
its tantalizing flavor came from the unique idea of sprinkling it
with cinnamon. She turned to me at this point. Would I like to
have the recipe?

I would, of course. So then and there, while space was being
cleared among the dishes by the little hired girl assisting in the
kitchen, I got out my trusty pencil and meticulously wrote it
down. It went like this:

TOMATO SALAD

6 tomatoes	¾ cup sugar
2 stems celery, cut fine	salt
¼ cup vinegar	cinnamon

Slice tomatoes thin, salt and let stand for 10 to 15 minutes. Then
drain away the juice, add vinegar, sugar, and celery, and sprinkle
thinly with cinnamon.

But, fascinating as this salad sounded, even more intriguing to
my way of thinking was the question of just how those luscious
fritters had been made. And once again Miss Mollie cheerfully
revealed her secret. First, you made corn pudding, she informed
me. Then, when it was cold, you sliced it down and fried it in
deep fat—and there you were! But surely, I protested, not just
any pudding would make fritters like the ones I'd eaten in such
shameless quantity? Miss Mollie smiled. Well, this was how she
made hers, she obliged:

CORN PUDDING

2 cups fresh corn, *or*	1 tablespoon butter
1 can whole-kernel corn	2 eggs
2 tablespoons sugar	1½ cups milk
1 tablespoon cornstarch	salt

Put corn through coarse food chopper (to keep it from settling to bottom). Be sure to save the juice, which should be included in the 1½ cups milk. Add sugar, cornstarch, butter, eggs, and salt, and beat well. Add milk and bake in moderate oven for 30 minutes.

By this time the last crumbly morsel of our custard pie had disappeared, and with that feeling of ineffable content which only such a meal can bring, we moved back to the living-room. The other guests, replete and happy, lingered for a short time and then said good-bye. With smug delight at having all three sisters to ourselves at last, we lost no time in plying them with questions. How long had they been living in this ancient house, we asked? How many people did they have as guests throughout the year? And did they really carry on the work that such a place entailed with only Henner and young Annabelle, the kitchen helper, to assist them?

The trio answered readily, each chiming in to supplement the others' words. Their father, we were told, had come here at the age of ten, and all of them, including a fourth sister who was married and lived elsewhere, had been born at Waldeck Farm. The peaceful-sounding German name, whose English meaning is a "corner of the woods," was taken from the principality of Waldeck, Germany, we learned. From there four Gable brothers, back in 1739, had emigrated to this country. All four had come to Pennsylvania, one to Lebanon and one to Lancaster, another to Montgomery County, and a fourth—well, somehow that fourth brother wasn't listed in the family records. But the one who settled down in Lancaster, the sisters said, was their direct ancestor. Grandpop, third in line, had bought this farm in Lebanon County, then a tract consisting of a hundred acres, only six of them cleared land that could be ploughed. Their father had grown up at Waldeck and eventually become a teacher, but he'd always spent his summer months upon the farm. And finally its call had proved too strong to be denied. So, giving up his teaching altogether, he'd devoted the remainder of his life to its demands.

Miss Lottie and Miss Mollie, following in their father's footsteps, had both studied to be teachers, too, they told us. The elder of the pair had realized her ambition, and the June before had reached the end of a professional life that lasted only five years short of half a century. But Miss Mollie's plans had been disrupted by an accident. For half a dozen years she'd been a semi-invalid, and when at last she'd gotten better, on her shoulders there had fallen the full burden of a family left without a mistress by her mother's death. And then it was, in cooking for a household that included her three sisters and her father and six husky hired men, that the amazing culinary talent which she now possessed had first been born.

"I'll say one thing for Mollie, anyway!" Miss Emma's tone, though marked by sisterly restraint, was not quite able to conceal a note of pride. "She never burns or scorches anything from one year to the next! She never tastes things while she's cooking, either. And—" again Miss Emma's voice bespoke unqualified approval—"she doesn't use a recipe. Not ever! Sometimes she cooks on an electric stove, and sometimes on coal-oil or wood. But I've yet got to see a single pan that Mollie's ever burned!"

This noble record, unbelievable enough to start with, took on added lustre when we learned that in the two months just preceding, 2,700 meals had been prepared by this consummate cook. All through the spring and summer seasons eager gourmets came from far and near, it seemed—a score or two a day, and sometimes twice that number—to enjoy the palate-tickling fare and simple hospitality served up in equal measure by the sister trio. With only thirteen-year-old Annabelle to help them in the kitchen, and faithful Henner carrying on the heavier work about the farm, their lives were filled to overflowing with a never-ending list of homely tasks. Six bedrooms on the second floor, we learned, accommodated paying guests—at least two guests to each of them —throughout the season, not to mention that continuous stream of transient diners whose requests for reservations often poured in five or six weeks in advance. And yet with all this ceaseless work the sisters still found time for other interests, too, they told us. For when finally the busy season dwindled to a close, and some five hundred jars or more of home-canned fruits and vegetables were safely stored away on pantry shelves, the sitting-room replaced the kitchen as main center of activities. Then through the winter evenings crochet hooks flew in and out of brightly colored silks and yarns, while rockers creaked and needles flashed and many a cushion top or washcloth, fancy apron or potholder destined to be bought by future guests took shape beneath the sisters' fingers.

Miss Lottie's special hobby until recently had been the sale of dahlia bulbs she raised herself, she said. Miss Emma, on the other hand, found outlet for her love of beauty in a rare collection of old buttons. Close to sixty thousand of them, ranging all the way from blown glass and cut steel to paperweight and silver lustre treasures, had been mounted neatly on the cards she proudly showed us. A member of the National Button Society and the Pennsylvania Dutch Button Club, she thoroughly enjoyed the fun of trading and comparing specimens with other members of those groups.

We marveled at the boundless energy responsible for all these varied enterprises as at last we bid our hostesses good-night and went upstairs. The country air had made us sleepy and we yawned in drowsy satisfaction as we slipped between our cool, fresh sheets. Miss Emma had assured us we could sleep late in the morning since the day was Sunday—but her definition of the word "late" evidently differed slightly from our own. For, promptly on the stroke of seven, we were wakened by the sound of thunderous music from the radio below (the customary rising signal in the Gable household). Our stifled moans of anguish faded into shamed activity, however, when we learned that all three sisters had been up and doing for at least an hour or more. Already there was bustling action in the kitchen, where preliminary preparations for the midday meal were getting under way.

With a wisdom born of recently acquired knowledge, we ate a very modest breakfast in anticipation of the dinner to be served at noon. And it was well we did. For when we sat down, with some twenty-two additional guests, to that "full" chicken dinner we'd been promised, our capacity was taxed to its elastic limit. The chicken, crisp and brown and tender, was of course the center of the menu—but a center almost lost in the abundance of surrounding dishes. A few repeats—the mashed potatoes and the candied sweets, the lima beans and (with a meaning glance in my direction from Miss Emma) the corn fritters—were among them. But such additional features as fried eggplant, cauliflower, apple fritters, coleslaw, buttered beets, and applesauce supplied a new and varied list for hardy appetites to sample. The apple fritters, though—to me, at least—proved the outstanding highlight of the whole Gargantuan repast. I'd thought those crisp and ravishing corn fritters of the night before the final word in eating, but this latest offering, golden brown and tempting, with a flavor delicate beyond compare—! I sighed and gave up all attempt to choose between the two. I had the recipe for one already, and perhaps a little later on, I thought, Miss Mollie would oblige me with the other. She did, explaining that the secret of their luscious savor lay in using Summer Rambo apples. This is how they're made:

APPLE FRITTERS

Cut each apple in four slices across and dip in the following batter:

1 egg	1 cup milk
1 tablespoon sugar	salt
1 teaspoon baking powder	flour

Beat the egg well, add the sugar and salt, then the milk alternately with the baking powder, which has been sifted into enough flour to make a heavy batter. Fry in lard ½ inch deep.

As special treat for Mabel and myself, a heavenly concoction known as "Amish pie" was served us as dessert, while other guests not quite so favored happily consumed the coconut custard pastry that we'd had the night before. The recipe for Amish pie, Miss Mollie told me, went like this:

AMISH PIE

¾ cup sugar	1 teaspoon vanilla
1 cup molasses	2 cups hot water
1 egg	3 tablespoons flour

Mix thoroughly all ingredients, boil the mixture till it thickens, then pour into 4 unbaked pie shells. Sprinkle on top crumbs made by rubbing through the hands the following:

1 cup flour	1 tablespoon lard and butter
½ cup sugar	½ teaspoon soda

To me that toothsome pastry—sheer ambrosia if I ever tasted any—proved the final, crowning touch that placed our week-end in the foremost rank of my most cherished recollection. For a rare adventure in the art of eating—and a shining sample of the kind of hospitality that's practised by the Pennsylvania Dutch—commend me to the Gable sisters and that peaceful little pocket in the hills of Pennsylvania Dutchland known as Waldeck Farm!

September

IT'S DONE WITH MIRRORS

IT WAS a gorgeous day, with a fresh breeze blowing steadily and everywhere you looked dark shadows standing out in sharp relief against the golden sunlight. Along the roadside huckleberry bushes and Virginia creeper, sassafras and dogwood branches all were turning red. In little country schoolrooms on the way to town I saw long rows of tin lunchboxes on the windowsills and heard the drone of childish voices telling to the world, reluctantly, that lesson time was here again. Yes, fall, I thought, was definitely on the way.

[63]

Before I turned the Rat toward home I stopped off for a little visit with a lady whom I'd never met before. She'd called me on the 'phone one day to tell me that she thought I might be interested in two old mirrors that she owned. Wouldn't I like to stop and see them next time that I came to town, she'd asked?

And so I did—and she was right! They certainly do interest me. Her ancient relics, as it turned out, were *Erdspiegel*—mirrors used by superstitious people to locate all sorts of treasure hidden in the earth. (That's why they're called *Erdspiegel*, which is German for "earth mirrors.") Naturally, they're magic implements, and anyone who knows just how to handle them can learn all sorts of useful secrets—like the name of his most deadly enemy, or who *ferhext* his cattle, or where Grandpop hid the family silver, or other fascinating little items of the kind.

The owner of the two *Erdspiegel*, Mrs. Erdman, told me they'd belonged originally to her father and grandfather. Often as a little girl, she said, she'd seen the two men start out in the evening from their home near Reading, sitting in the old spring wagon with the iron box that held the mirrors laid tenderly across their knees. It had to be a *"dunkle, dunkle Nacht"* (a dark, dark night), she said, without a trace of moon or stars to light the distant hills. And as they started off, her mother always wept and pleaded with them not to go, thus planting firmly in her daughter's mind the thought of something dark and dangerous and malign connected with their little journeys. They'd be away all night, my new friend told me, and when finally they got back on the following morning, they'd conceal the two *Erdspiegel* in a secret hiding-place and never tell their womenfolks just where they'd been or what they'd been about. But, Mrs. Erdman added, she was sure they'd visited the mountains back of Reading where, supposedly, large hoards of gold and silver had been buried during Civil War alarms.

For almost an hour we pored eagerly above the ancient relics.

The larger one, rectangular in shape, with fluted edge and metal handle, was a mirror of the hand variety. The other, almost square and somewhat smaller, had two separate parts that hinged together like a little book. The quicksilver on the back of each was much the worse for wear, but sometime, somehow, in the dim and distant past a dozen mystic words and letters had been scrawled upon it—scrawled with something sharp and pointed, evidently. The years, of course, had made the letters faint and hard to read, almost impossible to disentangle from the little lines and blotches that old mirrors always seem to have. But—there they were. There wasn't any doubt that they *were* words. But *what* words? How to separate them from the spots and scratches all around?

Try as we would, we had no luck at all—the lettering still eluded us. And finally my hostess heaved a sigh and gave up in defeat.

"Why don't you take the mirrors home with you?" she offered trustingly. "Perhaps when you have plenty of time to give them, you can figure out just what the letters really are."

And so I did as she suggested. All one evening I spent struggling with my newest acquisition, using up a lot of patience, and a lot of eyesight, too. But it was worth it. For I made a real discovery! By holding the folding mirror to the light in such a way that one side was reflected in the other, I made out that both *Erdspiegel* had the selfsame letters on them. In the center of the larger one, however, was a five-point star surrounded by the three words: *Heilig, heilig, heilig* (Holy, holy, holy). The smaller mirror had no star, but the letters scratched across it were a repetition of the letters on the other one. And here they are:

> S Solam
> S Tattler
> Echogartner
> Gematar

A magic formula of some sort—there could be no doubt about it! But, how, I wondered, was I going to find out what it meant?

THE MYSTERY DEEPENS

THE plot was thickening! I'd discovered someone who knew something about magic mirrors. Not too much, unfortunately, but enough to cheer me on the search for knowledge that began when Mrs. Erdman hopefully entrusted me with her *Erdspiegel*.

The gentleman who gave me new incentive was no less an expert on occult goings on than my old powwow doctor friend, Grandpappy. I've paid Grandpappy several visits since the day I first became acquainted with his supernatural powers,* and he never fails me when it comes to handing out amazing bits of lore about the spells of witches and unearthly incidents in general. So it struck me suddenly that he was just the one to tell me what the lettering on my magic mirrors meant!

I found my white-haired connoisseur of witchcraft sitting in his workshop, with an oil stove burning cozily beside him and a cuspidor, as usual, standing within easy range. His hands were busy with an intricate and quite impressive-looking wooden lamp —which called to mind the fact that, in addition to his talents as a powwow artist, Grandpappy is a very clever cabinetmaker on the side. No matter where you look, his house is always full of chairs and clocks and chests and various other articles that prove his skill.

In younger days, I've heard it said, he also went in for inventing. His most spectacular contrivance was a railroad coupler, but he never made a penny from it, I've been told. It seems he showed it trustingly to certain city gentlemen one day—and shortly afterward another coupler which included all the new and special fea-

* See Chapter III, *Hex Marks the Spot*, by Ann Hark.

tures of his own made its appearance on the market. Which simply goes to show the depths that certain city slickers will descend to!

Grandpappy looked up vaguely from his labors as I entered. Though he never seems to know me from one visit to the next, he always winks at me on general principles. I wink back sociably, of course.

"Look!" I began without preamble, and untangled Mrs. Erdman's mirrors from the swaddling clothes in which I kept them. Eagerly I poked them underneath his nose.

The bearded little brownie on his high, round stool looked mildly interested. With eyes a trifle bleared by age, but guiltless still of spectacles, he peered intently at my two *Erdspiegel.*

"See!" I pointed to the mystic lettering. "Can you tell me what this magic writing means?"

Grandpappy shook his head and aimed a stream of dark brown liquid at the cuspidor. No, he replied, he'd never seen a mirror of that kind before. But still—he thought a moment silently— he'd heard of them. Yes, he remembered now! A fellow once had even told him how you made one! First, it seems, you have to find a crossroads. Not just any ordinary crossroads, either, but a real right-angle one. Then— Suddenly Grandpappy stopped. Perhaps he couldn't quite remember what the "fellow" had said next —or maybe he decided that the knowledge wasn't for a layman's ears. At any rate, he handed both the mirrors back to me. His air was that of one no longer interested.

"Yes, well!" he muttered thoughtfully. "I knew a fellow onct that had an earth glass. When you looked in it, you put a black cloth on your head like a photographer's. (Grandpappy pronounced it *pho*tographer's.) "Onct there was a man near Newmanstown whose barn burned down, and so he went to see this man that had the glass, to find out who'd set fire to his barn. He put the black cloth on his head and looked right in the glass, and

there he seen his house. So he looked and looked some more, and
pretty soon he seen his barn, and from the barn a little thread
of smoke was coming out. And then he seen a man jump out the
window, climb the fence, and run away! That man," Grandpappy
finished darkly, "was his neighbor!"

With a practised twist, he shifted his tobacco quid and spat
again. "Now, if only someone else had looked in that there glass
and seen it, too," he added, "he'd of had a witness! Then he
could of gone to court and proved his neighbor done it all!"

Grandpappy's reasoning seemed a bit obscure to me, but I decided not to press the point. "Do you know what other things,"
I asked, "can be discovered with a glass like this?"

He nodded. Sure—he knew of people who'd found money with
them. Only finding it, it seems, is fairly easy—holding on to it
is something else again. Unless you follow out a certain set of
rules, Grandpappy said, you lose the money in the end. For instance, first of all you have to make a cross above the spot that
holds the hidden gold. You do this just exactly on the stroke of
noon, he added. Then, in the very center of the cross you make
a little hole, and when the sun shines down directly in the cavity
you start to dig. But the most important thing to keep in mind is
not to say a single word throughout the whole procedure.

"I knew three fellows onct," Grandpappy illustrated, "who
found a place where money had been hid. They dug and dug,
and finally their picks struck something hard, and they began to
pull at it with all their might. They pulled and pulled, but still
they couldn't pull it out, so one of the fellows motioned to the
others with his pick to pull a little harder yet. But that there
wasn't right!" My powwow doctor's beard wagged to and fro in
emphasis. "The spirits held on after that and wouldn't let it go.
And so it sank back in the ground again, and the fellows didn't
get it!"

"But they didn't *talk!*" I said in some confusion.

"Yes, well!" Grandpappy granted that. But still, the gesture with the pick was strictly out of order, he insisted. Making motions evidently means the same to spirits as the use of words—you've got to play the game according to the rules or not at all.

The little story had apparently touched off a train of thought in my instructor's mind. His blue eyes peered at me intently now. He raised a warning finger. "If you see a fire burning on the ground somewhere," he said, "and don't know where it comes from, then you know for sure there's money buried at that spot! My uncle's wife seen such a fire burning in a corner of the hayfield onct. She didn't tell her husband right away, though, and he blamed her awful for it. '*Ach*, you should of called me, Sal!' he said. 'Then I'd of come and throwed my coat on it and we'd of had the money!' "

A trifle dazed by this peculiar tale, I pondered deeply for a moment. "You mean that if you throw a piece of clothing on the fire, then the spirits have to let the money go?" I asked.

Yes, that was it, it seemed. But still, not *any* piece of clothing, either. A coat or vest was perfectly all right, Grandpappy said, but not a shirt. From which I gathered that it had to be a garment not worn next the skin.

"How do you know so much about these things?" I asked.

Grandpappy grinned a toothless grin. "I know a lot of things!" he told me meaningly. "For sixty-five years now I been powwowing, and I know a lot more than the doctors do! If people only come to me, I fix them! But instead, they go to doctors and they keep their troubles. Yes—" he nodded wisely—"if they come to me I cure them! And I fix it, too," he added with a crafty wink, "so you can win a lawsuit, even!"

But I hadn't any lawsuit on my hands—the only thing I had was two *Erdspiegel* with some cryptic lettering scratched across their backs. So, since my powwow friend in spite of all his supernatural knowledge couldn't tell me what that writing meant, I said good-bye and took myself away.

It looked as though I'd have to find the answer to my riddle in some other field.

SIDETRACKED

I'M not a thing if not persistent. So—I took my two *Erdspiegel* to another expert. Not a powwow doctor this time, but a gentleman whose knowledge of the Pennsylvania Dutch should certainly, I thought, include a gem or two about the subject that was fast becoming an obsession with me.

Mr. H. K. Landis and his brother George are guardians of a treasure-trove of Pennsylvania Dutch antiques that's probably the largest in the country. For more than a quarter of a century they've been gathering it together—from country sales and private homes and various other sources. Almost every day sees some addition to the huge collection that began inside their home, then spread out to the nearest barn, and finally from there to several other buildings.

The elder Landis—or *der Grosser Henner* (fat Henry), as he's better known around the country—has a slogan that he's very fond of quoting. "To have something you can do when you stop work, and something you can do it *with*—that's satisfaction!" And *der Grosser Henner* really has it—there's no doubt of that. The job of studying and tabulating all that wealth of rich material there at Landis Valley is enough to keep not two but half a dozen brothers satisfied and busy all their lives.

I'd visited this place of theirs quite often, but till now I'd never taken time out for a really thorough tour. As usual, I was there on a specific errand—my *Erdspiegel*—but for once, I thought, it wouldn't do a bit of harm to get some extra education on the side. However, first I had to find out if *der Henner* couldn't help me solve the puzzle of my mirrors. So I got them out and laid them on a rustic table underneath the maple trees that shade the Landis lawn. The leaves had started falling, and the sunshine filtering through the semi-naked branches struck our heads with pleasant warmth as we bent earnestly above my prizes. Once again I pointed to the words that baffled me—and waited.

The keen eyes of my host lit up with interest, and he nodded slowly. Yes, there wasn't any doubt about it, he declared—these certainly were magic mirrors! He'd seen and heard of others like them, but he couldn't quite remember where or when.

"And did they have this sort of lettering on them?" I inquired. *Der Grosser Henner* shook his head. No, there was nothing in the way of writing—he was sure of that.

"You mean you never saw these words before?" I persevered. "You haven't any idea what they stand for?"

Again he shook his head. "They might mean almost anything," he said. "Let's see now!" He picked up paper and a pencil from the table. "I'll write them down so we can see exactly what they are. Then maybe we can figure out some plausible interpretation."

Slowly and clearly, taking pains to add the five-point star appearing on the larger mirror and the *Heilig, heilig, heilig* that surrounded it, he copied down the words. In silence we both studied them intently.

"Now, let me see—'*S Solam*' and '*S Tattler*.' " I was thinking deeply. "Could it be—?" I hesitated. "Could the *S* be an abbreviation for the title Saint, perhaps?"

The gentleman across from me looked skeptical. "Saint Solam and Saint Tattler?" he repeated. "Well, I never *heard* of any saints named that. However—" and he chuckled—"in the olden days handwriting wasn't very accurate, you know. They used their capitals in odd and unexpected places, and their spelling wasn't all it should have been, besides. For instance—" and he pointed to the second row of letters—"take *S Tattler*, now. It might be just one word, of course, instead of two. *Statt* is Pennsylvania

Dutch for 'town' or 'city,' and so *Stattler* might be 'city dweller.' "

"And *S Solam?* What would that mean?" I was suddenly excited. Was it possible the trail was getting warmer? "Could it be a man's name, do you think?" I asked. "And *Echogartner—? Eck* means 'corner,' doesn't it? And *Gartner*—could that be a misspelled version of the German *Garten?*"

Almost as excited as myself, my fellow sleuth looked up. "Why not?" he asked significantly.

"And how about *Gematar?*" Suddenly my mind flashed back to certain ancient tombstones that I'd studied in deserted graveyards. Several, I remembered, bore the line, *Gemordet von Wilden* (Murdered by the savages). "*Gemordet—Gematar?*" I pronounced the words aloud. "Could they, perhaps, bear some relation to each other?"

Mr. Landis nodded. "It's possible," he said. "Allowing for the carelessness of spelling and pronunciation both."

"We've got it, then!" I gloated. " 'S. Solam, city dweller, murdered in a corner of the garden.' Only—" and my face fell suddenly—"just why would anybody write that on a *mirror?*"

There was a little pause. I shook my head at last, reluctantly. "It doesn't make so much sense, after all, I guess."

My host apparently agreed. "Well," he consoled, "we'll keep it as a *possible* solution, anyway!"

Approaching footsteps on the lawn distracted us at this point. When I'd first arrived, George Landis had been absent—tracking down, no doubt, some new addition to the multitude of articles inside the house. He joined us now and we included him in our debate. But one look at my two *Erdspiegel* was enough. He shook his head. Those mystic words were something that he'd never seen before, he said, although of course he'd heard of magic mirrors of the kind. "Where are the bags?" he added curiously.

"What bags?" I asked.

Der Henner came to my assistance. "These *Erdspiegel*," he explained, "are usually accompanied by a bag or cloth of dark material. When a person wants to find the answer to a question, he puts the mirror in the bottom of the bag and sticks his head in after it. The cloth, of course, keeps out the light—except the little bit that seeps in near the top."

So this, I thought, was what Grandpappy had referred to when he spoke of that black "*pho*tographer's cloth"!

"Within the semi-darkness of the bag," *der Henner* went on, "the inquiring person peers into the glass' depths. And, if he keeps on peering long enough, he starts imagining that he sees things there—the things, of course, that he's been hoping and expecting that he'll see."

"I heard a story once," the younger brother put in suddenly, "about a man who found out with a magic mirror where some gold was buried. So, with a friend of his, he went there at the stroke of midnight and began to dig, and pretty soon they struck a heavy box. 'We've got it!' one of them exclaimed excitedly. 'Now we'll be rich!' But even as he said it, a terrific crashing sounded in the woods near by, and out came plunging a huge animal that leaped into the hole they'd dug—and box and animal together sank back into the ground!" He laughed. "You see, the man had broken one of the most vital rules of these performances. You're not supposed to talk at all while digging. So of course the Devil, in the form of the huge animal, rushed out to claim the gold himself!"

I thought again of Grandpappy and the similar tale *he*'d told. Apparently these various stories have some bearing on each other. Whether noon or midnight is the proper time for digging, whether His Satanic Majesty or some less sovereign spirit guards the treasure, doesn't seem to matter much—the main point, evidently, is to hold your tongue!

Well, it was interesting, of course, but still—it threw no light whatever on the riddle that I'd come to solve. Perhaps, I thought, it might be well to turn my mind to something else. The contents of the Landis house and barns, for instance.

So I asked permission to go through them, and *der Henner* with his usual willingness said he'd escort me personally from place to place. We started in the house—a house completely crammed with objects of the sort to make an antique dealer tear his hair with envy. First, the red ware—earthen plates and jars and crocks and other vessels made of red clay from the hills of Pennsylvania. Wavy lines of yellow slip in rows of three adorned the pie plates, and my guide called my attention to them with a Pennsylvania German proverb: *Alle gute Dinge drei* (All good things come in threes).

There was *Sgraffito*, also, in abundance—that particular variety of slipware that's engraved or scratched instead of traced or painted. And long shelves of china—spatter, lustre, ironstone, and Gaudy Dutch—plus endless other types beyond my meagre knowledge to identify. I picked out with especial interest one small spatter plate reposing in the midst of several lustre pitchers —silver, copper, pink, and lavender—because it bore a six-point star of red and blue and green exactly like those baffling symbols that I'd seen so often on my favorite barns.

I turned away at last from the Dutch cupboard housing this amazing wealth of chinaware, and found myself confronting an old walnut dresser with the slots along the front edge of its shelves containing an array of ancient brass and pewter spoons. More china loomed behind them, and on the bottom shelf a pile of painted wooden boxes that had once held spices, pepper, salt, and other kitchen condiments.

"Lehn ware," my guide explained the latter. "Made by Joseph Lehn, a Lititz farmer, in the 1880's. Lehn got tired of farming, so he set up in his home a little workshop and equipped it with a wooden lathe. He started making decorated ware like this, and later on, when he became successful, people got to copying him."

Not far away there stood a table crowded to capacity with tôleware—gaily painted canisters and pitchers, coffeepots and fruit trays, tall, lipped measures and small lidded chests of untinned iron. Next came ABC plates for the children, with their Franklin proverbs in the center and their alphabets around the edge, then delicate waxed flowers under rounded domes of glass, and endless flasks of every size and shape conceivable.

The room next door was filled with furniture—all reminiscent of those thrifty years when articles were made to last not for a lifetime merely but for generations. Several antique stools, a solid walnut corner cupboard, three or four settees of varying designs and woods, a Windsor chair with broad "cheese cutter" rockers— these stood out among the rest with quaint appeal.

Shelf after shelf of pewter lined the walls of still another room —dull-gleaming plates and coffeepots, old candlesticks and lamps and ladles, spoons and bowls—a vast array of objects such as any connoisseur would give his very soul to own. I saw old mirrors, too, with painted scenes across the top, a shaving mug of red ware made with two compartments, one for soap and one for water, patchwork quilts and woven spreads galore, long-barreled guns, and pistols by the dozen. We went upstairs and found large desks and drawers and shelves and boxes filled to overflowing with all sorts of books and manuscripts—*Geburts und Taufscheine* (birth and baptism certificates), *Himmelsbriefe* (letters from heaven), almanacs, *Haus Segen* (house blessings), and all sorts of other documents.

By this time I was slightly dizzy—and we hadn't even reached the barn! Long since I'd given up all effort to express my feelings, and at last, completely dazed, I followed close at Mr. Landis' heels across the yard and toward a building on the left. We started up a flight of steps—and for the dozenth time I gasped incredulously. On the wall beside us hung a cumulation of wrought-iron hardware that would tempt the honesty of any expert. It included locks and keys of all descriptions, toolbox lids from Conestoga wagons, with their hasps and hinges delicately wrought in tulip shape, door handles with that same beloved flower of the Pennsylvania Dutch adorning them, axe sockets, two in fish design, and various other samples of the ironmaster's art too numerous to list. What wouldn't I give, I thought, for two of those strap hinges ending in a three-point tulip, to replace the broken ones on my old bedroom chest!

We mounted to the second floor, and I discarded altogether my attempts to keep a mental record of this huge collection. It simply wasn't possible! For there before me all the riches of the ages seemed to be spread out—including everything that ever had to do with Pennsylvania German life. I saw a vast array of iron pots and trivets, wooden barrel scoops and shovels, candlemolds, and early basketry in fascinating shapes. I saw tin lanterns punched in decorative patterns, and large cabbage slicers made of wood, with heart-shaped fingerholds cut in the handles. There were wafer irons with long hafts that measured three feet at the very least, and cookie cutters one of which, for gingerbread, was fashioned like a man and all of two feet high, with others in the forms of animals and tulips, hearts and birds and stars, and various other shapes.

Then, there was stoneware—gray, with deep blue decorations. And additional red-ware butter crocks and pitchers, flowerpots, tobacco jars and pie plates, sugar pots and mugs and baking dishes. There were even cuspidors, and one strange-looking vessel which, I learned, was meant for catching roaches. First, my guide explained, the insects crawled along the inside till they reached the top, then slipped down through a cleverly provided hole to find a watery grave inside the jar.

Grandfathers' clocks of various types and dates were also there, as well as powder kegs and water kegs, spinning wheels and iron fishing gigs, bellows for the fireplace, hearth brushes, wood and iron tools of every possible design. And, lining all the walls and piled up on the floor, huge stacks of books—a trifling twenty thousand of them, I believe my pilot said.

Farm implements had been collected in another barn, with a towering Conestoga wagon in the place of honor. Its twelve-ribbed top and high, red wheels, its boat-shaped body painted the inevitable blue, its toolbox at the side and feedbox at the rear, brought back an old-time scene that needed only half a dozen stalwart horses and a booted, stogie-smoking driver to complete the picture.

Next door another barn held stoves and stoveplates of all types and periods. There were cannon stoves and ten-plate stoves and Franklin stoves and various others that escaped the somewhat glassy stare I turned in their direction. For my powers of observation weren't as keen and penetrating as they'd been to start with. Still, a stoveplate dated 1769 and manufactured by the famous ironmaster, Henry William Stiegel, founder of the town of Manheim and maker of the marvelous glassware that still bears his name, did manage somehow to impress me. I noted, too, the date of 1726 on still another plate—the oldest made in this part of the world as far as known, *der Henner* told me.

I staggered out at last, replete with knowledge but a bit befuddled by the generous dosage given. Patsy, waiting patiently inside the Rat, jumped out to greet me and exchange a wary sniff with Mr. Landis' dog. The latter's name is *Wasser* (Water), chosen by his master with deliberate cunning. For everybody knows, of course, that *Hexe* (witches) love to weave their evil spells around a farmer's barns, and only water somewhere on the premises can frighten them away. So—*Wasser* keeps the witches from the Landis barns.

I said good-bye eventually, attempting rather lamely, I'm afraid, to voice my thanks. Of course, I hadn't gotten what I came for—the inscription on my mirrors still remained a mystery.

But I'd gotten such a wealth of other information that the matter didn't seem so vital at the moment as it had before.

Besides, I still could take them to some other expert for deciphering!

ANOTHER DISAPPOINTMENT

So FAR I'd gotten just exactly nowhere in my quest for information. But despite that fact, the only thing in all the world that really held my interest was those baffling, maddening, altogether fascinating mirrors. My avid curiosity had proved a trifle hard on my Chauffeur, however, and at last he took a stand.

"Come on!" he said in a tone that brooked no opposition on my part. "We're going to find out *some*thing on the subject of those mirrors if it takes all day! You haven't been to see your favorite expert yet, you know. Jump in the car—we're on our way!"

Far be it from me to argue when he talks like that—especially when the thing he's set his mind on happens to be exactly what I want myself. So off we started. The afternoon was warm and balmy—one of those leftover days from summer when the sun and air and temperature all get together in a little game to prove the calendar is wrong. The sound of thunder rumbling in the distance had been followed earlier by gentle rain that misted the far hills and spattered on the shiny surface of the lake like little pebbles. It passed, however, leaving in its wake an intermittent breeze that ruffled softly through the trees and made small, dancing ripples on the water.

The sweet-gum tree beside my little house was wholly colored now—a soft and dusty brick. The oak was gorgeous in a mottled dress of green and crimson, and across the lake the meadow grass had taken on a pinkish hue. Along the roadside goldenrod and asters were in full possession, and the dogwood leaves, already tinged with red, were speckled lavishly with tiny scarlet beads.

The road we traveled ran beneath the shadow of the hills—my beautiful blue hills that now had suddenly become a changing tapestry of green and red and gold, forerunner of the greater glory yet to come. They separated at one point, and through the gap we came out on a vista soft and lovely as an old oil painting. There before us stretched out hills and still more hills—those hills of Pennsylvania Dutchland which to me spell home and all the sweet content that word implies. What other land can still the heart and fill the soul with such a glowing warmth of satisfaction?

We reached the outskirts of the city, and I roused from my delicious torpor. This was where my favorite expert lived—a gentleman whose knowledge of things Pennsylvania Dutch had always left me humble and abashed at such a treasure store of learning. Surely, I thought, *he* wouldn't fail me like the others had!

With both *Erdspiegel* cradled gently in my arms, I followed at the heels of my Chauffeur as he alighted, and together we advanced upon my expert's door. As usual, he received us cordially. With a twinkle in his eye at my excitement, he watched attentively as I unwrapped my baffling treasures. A friend of his who'd dropped in just before us—quite apparently a Pennsylvania Dutchman by his accent—also seemed intrigued. Both bent above the mirrors silently, and my Chauffeur and I forgot to breathe.

At last they straightened up. "Most interesting!" my expert murmured. "They're the first I've ever seen!"

"Me, too!" his friend put in. "Although I've heard of them, of course."

Our white-haired host inclined his head. "Of course!" he said. "*Erdspiegel*, like the semaphora or divining-rod, were widely used among the superstitious—and still are today, I wouldn't doubt."

The other chuckled. "Well," he said, "I've never seen a mirror used. But a divining-rod—!" He laughed again and leaned back in his chair. I sensed a story coming and pricked up my ears.

"Some years ago I bought a farm not far from here," the gentleman began. "I had to have a well, of course, but didn't know just where to dig it. So when suddenly a man appeared with a divining-rod one day and told me he'd locate some water for me, I agreed to let him go ahead." He stopped and looked at my Chauffeur and me. "You know what a divining-rod is like?" he asked.

We nodded, somewhat doubtfully. "I've *heard* of them," I said.

"Well, a divining-rod," he told us, "is a V-shaped twig or branch cut from a tree or bush. It's got to be a hazel, or a cherry, or a white-thorn branch of this year's growth, remember, and each arm has got to be about a foot in length. The man who operates it holds a section of the V in either hand, with the long, straight handle upright. He paces back and forth, and when the handle starts to move and turn till finally it's pointing downward, then he knows there's water at that spot—or possibly a lode of ore."

He looked at us to see if we were following his description, and we nodded eagerly.

"Well, anyway," he went on, "this man walked around my farm with his divining-rod until it started to turn downward. Then he stopped. He asked me for a glass half full of water, and I fetched it for him. Then he took a button from his pocket —just an ordinary button made of brass, that had a red silk string attached to it. He dangled it inside the glass above the water line, and after several minutes, suddenly, to my surprise, I heard the button tinkle on the glass. His hand was very steady— I took special note of that. It didn't move a fraction of an inch, I'm sure. But the button waggled back and forth, back and forth, and as it hit the glass each time he started counting. Every stroke, he said, meant one more foot I'd had to dig my well before I came to water."

"And how often did it hit the glass?" I asked.

"Exactly forty-three times!"

"Did you dig that many feet?"

He nodded solemnly. "We came to water just six inches from the depth he'd said!"

We all laughed simultaneously, the teller of the tale as heartily as any of us. But deep down in his eyes I glimpsed a silent and uncertain question—that same question which I've seen so often in the eyes of other scoffers at occult beliefs. "All foolishness!" they always say. "It's pure coincidence, of course!" Yet in the mind of each I sense a lurking doubt that still persists in spite of everything.

I brought the conversation back to my *Erdspiegel*. After all, divining-rods, though fascinating in their implications, threw no light whatever on the puzzle that we'd come so far to have explained. "These letters on my magic mirrors," I reminded our politely listening host. "Have you a theory as to what they possibly can mean?"

He smiled—the slow and philosophic smile of one who's grown accustomed to the unexplainable. "A theory—yes," he said. "But only that. I have no real solution to your mystery, I'm afraid. But this much I can tell you: Back in olden times, when necromancy and black magic flourished and the ignorant were preyed upon by those more highly lettered, charms and incantations were the order of the day. The wise men who dispensed them—at so much per charm, of course—were learned priests, well-versed in Latin, who would use that language as a mask to guard the secret meaning, or perhaps the lack of meaning, of the hocus-pocus that they handed out. For mystery was their stock-in-trade, you know —the more mysterious their weird spells and exorcisms were, the more the dupes who bought them were impressed.

"At times," he went on, "to conceal their sense, if any, more completely still, they'd use a species of hog Latin for their little runes and talismans. And sometimes, just to make assurance doubly sure, they'd use abbreviations, too." He pointed to the smaller of the two *Erdspiegel*. "This S *Solam*, now," he said, "and this S *Tattler*. It's quite possible they don't mean anything at all, you know—just cabalistic jargon purposely designed to fool the simple-minded. And I must admit," he added with a smile at my disgruntled face, "that's what I think this writing really is!"

I sighed profoundly. What an unromantic ending to my quest! Just random words and letters scribbled by a medieval faker, with no awe-inspiring message locked within their wavering lines! I didn't even try to hide my disappointment as I said good-bye. Sadly I reached out for my mirrors and returned them to their wraps. Dejectedly I rose to go. Our host smiled after us apologetically as he watched us out of sight.

It certainly was most discouraging. I couldn't merely brush aside my expert's theory—it sounded far too plausible. And yet— He'd said it was a theory only, hadn't he? Well, then—he *could* be wrong! And if he were? Well, if he were, the answer to my riddle still remained to be tracked down!

AT LAST A CLUE!

As IF to spur me on in my renewed endeavors, the next day brought a real discovery.

As a last resort I'd started leafing through the pages of Albertus Magnus' book of dark and dire magic called *Egyptian Secrets*, one of three such esoteric works that superstitious Pennsylvania Germans used to set great store by in the olden days—and still do, possibly, in certain quarters. I have all three of them—the *Sixth and Seventh Books of Moses*, John George Hohman's *Long Lost Friend*, and Albertus' little work entitled modestly:

ALBERTUS MAGNUS

Being the Approved, Verified, Sympathetic and Natural
EGYPTIAN SECRETS
or
WHITE AND BLACK ART, FOR MAN AND BEAST
*The Book of Nature and the Hidden Secrets and
Mysteries of Life Unveiled; Being the*
FORBIDDEN KNOWLEDGE OF ANCIENT PHILOSOPHERS.
*By that celebrated Student, Philosopher, Chemist, Naturalist,
Psychomist, Astrologer, Alchemist, Metallurgist, Sorcerer, Ex-
planator of the Mysteries of Wizards and Witchcraft; to-
gether with recondite Views of numerous Arts and Sciences
—Obscure, Plain, Practical, etc.*

Surely, I thought, a gentleman as versatile and learned as this
famous thirteenth century monk should offer something helpful
in the way of solving riddles!

And suddenly, between two pleasant little remedies—"To Fix
a Thief" and "When a Person has taken a Fatal Step, how to
Help and Alleviate"—I came upon these thrilling words: "To
Make a Mirror in which Everything may be Discerned." I gasped
in real excitement. "To make a Mirror—!" Could it really be—?
I read on breathlessly:

Procure a looking glass, such as are commonly sold. Inscribe
the characters noted below upon it. Inter it on the crossing of
two pathways, during an uneven hour. On the third day thereafter, hie to the place at the same hour, and take it out: but you
must not be the first person to look into the glass. It is best to
let a dog or cat take the first look into the mirror.

And then—my heart stopped beating almost—at the bottom of
the page I read these magic words, now so familiar to me:

S. Solam   S. Tattler   S. Echogardner   Gematar.

The self-same words inscribed on my *Erdspiegel!*

I read them over carefully. Of course, the *d* in *Echogardner* was a *t* on Mrs. Erdman's ancient treasures, and there wasn't any *S* before the word. But why be fussy? After all, in old-time German writing *d*'s and *t*'s were practically interchangeable. The missing *S*, I reassured myself, had no doubt been obliterated by the wear and tear of years. So actually—at last—it seemed as though I'd come upon the answer to my tantalizing problem!

It seemed that way, at least, until I read on further—only to discover that Albertus hadn't bothered to explain the meaning of his magic formula. And so I found myself no wiser than I'd been before! But still, I thought, I *had* learned something. For I knew now how to make a mirror. And perhaps such ordinary mortals as myself weren't *meant* to understand the cryptic words that gave them their mysterious power. In fact, another horrid thought occurred to me. Perhaps my favorite expert on these things was right—Albertus and his brethren might deliberately, with tongue in cheek, have made up such high-sounding jargon just to fool poor, trusting souls like me!

The whole thing was a bit confusing. Somehow, I could feel my pristine faith in being able finally to reach a definite solution fading miserably away. Could I be wrong? Perhaps there *wasn't* any answer, to my riddle, after all!

THE PLOT THICKENS

AND then my cleaning woman, Mrs. Nissley, paid her weekly visit and let drop a piece of news that sent my hopes of finding out the whys and wherefores of my magic mirrors soaring once again. A few days back, she said, an old man had turned up at her house with the startling information that he knew where $18,000 had been buried on her property! He'd seen the pot containing it, he said, in "such a glass"—meaning, of course, a mirror—and the pot was buried underneath the lilac bush beside the Nissleys' porch. If they'd agree to let him dig it up, he said, he'd share the money with them and they'd all be rich for life.

"He's coming back a little later on—some evening when the moon's just right," my cleaning woman told me. She laughed indulgently and let the matter drop. Apparently she had no further interest in the stranger and his weird disclosure.

But *I* had. The old man evidently owned a magic mirror, and I wanted to find out if it were anything like Mrs. Erdman's. So I asked his name and where he lived, and just as soon as possible I went to see him, with the two mirrors tucked beneath my arm as an excuse.

To my surprise, the gentleman seemed only mildly interested in my *Erdspiegel*. No, he'd never seen a mirror like them, he admitted, and he didn't have the least idea of what the lettering on them meant. *His* mirror, now, was dark, he said. (And incidentally, it turned out it wasn't really his, but had been lent him by a friend.) At my request, a bit reluctantly, he got it out and showed it to me. At first glance it was a little disappointing, for it wasn't actually a mirror but a double piece of glass, rectangular in shape, about six inches long, and bound together by a metal frame. In fact, it looked more like a photographic plate that's been exposed to light than like a mirror—and it had no lettering on it whatsoever.

I asked him how he knew the $18,000 lay beneath my cleaning woman's lilac bush. He smiled complacently. "I seen it in the glass!" he said.

"But *I* can't see a thing when I look in it!" I objected.

Well, it had to be a dark, dark night, it seemed—the darker night the better. And besides, a woman friend of his, now dead, had told him all about the hidden money. Her grandpop once had owned the Nissley farm, he said, and it was he who'd dug beneath the lilac bush and stowed away the cash to keep it safe for her until she came of age.

The old man seemed to get more friendly as his little tale progressed. There was a right way and a wrong way when it came to burying money, he informed me solemnly. The right way was to put a "seal" upon it by reciting certain magic words. Then, if a body should attempt to dig it up, the spirits would get after him. "You'd see the Devil and all sorts of things!" he added grimly. But if you'd hold another "seal," passed on to you for that especial purpose, tightly in your hand while you were digging, then you'd be quite safe from any sort of harm.

"And have you got the seal?" I asked in some anxiety. He seemed a nice old soul—I didn't like to think of his succumbing to the powers of the Devil.

He nodded cheerfully. Oh, yes—his friend, he said, had never bothered to dig up the money. She didn't need it (lucky friend!), so when she died three years ago she'd passed the secret on to him. Just why he'd waited all this time before deciding that the gold should be unearthed was something that he failed to tell me.

I asked him next about the proper time for digging. Should you start at midnight, or exactly on the stroke of noon? Grandpappy, I remembered, had insisted that it must be midday, while the story Mr. Landis had related seemed to indicate that midnight was the witching hour. Apparently, however, you can take your choice. It doesn't really matter when you start, the old man said.

"And will *you* start soon?" I queried boldly.

He hesitated for a moment, and then shook his head. He didn't know right just *how* soon, he answered. He might start tomorrow evening, maybe—and perhaps he mightn't, either. His rheumatism got him pretty bad sometimes—especially when he worked out on the road.

I took a deep breath. "When you do," I said persuasively, "perhaps you'll let me come and watch you? I've never seen a pot of gold unearthed!"

He hesitated once again. "Yes, well!" he said at last, resignedly. "I guess it won't hurt none! Remember, though—" he shook a wavering finger underneath my nose—"you ain't to do much talking—and especially no high language!"

So I promised that I'd make a noble effort to refrain from swearing, and betook myself away. I told the Nissleys to be sure to call me just as soon as he appeared, so I could rush right over and be present at the fateful moment when a fortune was unloaded in their laps. The only thing remaining, then, was simply to possess my soul in patience till the happy day arrived.

But still, I wondered, would he ever actually show up? To be quite honest, I was getting just a trifle skeptical. My early optimism on the general subject of *Erdspiegel* wasn't what it once had been!

DEAD END

I THINK I'll write a book some day and give it the dramatic title of "The Mirrors' Dire Secret"—or perhaps "The Great *Erdspiegel* Mystery." For that's exactly what it has remained—a mystery as deep and dark and dire as on that first day when I started out so hopefully to find the answer to the riddle they contain.

I played my last card in the little game with something less than my original confidence. I went to see the owner of the mirror in which Mrs. Nissley's caller spied that $18,000 underneath her lilac bush. Of course I took my two *Erdspiegel* with me, in the weary hope that this new gentleman *might* prove to be the person I'd been looking for.

He wasn't. One glance at the mirrors was enough to prove it to us both. So, as the next best thing I started asking him about his own *Erdspiegel*. Just at first he seemed a little loath to talk. But my persistent interest in the subject wore him down at last, and soon we were discussing various phases of occult affairs quite sociably.

The facts I gleaned, however, didn't always tally with the ones his friend had given me. Both were agreed the proper time to use a magic mirror is at night—a dark and moonless night, at that. And both were definite about the veto on "high" language (swearing). But my second host was sure that there should be no talking whatsoever while the treasure digging was in progress. And the diggers mustn't say a word until they'd made it safely back inside their own front door. "The Old Fellow," as he warily alluded to the Devil, followed you the whole way home, it seemed, and not until you'd shut the door behind you dared you speak a word without the danger of his snatching back the money that you'd wrested from his grasp.

I asked my new acquaintance if the mirrors could be used for other things than finding money. If you had an enemy, for instance, or had lost a certain object, could you find out from the glass just who or where they were? Unlike Grandpappy, whose intriguing story of the man whose barn had burned down seemed to signify you could, he shook his head. No, money was the only thing he'd ever heard the mirrors could locate, he told me.

I asked him next about the placing of a "seal" upon the buried treasure, and this time he went along with what the other man had said. In fact, he went still further—it was customary, he informed me, that a "curse" be put upon the money, too.

"A curse?" I echoed. "Just what kind of curse?"

Well, it could be a cat or dog or snake, he said—or even a wild animal.

I puzzled over this peculiar answer for a moment, but it didn't seem to make much sense. However, after patient questioning I gathered that the snake or animal selected for this pleasant little job was buried with the money as a sort of sentinel. If anyone without the necessary "seal" should start to dig it up, the creature would then leap upon him and the digger would immediately lose interest in the whole proceedings.

This added feature of a supernatural guardian of the treasure brought to mind the story Mr. Landis had reported, of the huge, dark beast that bounded from the underbrush to leap upon the money and sink back with it into the ground. I told the story to my friend, and at its end he nodded solemnly. Yes, he agreed, that animal no doubt had been the "curse" laid on the treasure by the man who buried it. And since the diggers evidently didn't have the proper "seal" to counteract it, the spirits had been able to reclaim the money for themselves.

My host got up at this point, and I saw him shudder. "*Ach*," he said, "it sure gives me the creeps!"

A little silence fell between us. Evidently he preferred to drop the subject, so I thanked him for his information and departed with a baffled sigh.

It's quite a tricky business, this gold digging, I decided. Possibly it might be well to let the whole thing drop. Besides, my utter and humiliating failure to find *any*one who could interpret that outlandish writing on my magic mirrors—well, my pride was dragging in the dust. So I resolved to take those thoroughly exasperating objects back where they belonged. I'd tell their owner that from this point on she'd better count me out. I might as well admit it—I was just plain licked!

I guess there *isn't* any answer to my riddle, after all!

October

APPLEBUTTER TIME

OCTOBER is and always was, I think, my favorite month of all the year. For then come blue and white and golden days whose beauty fairly clutches at the heart. Days when the lake below my little mountain cottage is an eye-arresting palette daubed with ever changing, ever more resplendent hues. The scarlet of the sumac mingling with the gold of tulip-poplar, the bright vermilion of the maple and the rich, warm rust of chestnut oak, the dusty rose of rippling grass upon a distant hillside, and the mottled brown of meadows pied with blobs of fairy white—all form a pattern of pure gorgeousness beyond the tongue or brush of any man to picture.

It was on such a day of pure enchantment, as I lingered on the porch bemused by all the loveliness around me, that the 'phone rang suddenly and Katie Spangler's voice inquired hurriedly if I could drive right over? They were boiling applebutter, she informed me, and I'd asked her once to let me know the next time that they did. Could I come over *now*? she urged.

I could. Without a moment's hesitation I accepted. To begin with, it was far too beautiful a day to spend indoors. Besides, a bright idea had suddenly occurred to me. It might be possible that Katie, with her countrywoman's knowledge of the neighborhood and its inhabitants for miles around, could help me in a little problem I'd been struggling with for some time past. It had to do with a dilapidated quilt of mine—an heirloom dating back at least a century and a half. Repeated launderings had worn my treasure down, and though the tiny stitches running back and forth on homespun linen had withstood the years in splendid shape, the red and green and orange of its raised sunflower pattern had succumbed at last. Large wads of cotton used to pad the buds and blossoms oozed alarmingly in all directions, and a hand more skilled than mine was needed to restore it to its pristine bloom.

Not long ago I laid the case before a Dunker neighbor living several miles from me. Her tidy red brick house and glowing flowergarden lie beside the road that leads me to my cleaning woman's home, and more than once, with Patsy at my heels, I've stopped off for a little visit with her. Mrs. Schenk, I have a feeling, doesn't quite approve of dogs. Especially in that scrubbed and spotless shrine she calls the kitchen. But with never-failing Dunker hospitality—and, I suspect, a secret shudder at her heart —she asked us both inside the day we first appeared. And Patsy, to her everlasting credit be it said, lived up in noble fashion to the honor done her. Parked patiently upon the chair on which I'd placed her, she sat motionless throughout our visit—thereby earning from our hostess a surprised and almost unbelieving approbation that has lasted ever since.

The problem of my quilt inspired Mrs. Schenk to offer a suggestion. Why not bring it to her church's Ladies' Aid, she asked? They made a lot of quilts, she said, and sometimes renovated them, besides. Perhaps they'd know just what to do with *my* old masterpiece. And so I did as she suggested.

With Patsy left reluctantly inside the Rat—for after all, there's such a thing as putting *too* much strain on Dunker hospitality— I stopped off at the little one-room building where a dozen white-capped figures sat around a sturdy quilting frame. They made, I thought, a quaint and rather charming picture. Overhead a line of aprons and sunbonnets—products of past industry, to be disposed of at the next church sociable—supplied a pleasant contrast to their plain, dark dresses, utterly devoid of decoration. For the Dunkers don't believe in "show," of course, and gold and silver are forbidden by the tenets of their church. The "prayer veil" on the head of each was sheer and crisp and spotless, and I wondered as I have so often just how many of these little caps each Dunker woman owns. For never from the day of their "conversion" till the time they die, it seems to me, do they appear without them. Yet I've still to see a single cap that isn't scrupulously neat and clean, as smooth and sleek and fresh as if it came that very minute from the owner's ironing-board.

In casual fashion Mrs. Schenk got up to greet me. She presented me to her companions and they nodded primly. Then, as I unfolded the sad tale of my disintegrating quilt, a couple of the women rose and helped me spread it on the well-scrubbed floor. In sober bafflement they looked at it. Their heads shook doubtfully. It meant a lot of work, they murmured—yes, and time besides! They had so many new quilts on their hands now—!

Suddenly a thought appeared to strike one woman at the far end of the quilting frame. "Why don't you let us make a *new* one for you?" she inquired brightly.

But I shook my head. I didn't want a new quilt. All I wanted was my precious piece of homespun with its big, fat flowers blooming in renewed resplendence on its ancient front. And so at last it ended with my bundling up my problem child and, to the tune of deep regrets from the Ladies' Aiders and myself, departing thence in some disgruntlement.

But now, with Katie's 'phone call, I was suddenly an optimist again. Perhaps she could discover for me someone who'd be bold enough to tackle my poor quilt! So, with Patricia curled up happily beside me in the Rat once more, I trundled off toward Katie's house, through an unrolling panorama of sheer loveliness that left me breathless with delight. Slowly I idled through the countryside, past open spaces dotted with the silver down of milkweed, through woodland patches all aflame with red and gold. Here stretched a field of ripe tobacco, with its crop long since removed except for scattered plants left flowering for next year's seed. There spread a meadow richly splotched with autumn's final priceless gift of goldenrod. And everywhere—in woods and fields and by the roadside—floated those clouds of fairy lavender the literal-minded know as asters.

Breathless from the pageant of pure loveliness spread out on every side, I turned the Rat at last into the lane that leads up to the Spangler barn. Once more Patricia sank down with a disappointed sigh as I got out without inviting her to follow me. For just behind the picket fence surrounding Katie's vivid flowerbeds I'd caught a glimpse of Mom and Puppy waiting for me, and the latter, as I knew from past experience, wasn't one to welcome canine strangers. He was standing on his hind legs now, his small paws clapping violently together—an ingratiating trick he'd picked up in the days before he joined the Spangler clan. For Puppy hadn't always been a member of the family. On a scorching summer day a year or two ago he suddenly came trudging up the lane from nowhere—straight into the Spangler hearts. They never did learn who his former owners were, or why he'd left them, or what special canine Providence had prompted him to choose *their* lane from all the others branching off the road. But there he was—a small, bedraggled figure at their gate, his pink tongue lolling wearily, his dark eyes gazing from behind the straggly fringe that veiled them, with a patient trust and confidence that wouldn't be denied.

He'd been there ever since. And though they wouldn't for the world admit it, all three Spanglers—Katie, Mom, and brother Will—are his adoring slaves. Not even a distressing incident that happened two weeks after his arrival could discourage them. For some mysterious reason—linked up in his doggy mind, no doubt, with an unpleasant memory of his past—the little stray went berserk suddenly one night when Katie tried to move his bed from its accustomed place. With sharp teeth bared and lips drawn back in vicious snarls, he launched himself upon her like a small tornado, tearing both her hands so badly that for six long weeks she had to keep them swathed in bandages, completely useless for the never-finished chores that pile up on a well-kept farm. The strange attack had never been repeated, though, and the diminutive attacker, long since pardoned, had become the unacknowledged ruler of the Spangler home. With winning ways and iron paw he governed all the family—and their work-filled lives were brightened indescribably because of it.

His plumy tail was wagging now in hospitable greeting as I entered through the opened gate. Behind him on the porch there lay a freshly emptied plate. "He chust now et his dinner!" Mom explained, and with a swift, accustomed motion scooped the plate up and deposited it on a near-by bench. "We give him salad, still—he's awful *for* it!" she confided, adding with a certain naïve pride: "He likes it sour!"

The little tyrant's startling preferences, I learned, included fried potatoes also—and I shuddered at the thought of what such strange, undoggish food must do to his digestion. Unconcerned, however, and so far at least quite unaffected by the eccentricities of his peculiar diet, Puppy gamboled on ahead as we sedately followed him along the concrete walk. Beyond another gate that led out to the chickenyard I saw the master of the Spangler household standing guard above a mammoth cauldron hung above a roaring fire. Alternately he threw another log upon the blaze and stirred the contents of the bubbling kettle, while a rain of perspiration trickled down his forehead and his pale eyes winked and watered in the acrid smoke that wafted upward, mingled with a cloud of wondrous fragrance such as never was on either land or sea.

Entranced by this my first encounter with the rite of apple-butter "stirring," I was filled with questions. What, I asked, made up the contents of the kettle in addition to the apples? When had they begun the boiling process, and just how much longer would it last? And when it *was* completed, how much applebutter would they have? Attracted by our voices, Katie joined us in the chickenyard, and while her brother kept the wooden stirring paddle with its perforated blade in rhythmic motion, she explained to me the mysteries of this favorite outdoor sport of country people in the fall.

It seems the process starts quite early in the morning. Seven o'clock or so, she told me, is the usual hour. First, you pour the cider in the kettle, let it boil down to one half its quantity, then add the water and allow it to boil down again. Next come the *Schnitz* (sliced apples), to be added with a bag of sassafras to give that rich and spicy taste. But, Katie pointed out, you add

only the sweet apples now—the sour apples have to wait until the
whole thing once again has reached a rolling boil, and then they,
too, are dumped into the scalding broth. For hours then—until
late afternoon, she said—the boiling and the stirring go on
simultaneously, and not until the dark, delicious-looking mess is
almost finished do you add the sugar as the final, crucial touch.

A sudden question popped into my mind at this point. Applebutter kettles, as I've noted many times, are always made of
copper—black and sooty on the outside sometimes, but as clear
and shiny-bright within as endless scrubbings possibly can make
them. Why, I asked my hostess, is this special metal always used?

But Katie shook her head. "They're *always* copper!" she replied
as through that were sufficient reason, and went on to tell me
of the net results to be expected from this season's crop. Four
other batches had already been turned out, she said. They'd used
six bucketfuls of apples for the last one—four of sweet and two
of sour ones—plus eighteen pounds of sugar, more than thirty
gallons of cider, and two bucketfuls of water. Fifteen crocks of
applebutter, or some forty quarts or more, was the result. "And
till we're finished," Katie added with a modest glow of pride,
"it'll give five times as much again!"

It sounded like a lot of applebutter to my inexperienced ears.
But my astonishment was lessened somewhat when I learned a
little later of the truly mammoth quantities turned out at other
stirrings of a bygone day. I'd had a try by then at wielding the
enormous paddle, back and forth and round and round the
steaming cauldron, while I choked and coughed and spluttered in
the scorching smoke and heat. It hadn't been as easy as I'd
thought, however, and when Katie started for the house I was
content to follow meekly, leaving Will to carry on the endless
task in solitary state.

We entered on a lull inside the kitchen. Little Mom, assisted
by two neighbor women, had the heavy earthen crocks all washed

and ready for their spicy contents, and the three were now enjoying a short breathing spell before the next activities began. The older of the women was recalling other applebutter boilings as we joined them, and I sat down eagerly to listen, with my ears agog to catch the last detail. When she was young, she said, they'd had as many as a dozen stirrings in a season, always held inside the summer kitchen that adjoined the house. From dawn till dark the stirring lasted, while the low-slung stove, a half a century old or more, glowed red and angry from the heat within its rounded belly, and two mighty paddles with long handles held by leather straps that fastened to the rafters were in constant motion. Two mammoth kettles simmered simultaneously, she said, and into each of them there went a hundred gallons of cider, eleven bucketfuls of *Schnitz*, and thirty-five pounds of sugar, not to mention cloves and cinnamon and sassafras to suit the family taste.

It sounded fascinating and I listened avidly. But to my disappointment Mom had other subjects on her mind. A slight pause in the conversation offered her her chance, and with a childlike zest she plunged into a discussion of more up-to-date affairs. Will, she informed us dolefully, had cut his finger bad last week. Let's see, now—and she pondered deeply—it was Mondays, wasn't it? Or maybe Tuesdays? Anyhow, he'd gone on working, still—she shook her head in earnest deprecation—but it made it so *un*handy for him! Old man Sensenig, she went on with her list of harrowing events, had died a few days back. *Ach,* he'd been wonderful sick, she added with a certain artless gusto, and proceeded to enlarge on all the sad details.

Her somewhat grim recital seemed to stir a memory in the second neighbor's mind. A gray-haired Dunker woman, plump and comfortable, with gold-rimmed spectacles and filmy prayer veil perched securely on her head, she swayed sedately back and forth in the worn kitchen rocker as she told her little tale. One

winter, she informed us, there had been a woman in her neighborhood who'd had pneumonia awful bad—she'd been so sick
the doctor thought that she was going to die. The woman hadn't
joined a church yet, but she'd made her home with an old Dunker
couple and had learned to like the way they lived, she said. So
she insisted that before she went she had to be baptized according to their church's custom.

The minister, I gathered, had his doubts about the matter, and
the doctor, too, was open in his disapproval at the thought of
dipping a sick woman in the icy waters of an outdoor stream.
But still the patient wouldn't be denied, and finally they all decided she should have her dying wish. Accordingly they wrapped
her tenderly in blankets, placed her on a chair, and took her in
a covered wagon to the scene of the baptismal "dunking." There
the two men, clad in hipboots, waded in the water with the chair
slung carefully between them, and immersed its occupant three
times, according to the Dunker rite. And, much to everyone's
surprise, the patient from that moment on proceeded to get well!

"Her faith," our Dunker storyteller finished piously, "was greater
than the minister's!"

The conversation turned to other subjects now, and Mom re-
sumed her recitation of events a trifle nearer home. They'd put
away two bags of sweet potatoes yesterday, she told us, and besides
she'd helped Will with the shelling of the corn. The week before,
she added, she and Katie had got in their white potatoes—a hundred and fifty bushels of them—and had baked their usual batch
of thirteen dozen cakes and endless bread and pies to be disposed
of on their weekly peddling jaunt. It hardly seemed surprising
that she now complained of being "all played out."

"Suppose you let me take you for a little ride?" I offered helpfully. But at the look of horror on her face I realized how un-
thinkable such wanton waste of time would be.

"*Du yammer!*" she exclaimed, and both her work-worn hands

flew up in protest. "Why, I've got my dirt to make away yet—and my supper, still, to get besides! I don't know right," she added worriedly, "chust what to give them! They had fried potatoes for their dinner." She stood a moment wrapped in thought. "Yes, well!" she said at last. "I guess I give them apple upside-down cake," and she started purposefully toward the stove.

The afternoon was growing late and I bethought me of my own and Patsy's dinner still to be prepared. I rose to go, then hesitated briefly as I reached the door. That apple upside-down cake which she'd mentioned—would she tell me just exactly how it should be made?

She nodded readily. "Why, sure!" And so, with Katie prompting from the sidelines, she proceeded to set forth the whys and wherefores while I wrote them down. She made me read it back to her to be quite sure I had it right.

"And when it's done," she finished earnestly, "go out around it with a knife to make it loose, and turn it upside-down out on a plate!"

With this confused but nonetheless intelligible explanation ringing in my ears, I said good-bye and stepped out on the porch.

"I'll ride along with youse down to the road, still!" Katie volunteered. "It'll save me walking down to fetch the cows."

We strolled together through the garden's freshness, and suddenly I saw a smile tug at the corners of my hostess' tired mouth. She turned to me and archly put her usual question: "Could you use some flowers?"

I could, of course. But as I watched her reddened fingers linger lovingly on every blossom—aster, zinnia, "red-hot poker," canna, and chrysanthemum, all bright and fresh and still untouched by autumn frost—I thought that even if I couldn't "use" them I'd most certainly accept them just the same. For watching pleasure such as this appear on someone's face was an experience not to be rejected lightly. To Katie, her flamboyant garden is her special joy and pride—the outlet for her secret hopes and sorrows, the comfort of her beauty-loving heart. A chance to be with her beloved posies was, I knew, the compensating highlight of her whole work-weary day.

We climbed aboard the Rat at last and started off, just as a ruddy sun was dropping leisurely behind the hill. Its gaudy red and orange tints reminded me of what I'd come to ask, and hastily I broached the subject of my poor, dilapidated quilt.

And Katie didn't fail me. "Sure!" she said. "I know where youse can get it fixed! Chust take it, now, to Mrs. Gantz and say I sent you, still. She's wonderful good at fixing quilts!"

So, richer by an answer to my vexing problem, plus a recipe for apple upside-down cake and the memory of a nostril-tickling odor wafting from a copper kettle outlined unforgettably against a blazing autumn sky, I left her at the bottom of the Spangler lane. With Patsy snuggled up beside me comfortably, her smooth, black head pressed trustingly against my knee, I turned my rattling equipage toward home. The afternoon, I thought contentedly, had been a great success.

Some day I'm going to put to work the knowledge that I've gained and have a try at boiling applebutter on my own.

KNEE-DEEP IN INDIANS

My driver had arrived in time for breakfast, looking like Santa Claus with both arms full of gifts. He'd been to market in the city just before he left, he said, and the rich armful of fall beauty that he brought had been the outcome. I smiled in silent understanding. Even city markets burst forth into glowing bloom at this time of the year, I thought, and color-loving souls like his fall easy victim to the charms they offer.

One parcel that he carried held a bunch of gay strawflowers which I promptly settled in a small, round, yellow bowl of Virgin

Islands pottery just made for them, it seemed. Two other packages contained a dozen long, straight spikes of orange-colored "love apples." These I arranged, appropriately, in the brass loving-cup that stood atop my secretary, where their brilliant hue was echoed by the candles in the seven-branch candlestick across from it.

It was a perfect day—too perfect, we agreed, to spend indoors. So we ate a modest breakfast on the porch, with lake and hills and fields in all their gorgeousness stretched out before us, and then departed on the tour of near-by beauty spots that I'd been planning all week long. I'd made a note of certain vantage points from which the pageant of the autumn woods could best be seen, and my poor, underprivileged city-dweller must, of course, be introduced to them.

There was that meadow where Patricia and the Rat and I had gotten stuck, for instance. The view from there was something guaranteed to stop the heart. And a special spot across the lake from which the mottled glory of Bull Mountain showed in rounded symmetry against the sky. My favorite maple, too, was waiting, richer far than rubies in its dress of glowing red, and a small sassafras whose blazing gold had warmed my heart each time I'd passed it—these and many other sights whose splendor must be shared to be appreciated to the full.

The gentleman's reactions proved as satisfactory as I could have wished. We "ohed" and "ahed" together till at last, sated with beauty for the moment, we came home to eat some lunch. But still the day was far too marvelous to waste, and shortly after, with my little dog as usual curled up on the seat between us, we were on the road again.

"Where are we going?" I asked in lazy curiosity. It didn't matter, but the question seemed in order.

My companion shrugged. "Nowhere," he answered from a lethargy of pure content as deep and satisfying as my own.

We drove in silence for a little while. Along the roadside an occasional cricket chirped its plaintive song, and from a cornfield in the distance came the drowsy cawing of a pair of crows.

"Of course," I mentioned casually, "I know somewhere we *could* be going!"

A muffled grunt came from the seat beside me. "Where?" my driver asked.

"Remember that old fort we heard about last week?" I hesitated. "It was called Fort Zeller, wasn't it?"

He nodded.

"Well—how far is it from here?"

"Not far." The car was slowing down already. My Chauffeur, with his uncanny knowledge of directions, spun the wheel about, and in a moment we were headed for a brand-new goal.

"I've learned a lot about the Zellers lately," I informed him as we bowled along. "I've looked them up, and asked all sorts of people, and discovered various fascinating things. Take Christine, now—"

"The gal who killed the Indians?"

"Yes." I nodded. "She was David Zeller's wife. He was a grandson of Clotilde—remember? But John Heinrich was the one who really built the fort. That is, the second fort, I mean. The first one—"

"Whoa!" My driver seemed a bit confused. "Let's start at the beginning, shall we?"

I smiled apologetically. "Well, it *is* a trifle complicated, I admit. But still, I think I've got it straightened out by now. Christine's ancestress, you see—the founder of the family—was the Lady Clotilde Zeller, a French noblewoman, formerly the Comtesse Clotilde de Valois. In her teens she'd married Jacques de Sellaire, who was Swiss. They had two children, Jean and Jean Henri de Sellaire—or John and Heinrich Zeller, as they later became known. They were all Huguenots, of course, and the Huguenots were very badly treated during the religious persecutions of the times.

So the family moved to Holland and took refuge there. And there the older son, Jean Henri, took a Dutch girl as his bride."

"French, Swiss, and Holland Dutch!" my audience commented. "Quite a combination! So—what happened next?"

I thought a moment. "Well, from Holland they moved on to England where Queen Anne was offering shelter to a lot of refugees from the Palatinate. And when the Queen invited all of them to settle in her colonies across the sea, the Zellers started for the new land with the rest. Meanwhile, however, Clotilde's husband died, and she was left to guide the family fortunes all alone. Things didn't go so well for them at first, and when they landed in New York they found the Governor of that state none too hospitable. So, when later on the Governor of Pennsylvania sent an invitation to the refugees to come and settle *there* instead, the prospect sounded pretty good to them. But Clotilde by this time had gotten just a little wary. She'd made up her mind they wouldn't move again until they had some first-hand information as to what the land in Pennsylvania would be like. So she dispatched John Henri on ahead to reconnoitre."

"Pretty smart of her!"

I nodded. "With an Indian guide, Jean Henri started down the Susquehanna River, up the Swatara Creek, across this very valley, and at last into the fertile country watered by the Tulpehocken. There they found a number of black walnut trees—and right away Jean Henri knew that this was going to be his family's home!"

"Why?"

"Because back home in France," I told him, "wise men always said that where black walnuts grew, the soil was rich and very fertile—and that's just exactly what Clotilde was looking for. So, back on foot and by canoe Jean Henri and the Indian went, and sure enough, the walnuts tipped the scales. Clotilde accepted them as a good omen and gave orders right away to build some rafts, assemble their provisions, and start off. And so at last, in

1723, they landed at Mill Creek, a mile or so from what today is Newmanstown, right here in Lebanon County. There they settled down and built their home. Of course, they didn't really own the land they built it on, but later, through the good will of James Logan, Chief Sassoonan of the Schuylkill Indian tribe presented to Jean Henri and three other men five hundred acres—"

"Why?" my listener asked again.

"Because Sassoonan and James Logan—he was counsellor to the Penns, you know—were very friendly. 'In consideration of the love and good will that I bear my friend, James Logan'—that's the way the deed begins. I've seen it."

"Very interesting, I'm sure. But how about Fort Zeller?"

"Well, I've found out lots of things about that, too," I answered. "It was built of logs to start with, but then later on the Zellers built another fort, of stone, above a stream of running water. That's the one we're on our way to see right now. It was John Heinrich, though, the son of Jean and nephew of Jean Henri, who was actually in charge of building it. John Heinrich had two brothers, Peter and David Zeller. Peter served as bodyguard to Washington throughout the Revolution. And David married Christine Horner. She's the one, you know, who killed the Indians."

"Well, at last we're getting somewhere!" My companion sighed. "I thought we'd lost Christine along the way! Go on, let's hear about her—I've forgotten most of the details."

I settled back and drew a long preparatory breath. "Well," I began obligingly, "the day this story happened, more than two whole centuries ago, Christine was in the fort all by herself. Her husband, David, had left early in the morning with a load of produce for the city market. Christine was getting supper, when she suddenly discovered that she needed milk to add to the concoction she was making. Now, the milk was kept down in the basement, in the water of that little stream which flowed beneath the house. So, with a kettle in her hand, Christine went out, around the corner of the building, and walked down the little flight of steps that led her to the cellar. Kneeling there beside the stream, she started to dip up the milk she wanted, when suddenly to her surprise she saw a moving shadow on the water! She knew she'd closed the door behind her when she entered, and the only light was coming from a small, square window halfway up the thick, stone wall. But now, she realized, something—or somebody—was obstructing it!

"Christine glanced up across her shoulder," I went on. "And then she gasped! For there, outlined against the brightness of the sky outside, she saw the head and shoulders of an Indian just about to struggle through! In horror she got up, and, though her knees were shaking, grabbed an axe that hung there on the wall nearby. With all her strength she brought it down on the intruder's head, then seized him by the shoulders, dragged him through the window, and dropped him on the floor. No sooner had she gotten him inside, however, than she looked up once again, and there framed in the opening was another painted face! Again the axe descended, and again a lifeless redskin sprawled at Christine's feet. Once more she glanced up, and for the third time saw an Indian just about to cross the sill. The sharp blade fell again, and three savages now lay upon the floor—then four— then five—then six—then seven. And at last, as she stood upright, practically knee-deep in dead Indians—"

"Wait a minute—whoa!" In patent disbelief my driver interrupted my blood-curdling tale. "You've added several Indians since we heard that story for the first time. There were three— remember? After all, enough's enough!"

I sat bolt upright. "Well—I've talked to other people since then!" I informed him haughtily. "Besides, what difference does it make? Christine got rid of all of them, you know. And when she'd finished off the last one, she leaned down and washed the axe blade in the water of the stream, then went back to her cooking."

A chuckle sounded from the seat beside me. "What are a couple of Indians between friends!" my driver muttered. "As it happens, though, you're wrong. There were just three!"

I stood my ground. "Seven!" I argued stubbornly.

"Three!"

"Seven!"

A deadlocked silence fell between us. It was broken finally by my companion. "Well, we're here!" he said, and turned the car into a rutty lane that branched off to the left. It led beside a muddy pond where several cattle waded, past a small, square, whitewashed building shaded by tall evergreens, and toward a large, red barn. A man on horseback was just entering the barnyard.

"Ask him if this *is* Fort Zeller," I suggested doubtfully. "And if it is—well, we'll find out how many Indians Christine *really* killed!"

Obediently a pair of long legs were unfolded from beneath the wheel. My driver stalked away in silence. He was back a moment later with the horseman, now dismounted, walking by his side. "This," he remarked, "is Mr. Harry Zeller. He's a lineal descendant of Christine, he tells me. Mr. Zeller doesn't live here, but he drops in now and then, he says, to visit the old place. He's going to show us through the fort."

Our new acquaintance nodded amiably. "There's quite a few that comes to see it," he observed. He led us through a picket gate flanked by a pile of golden pumpkins and a basket filled with purple cabbages. A pathway at the left led toward a rambling limestone house surrounded by a well-kept lawn.

"That's where the present owner lives," our guide explained.

The path we took, however, led us to the right. We followed through a formal garden, past a modest vegetable patch, and toward the neatly whitewashed little building we had sighted from the lane. We stopped before the open door.

So this, then, was Fort Zeller! Somewhat awed at the historic background that it summoned up, we stood regarding it in silence. It was hard to realize that this sturdy little house was really more than two whole centuries old. But sure enough, there at the level of the lintel, carved in somewhat wavering letters on the stone, we read the words:

J Henrich
Zeller 1745

I looked more closely at the door itself. Above the lintel a small shield bisected by a cross was carved—the Zeller coat of arms, our pilot said. "And look at this!" he added. Stepping through the doorway, he nodded upward toward the stone slab overhead. "See that depression on the inside of the lintel, several inches deep? Made by the sharpening of five generations' knives!"

I nodded, much impressed. But my Chauffeur's attention had been caught by something else. "Just look at *this!*" he said, and pointed to the wooden door. "It's made in two parts—see!" He swung the top half forward, pulling lightly at the old-time leather latchstring hanging from a small, round hole. "The planks are mitred in the middle panels, and the whole thing's put together with small wooden pegs instead of nails!"

"And look at this old latch!" I marveled in my turn. "Do you suppose it's the original one?"

"It sure is!" Mr. Zeller said. "The hardware on the building's never been replaced!"

We followed him inside. There in the dimness of the little room—a room with earthen floor and narrow steps that led up to a garret—we saw a fireplace at least ten feet in width. A copper kettle thirty inches in diameter was hanging from an iron crane inside the opening, and a huge, square beam, blackened and charred by countless roaring fires of a bygone day, supported the high mantel. On the left a neatly studded door with quaint old hand-wrought lock and long strap hinges opened on another room. A third door, fashioned in two parts like that by which we'd entered, led out to the back.

"But how about the basement room where Christine killed the Indians?" I inquired suddenly. "That's what we *really* came to see, you know!"

"Then come along!" The scion of the Zeller family led the way outside. We followed him around the corner of the building to some moss-grown steps that led down to another mitred wooden door. He opened it—and there before us lay the site of that intriguing Zeller legend. The room was lit by one small window on the left—the famous window where those Indian heads had popped up with such horrid repetition on that fatal day so many years ago. The feeble light that streamed in through the opening fell upon the water of a little pool so dark and clear and still I had to look again to be quite sure it wasn't empty. Moved by a sudden impulse, I knelt down beside the water as Christine had done and tried to summon up those savage painted faces that she'd seen reflected on its glassy surface. But all that met my eyes was one large frog—the largest, blackest frog I'd ever seen—sitting in silent meditation on the bottom.

I rose at last. My two companions were engrossed in a discussion of the pump which, most anachronistically, now supplies the farmhouse from the water of that little stream. The conversation lagged a moment, and I jogged my driver's elbow.

"Ask him!" I prompted in an urgent whisper.

"Ask him what?" He looked at me in masculine non-comprehension.

"About the Indians! You know—three or seven?"

He grinned and turned to Mr. Zeller. That gentleman stopped midway in his progress toward the door and listened patiently while our small disagreement was explained to him. And then he smiled.

"Well, if you really want to know," the great-great-grandson of the brave Christine replied, "the way *I*'ve always heard the story —there was only one!"

AUCTION PREVIEW

GEORGE GROSS, the watchman of the big hotel that stands deserted on the hill across from me, dropped in one day not long ago to tell me of a sale he'd heard about. It was to be held about five miles from here, he said, and since it sounded pretty good to me, I stopped off on my way to town and had a little preview of the objects to be sold.

The owner of the house—George called him "Old Man Gibble" —welcomed me with open arms. He lived alone, he told me, and I gathered that a visitor was something rare and thrilling in his humdrum life. No doubt the sale on Saturday would be the highlight of his whole career.

He took me through the place from top to bottom, and at last when we had covered every room, we went out to the barn. He had a treasure-trove of antique pieces scattered all around there, mixed indiscriminately with all sorts of trash. It would have taken quite a bit of time and energy to poke around them and discover what was what. Back in the house, though, there were several things that I'd already set my heart on. One was a covered butter crock with soft blue decorations on a gray background—the kind of sturdy pottery that filled the shelves of every Pennsylvania German home in days gone by. Another was a heavy yardarm scales like one I'd seen in a museum not long before. And there were other objects that I wanted, too.

I didn't say a word, however, till we'd reached the barn. There in a pile of helter-skelter odds and ends I saw a pair of barn door hinges and a hand-wrought lock that were exactly what I needed for the right touch on that century-old pine chest of mine. I *had* to have them, so I took my courage in both hands.

"I don't think I'll be able to attend the sale on Saturday," I said to Old Man Gibble, truthfully. (The Goods had asked my driver and myself for supper and to spend the afternoon that day.) "I don't suppose you'd let me have those hinges *now* instead?"

"Why, sure—just take them!" Mr. Gibble seemed a bit surprised that anyone would bother with such worthless trash.

I grabbed the hinges happily. "What do you want for them?" I asked.

"*Ach*, give me a quarter!" was the careless answer.

It didn't seem quite right, however, so I gave him double that amount. Then, rendered somewhat bolder by my luck, I took another plunge. "Back in the house are several other things I'd like to have," I told him. "Could you sell *them* to me, too?"

The old man hesitated. Well, it all depended on just what they were, he said. The larger things, like furniture and so on, had been listed by the auctioneer. He wouldn't dare dispose of them without that gentleman's consent. But smaller objects, now —perhaps *they* wouldn't matter. What did I want particularly, he inquired?

I told him, and he led the way back to the house. For the stupendous outlay of a dollar each, I got the butter crock and scales, plus a little ABC plate that intrigued me. It showed a rather dressy-looking youth seated beneath an overhanging willow tree, with a wicker basket, crock, and fishing-rod reposing on the riverbank beside him. The legend underneath read quaintly:

> Harry baiting is his line,
> For to fish he doth incline,

and the border, of course, was made up of the letters of the alphabet.

After this encouraging success, I found myself becoming even more ambitious. There were other articles I coveted—in fact, the more I looked around the more of them I saw. And Mr. Gibble seemed quite willing to co-operate—up to a certain point, that is. He let me have two wooden butter molds for ten cents each. But when it came to selling me the *Himmelsbrief*, Letter from Heaven, I'd discovered hanging on his bedroom wall, he shook his head. A *Himmelsbrief*, of course, is a very precious document to those who put their faith in its unearthly powers. And this, it said quite plainly on the yellowed paper, had been penned in golden letters and dropped down by God Himself from heaven back in 1783. The promise that it held out read like this: "That man who carries this letter with him, and keeps it in his house, no thunder will do him any harm, and he will be safe from fire and water."

Perhaps Mr. Gibble really believed it, or maybe, as he said, he valued it because it once had been his wife's. He failed to tell me *which* wife's, though, and I forbore to ask him. He'd had three wives, it seemed, and he'd survived them all. The first one lived for only eight months after they were married, and for several years thereafter he had been a widower. His second venture proved more fortunate, however, and for twenty-seven years he and Wife Number Two lived happily together. Then she also died, and once more Mr. Gibble found himself alone.

"I was fifty-two by then," he told me, "and I thought that was too old for getting married. But—" he grinned—"I changed my mind! For ten years after that, things went along real good. But then I had some more bad luck—my third wife had a stroke!"

With a certain morbid relish Mr. Gibble pointed to the spot where I was standing. "She fell right over there!" he said. A trifle hurriedly, I moved aside. "I caught her, though!" he added with some satisfaction, and went on to tell me how for ten

years after that she'd been an invalid, until at last, about a year
ago, she'd died.

He didn't say so, but I rather think the *Himmelsbrief* had been
her property. At any rate, he planned to take it with him when
he moved to Zion's Home, next week, he said. He had a nice
room all picked out—it measured twelve by twenty feet, he
added. "And I'm taking that there table with me, too!" He
pointed to a piece of furniture quite plainly of Grand Rapids
origin, embellished with a coat of gaudy purple paint. I glanced
at all the antique treasures piled about us, and shook my head in
silent bafflement. To choose a modern horror such as that in
preference to these lovely pieces that were going on sale—! Well,
everyone's entitled to his taste, I thought. And if that gay mon-
strosity he cherished represented fond association of some sort,
then it was only right to keep it with him, I supposed.

Before I left, I bought two other manuscripts that I'd dug up
from underneath a mass of china objects on the kitchen table.
One, quite old and brittle, showed the Twelve Apostles, done in
brilliant reds and blues. I didn't know exactly what it was, but
the bright coloring appealed to me. The other, a *Geburts und
Taufschein*, birth and baptism certificate, bore the date of 185–
(the final numeral was blank.) I had no such certificates among
my family treasures, but my mother had been born and baptized
in the 1850's, so I planned to have the empty spaces filled in with
her name and dates.

My arms were loaded with the treasures I'd accumulated as at
last I tore myself away. Already I was late for an appointment.
But as I started down the steps my eye fell on an object that I
coveted beyond all earthly loot—a trundlebed of rich, red cherry
wood! I'd always longed to own a trundlebed—and there it lay,
complete with wooden rollers and the little knobs along the sides
that held the ropes which served instead of springs! I turned to
Mr. Gibble.

"Oh!" I breathed, my voice as plaintive as a cooing dove's, "if you could let me buy that trundlebed—!"

The owner of my heart's desire looked at me regretfully. His voice was plaintive as my own. "I'd leave you have it if I could," he told me, "but I daresn't! It's on the list already!"

I heaved a heartfelt sigh. Well, if he couldn't, I supposed, he couldn't. But a trundlebed would fit so neatly underneath the curtains of my old four-poster bed!

"Come back on Saturday!" my host called after me as I departed. "Maybe you can get it then!"

But Saturday was promised to the Goods'. And oh, how sadly my poor heart was yearning for that little trundlebed!

November

YANKEE VERSUS PENNSYLVANIA DUTCH

A NEW and rather startling correspondent had appeared on
my horizon. It was a lady of New England background,
living in Ohio—squarely in the middle of a settlement of Plain
folk, so she said. Of course, that state, like Idaho and Iowa and
Minnesota—yes, and even California—has its colonies of Dunkers,
Mennonites, and Amish, too. Back in the first half of the nine-
teenth century the forefathers of these people gathered up their
patchwork quilts and favorite recipes, their tulip-painted dower

chests and *Fraktur*-decorated Bibles, their German almanacs and all their other best beloved possessions, packed them in white-winged Conestoga wagons, and set out across the mountains for the open plains beyond. And there they've lived and carried on their own peculiar customs and traditions ever since.

My correspondent's late husband was a Pennsylvania Dutchman, she informed me—and as if that weren't enough, a member of the Dunker sect besides. So after reading some of my descriptions of these people in my book, *Hex Marks the Spot*, she'd suddenly decided that she'd take her pen in hand and set down some of *her* experiences along that line. She has a gift for telling vividly what interests her, and I was favored with a graphic picture of the trials and tribulations of a stranger settling down among the Pennsylvania Dutch.

"It takes a lot of humor, patience, love, and grace," she wrote naïvely, "to be wed into a P.D. family. For so many situations can arise in daily life, both humorous and otherwise, to baffle and confound the uninitiated!"

But Mrs. Richards wasn't one to be confounded long, I gathered. Not with ancestors like the ones she boasted—stout New England judges and sea captains who endowed her with a stubborn, independent spirit that could more than hold its own. Her husband evidently had his troubles keeping up with her and here's a sample of what happened when the Yankee and the Pennsylvania Dutchman clashed.

To start with, Mrs. Richards was a staunch upholder of the right of woman suffrage, while her husband on the other hand was firm in his contention that no wife of *his* was ever going to vote! So, in the first year of their marriage, as election time drew near the Richards household was the scene of many a hot and vehement debate. And finally, the night before election day, the matter reached a head.

"You're not to vote tomorrow!" Mr. Richards gave his orders, glaring from behind the evening paper. "I forbid it—do you hear?"

Mrs. Richards nodded. "Sure I hear you," she acknowledged. "But I'm going to vote!"

In outraged dignity her lord and master disappeared once more within the manly sanctuary of his newssheet, and no more was said. A little later he got up and without speaking headed for the kitchen. Now, in the Richards family it was customary every night for wife and husband to imbibe a cup of coffee sociably together just before they went to bed. So naturally, when Mr. Richards reappeared a little later with the usual steaming beverage in his hand, his partner took it unsuspectingly and drank it down. Then, still in silence, they retired to the upper floor.

When she awoke next morning, Mrs. Richards had a queer sensation in her head. It ached abominably and her eyes could hardly focus on the clock. With dogged purpose, though, she kept on concentrating, and at last her vision cleared. And then —she screamed. Instead of five o'clock, her usual rising hour, it was ten!

In grim enlightenment the lady clambered out of bed. So that was it, she thought! Her husband, gentle soul, had drugged the coffee that he'd given her the night before! With a tremendous effort she stood up. Just wait, she promised silently—she'd fool him yet! And so, ignoring her revolving head, she rushed across the room and frantically threw the closet wide—only to find that her good man had taken all her clothes, and then to make the thing complete, had locked her in the room and left her there besides!

But Mrs. Richards was no spineless female subject to a mere man's whim. She'd sworn to vote, and vote she would or die in the attempt! And evidently Fate was with her. For although her own clothes had completely disappeared, her husband's Sunday garments still were hanging in their usual place. With breathless haste she donned a pair of knee-length socks and heavy, man-size shoes, put on her spouse's overcoat, and anchored firmly to her head his best fedora hat. The owner of the overcoat was tall and thin, his wife was very heavy, so the covering failed by several inches to connect across the front. But what, the lady asked with cogent reasoning, do such trifles matter when the constitutional rights of women are at stake?

So, tastefully arrayed in Mr. Richards' Sunday best, she hurried to the window and threw up the sash. Her lusty shouts attracted the attention of a paperboy who came to her assistance, and a short time later she was free to turn her manly footsteps toward the polling place. Triumphantly she voted—then, with vengeance in her heart, she called a cop to find her missing clothes. Result: Her husband and her first-floor neighbor, who had joined with him in carrying out his shameful plan, received a solemn warning from The Law about preventing honest citizens from getting to the polls!

Despite this little incident, however, and the scorn my correspondent cherished for such "stubborn Dutchmen" as her late lamented husband, there was *one* thing, she remarked quite frankly, that the Pennsylvania Dutch could do: They certainly could cook! And just to prove her point, she sent along for my enjoyment two old recipes for coleslaw that she picked up from her husband's people. I've sampled both of them and found them excellent—and here they are:

Hot Cabbage Slaw

Slice fine 1 medium cabbage, place in skillet with 4 tablespoons of heated lard, and brown slowly; add two-thirds cup vinegar. Mix pepper, salt, 1 teaspoon dry mustard, and 2 tablespoons of flour; add an egg well-beaten, and 3 cups of milk; then boil and stir till thick. Sprinkle the cabbage with 2 cups grated cheese, and pour the hot dressing over it. Serve hot.

Coleslaw

Cut fine 1 small cabbage, add pepper, salt, 1 cup sugar, and a grated onion. Blend together thoroughly. Mix 2 cups sweet or sour cream, two-thirds cup vinegar, and 1 cup sugar, and pour over cabbage. Chopped celery and sliced cucumber may be added if desired.

TILL DEATH US DO PART

FOR years it had been one of my most cherished aspirations to attend an Amish wedding. Very few outsiders, as I know full well, receive an invitation to these strictly esoteric functions, and I'd often wondered if I'd ever be considered worthy of the honor. And then it happened!

I'd stopped off rather unexpectedly to pay a little visit to the Yoders, whom I hadn't seen for several months. The Yoders, like most Amish people, have a good-sized family—nine in all, not counting one or two who've died. The oldest children are all married now, and only Christy, Rachel, and the youngest, Sadie, just sixteen, still live at home. Rachel, who's nineteen, had been "going steady" with John Stoltzfus for a good while back, but all my slightly teasing questions as to when they'd marry never brought forth any more explicit answer than a blush from Rachel and a matter-of-fact: "We need her here at home yet!" from her mother.

So it came as something of a shock when Mrs. Yoder asked me suddenly: "What are you going to do next Thursday week?" And when I told her that I'd made no special plans, announced in a significant half-whisper: "Rachel's getting married then— we'd planned to write you. Can you come?"

I gasped. Could I come! Wild horses wouldn't have kept me from it, and I told her so. She smiled in pleased self-satisfaction. There'd be about three hundred guests, she said—all relatives, of course, excepting me. The wedding would begin about eight-thirty

in the morning, Sadie added, and would last till midnight at the
very least. It sounded like a long and hectic day to me, and I
wondered silently if I'd last out the whole proceedings. It might
be wise to get there rather late, I thought.

And so, with this idea in mind, I timed my driving so that I
arrived upon the scene at ten o'clock or so instead of the eight-
thirty mentioned. As I turned into the Yoder lane I saw ahead of
me, lined up along the fence, inside the barnyard, on the sloping
ramp that leads to the tobacco shed, in fact, in every space avail-
able, a mass of gray "top wagons" and bright, shiny buggies of
House Amish vintage, with a scattering of autos, all of recent
make, attesting to the presence of a few Church Amish guests as
well. They'd started gathering before dawn, I knew, and many
of their occupants had risen in the wee, small hours to feed their
livestock and complete their chores before embarking on the long
drive to the Yoder farm.

I parked between two buggies, each with oilcloth covering
drawn up over open, topless seat in case of rain. I clambered out
just as a group of young House Amish boys approached from the
direction of the big, red shed whose basement room, I knew, was
filled with dried tobacco waiting to be stripped. The boys, I
thought with some amusement, looked exactly like a flock of
young crows in their Sunday black and white—tight trousers, short
coats closed with hooks and eyes, and broad-brimmed, flat-crowned
hats. They ambled briskly toward the house, and I fell in beside
them.

"So *you're* late, too!" I said by way of conversation.

"*Ach*, we been in already!" one youth answered. "But we had
to come out for a breath of fresh air, still!" He tossed his hat
atop a towering pile of headgear heaped in casual fashion on a
bench outside the door ahead of us. The other boys did likewise,
and I wondered fleetingly how anyone would ever find his individual property again in that amazing welter of identical apparel?

With no particular attempt at being quiet, the first youth turned the knob and entered. We followed him—and suddenly I understood why they had felt the need of going outside to get some air.

The whole first floor was one dense, solid mass of tightly packed humanity. Each inch of space inside the large, square kitchen, in the even larger sitting-room next door, and in two other rooms adjoining had been filled with benches—hard and backless benches ranged so close together that their occupants had barely room to move their feet. A stove inside the big washshed that opened at the rear was burning brightly, but except for that there was no heat whatever. Yet the temperature was eighty at the very least —and going up by the minute. The doors between the various rooms had all been taken from their hinges, and each stick of furniture except the kitchen stove had been removed.

A trifle dazed by the full impact of the scene before me, I stood still. At first glance it appeared to be a strictly masculine assemblage that stretched out on every side. The benches in the kitchen and the sitting-room were occupied entirely by men—old men and middle-aged men mostly, all of them with beards. So this, I gathered, was the husbands' section, since it's only married Amishmen, of course, who are permitted whiskers. No matter where I looked, it seemed, a perfect sea of beards confronted me—gray, white, brown, blond, and quite a few rust-red ones, too. It wasn't until several seconds later that I glimpsed the feminine contingent of the wedding guests packed tightly in a room that opened on the left.

The youths with whom I'd entered had by this time struggled somehow to their seats. Already they were lost to view. Somewhat abashed by all the stares directed toward me, and forgetting for the moment that a woman mustn't sit among the men, I started for the only seat I saw—a narrow space between two bearded patriarchs a little to my left. But, just in time to save me from this dreadful *faux pas*, a sudden movement in the doorway of the washshed caught my eye. A woman standing there was beckoning violently, and with a sigh of thankfulness I headed toward her.

The woman in a whisper introduced herself as Mr. Yoder's sister, Mrs. Esch. She had been watching for me, she informed me. "Here—let me have your coat," she added. "Then just come with me!" Meekly I did as I was bidden. Crowding between packed benches, stepping on protruding feet, and bumping into gnarled and cramped-up knees, we wormed our way back through the kitchen, through the sitting-room, through one of the adjoining rooms, and to a vacant chair at last, located in a doorway in between. The chair was one of very few, I noted, and had evidently been reserved for me. I sank into it gratefully and Mrs. Esch departed, leaving me to cope as best I could with my surroundings.

I looked about me eagerly. The room upon my left was jammed with girls and women, the one upon my right with youths whose beardless faces advertised the fact that they were single men. Within the women's ranks, however, there was no such guiding mark to go by, and I couldn't tell just which of them were married and which weren't. Their dresses, with but few exceptions, were of brilliant colors, and the room looked like a flowergarden that had somehow been misplaced. The favorite hues were blue and purple—sky-blue, turquoise, navy, lavender, magenta, and deep red—as well as various tones of green and gray. Each head, including those of several small girls just in front of me, was covered by a sheer, white prayer cap, and each woman wore a full, black apron, with a shoulder kerchief of the same shade as her dress.

There were, however, three distinct exceptions to the usual rule. For in the large, wide doorway straight ahead of me, connecting with the sitting-room, my eye fell on a trio of black caps that stood out strikingly in contrast to the white ones all around. The wearers were, of course, the bride and her attendants. Rachel, the bride, was wearing blue—that bright, rich shade of blue which

Amish people seem to love the best of all. Her dress was made along the same lines that all Amish dresses follow, with a high, round neck, long sleeves, a shoulder kerchief, and a full skirt covered by an apron. But instead of the accustomed matching kerchief and black apron, both these articles were made of fine and snowy white. Sadie, who sat beside her sister, with the bridegroom's sister on the other side, was also clad in blue, but of a lighter shade than Rachel's dress. Both girls, like Rachel, wore white aprons and white kerchiefs, and all three of them were clutching handkerchiefs at which they pulled in nervous fashion, with their heads bent low and eyes fixed modestly upon their laps.

The groom, John Stoltzfus, with his two attendants sat directly facing the three girls across a narrow vacant space, while on their right against a closed door leading out of doors the minister was stationed. He was a bishop, Mrs. Yoder had informed me, who had come from Iowa for several weeks to solemnize the numerous marriages that take place at this season of the year. November and December are the marrying months among the Amish. Crops are in then, and all farm work slackens for the winter, and everyone can take time out to give the all-day wedding celebrations the attention they deserve. By long-accepted custom, Amish weddings take place always on a Tuesday or a Thursday.

I set myself to listen to the bishop's long and passionate discourse. It had been flowing on for quite awhile, apparently, though Mrs. Yoder later told me that two other preachers also had held forth a little earlier. The bishop spoke in Pennsylvania Dutch, his rather high-pitched voice going on and on without a hitch or pause. At intervals the Bible in his hand was opened and he read some passages in German, then switched back immediately to Pennsylvania Dutch. Occasionally his voice broke with emotion and he blew his nose with frank and artless vigor.

Throughout the various rooms I noted others, too, who evidently labored under deep emotional strain. On all sides handkerchiefs were being used, with much nose blowing everywhere among the older men and constant sniffles coming from the women's section. At times a muffled sob was plainly audible, and every now and then a rumbling snore from some old brother, overcome by the combined hypnosis of the bishop's droning voice and the benumbing heat, rang startlingly upon the quiet air. Not far from me a girl was leaning forward with her head bent almost to her knees, her body shaking visibly. All down the line wet eyes and working hands told eloquently of the nervous stress that seemed to hold the gathering in its grip.

The bishop's monologue continued for another hour and a half. And then at last a sudden stir swept through the rooms. The bride and groom had risen. They were standing now before the bishop, silent, ill at ease, their heads bowed low, their eyes fixed straight ahead. The bishop put three questions to each one. With lips that barely moved they answered, and the syllables they uttered were inaudible three feet away. The bishop spoke again with slow and solemn emphasis. I couldn't understand the words, but there could be no doubt about their meaning. It was the Amish version of the old, old promise: "For better, for worse, for richer, for poorer," and it had a specially solemn implication here. For with the Amish there is no divorce. Once married, it's quite literally "till death us do part." No wonder, I thought silently, that Rachel's pretty pointed face beneath the crisp, black prayer cap looked so grave and pale.

A prayer came next, with the entire congregation kneeling on the floor and facing toward the back. Still facing thus, they stood up while the bishop said his final words, then turned around and joined in singing a slow-moving hymn. And now at last the wedding service was completed.

Immediately the rooms became a seething hubbub of brisk motion. The younger men streamed toward the open, followed by the vast majority of older ones as well. A few, however, stayed behind to move away the benches and prepare for the next part of the festivities—the midday wedding dinner. With rough-and-ready bustle windows were thrown wide and bearded members of the Yoder *Freindschaft* started laying tables, with long benches placed on either side. Unceremoniously they pushed aside all stragglers, and it wasn't long before the rooms which just a short time previously resembled a huge meeting-house had suddenly become a mammoth dining-hall.

One long, unbroken table ran the full length of the sitting-room, then turned abruptly at right angles and continued through the doorway to the room beyond. This, it developed, was the table where the bride and groom and all the single boys and girls would sit—a trifling sixty couples, I discovered later. Still other tables were set up in the remaining rooms, while everywhere the clash of cutlery and china filled the air with cheerful noise.

Meanwhile, inside the washshed, from which certain nostril-tickling odors had been drifting steadily throughout the wedding service, there was frantic animation. Mrs. Yoder, Mrs. Esch, and various female helpers rushed about in feverish activity, with certain masculine assistants in the role of waiters shuttling back and forth between the tables and the shed. Weddings, it seemed, were one time when the menfolks didn't let the women carry the full burden of the kitchen labors.

I joined the ranks of those inactive guests who lined the kitchen walls, waiting and watching hungrily for the ambrosial feast to come. And what a feast it certainly turned out to be! Just fourteen of us sat down at the table in the kitchen—two Church Amish couples and four Mennonites among the rest—but there was food enough for twenty times that number. A long, silent grace, with every head bowed reverently, came first—and then the battle of the knives and forks began!

Roast duck, with separate plates of stuffing, was the central dish, surrounded by a varied and plethoric menu that included mashed potatoes and stewed celery, cabagge slaw and applesauce, pineapple jelly and pear butter, apricot and cherry pie, all sorts of cookies, cakes, and doughnuts in profusion, tapioca pudding, and of course the usual coffee, bread, and butter as the final touch. Main dishes, entrees, and desserts were placed upon the table all together, and each person helped himself according to his individual taste, while busy servers hovered in the offing, filling emptied plates and urging everyone to greater effort. And when at last each valiant trencherman had done his best, and finally reluctantly admitted his defeat, a second silent grace was said, the table was vacated, and another group sat down to take take its turn at the replenished board.

Within the sitting-room next door, meanwhile, the long, right-angle table where the young folks sat had taken on an air of care-free fun and relaxation. To the Amish, weddings are the one occasion when the young quite frankly occupy the center of the stage. Their table, with the bride and bridegroom seated at the outer corner of the angle—a location designated simply as The Corner, I discovered—was the focal point of everyone's attention, and the youngsters were enjoying it immensely. Talking, laughing, eating, with hardly a pause for breath, they were living for the moment in a world all theirs, encouraged and approved of by their beaming elders.

At last, however, appetites were satisfied and youthful interest turned to other features of this gala day. The boys, and many of the older men as well, went out to the tobacco shed, where John, the bridegroom, passed around cigars in honor of the great occasion. Rachel, meanwhile, in her bedroom on the second floor had laid aside the black cap that she'd never wear again and placed a white one on her smoothly parted hair—the bride's traditional act of entering on the married state. Then, with her closest friends surrounding her, she started to unwrap the wedding gifts that certain of the guests had brought her. They were useful

objects mostly—dishtowels, linens, pots and pans, and such—
and numbered not more than a score or so. For Amish brides
receive the greater portion of their presents in the months that
follow marriage, when instead of taking a protracted trip somewhere they visit relatives throughout the neighborhood, staying a
night or two with each and picking up the gifts each family has
provided, at that time.

I took my turn with others at inspecting Rachel's presents, after
spending several minutes getting to the second floor. For the only
stairway leading upward was a shifting mass of girls and boys and
women and small children rushing up and down without cessation.
Time and patience both were needed to make any progress either
way. I got there finally, however, and with others grouped about
the bed admired the display of gifts. Then, making way for new
arrivals, I proceeded on a brief tour of the other rooms beyond.
Each had been gaily decked out for the festive day, I found, with
colored paper roses in large vases on the bureaus and lace-paper
doilies draped from every shelf. Each windowsill was filled with
painted pots and tins of blooming plants, and on the walls hung
decorated biblical quotations in the place of ordinary pictures—
which, of course, are never found in Amish homes. The beds in
every room, it seemed, were filled with babies, some asleep and
some awake and all attended by young white-capped mothers pat-
ting them mechanically as they gossiped with the other girls and
women in the room.

I made my way downstairs again at last, to find that the majority
of boys and girls had disappeared outside. Despite the chill November air, they hadn't bothered about wraps, I noticed. Probably
the games they played, combined with the high spirits that the
holiday had brought, would keep them warm enough. The old-
sters sat on chairs and benches ranged along the kitchen wall. I
circulated restlessly among them, now perspiring from the heat
that issued from the kitchen stove, now shivering from the waves

of cold that came in through the opened door as men and women,
boys and girls, kept going out and coming in continually.

With conscientious hospitality both Mrs. Esch and Mr. Yoder's
sister kept an eye upon my movements, introducing me to other
guests and entertaining me with friendly small talk in between.
At one point Mrs. Yoder bustled past us, pausing long enough to
smile at me and ask me how things went.

"You ain't seen Rachel's cakes yet, have you?" she inquired.
"Come along with me onct and I'll show them to you!"

I followed as she started for the cellar stairs. Below, upon a
large, low table underneath innumerable jars of canned fruit and
preserves arranged on shelves beneath the ceiling rafters, stood a
noble sight. Huge three-and four-and five-tiered cakes, with fancy
frosting and elaborate decorations, elbowed overflowing baskets of
mouth-watering fruits and candies—gifts of friends and relatives,
my hostess said, to be included in the wedding feast. But Rachel
hadn't seen them yet, she added. Her first glimpse would come
when they were borne in triumph to The Corner at the afternoon
repast.

She hadn't long to wait, it turned out. For we'd hardly reached
the first floor after our inspection of the cellar offerings than once
more the tables were piled high with food and for the second
time the guests assembled for a hearty meal. Raw celery, apples,
pickled cantaloupe, potato chips, a chocolate layer cake, and a black
walnut cake were added to the menu at our special board, with
custard pie replacing the two other kinds that had been served
before. But at the young folks' table there were other dishes, too.

First, though, Mrs. Yoder told me, all the boys and girls had
gathered in the upstairs rooms, where each young man had picked
his special partner for this portion of the celebration. Hand in
hand, the couples then streamed down to take their places at the
table, where all sorts of extra treats, including several of the masterpieces from the cellar, were set down before them. And when

finally young appetites had once again been sated, suddenly the strains of an old German hymn rose slowly on the overheated air.

I hurried to the kitchen doorway for a closer view of what was going on. Behind the boys and girls, still seated, many of the older guests—especially men—had gathered now. Some carried hymnbooks—copies of the ancient *Ausbund*, oldest hymnal in continuous use here in America. First printed back in 1564 in Switzerland, it bears upon its title page these simple words: "These are some of the Beautiful Christian Hymns as they were composed here and there in prison in the castle or dungeon of Bassau by the Swiss Brethren and other believing Christians." The tunes are said to be descended from the old Gregorian chants, and though the Amish never have seen fit to write them down, they've passed them on from ear to ear for two full centuries and a half.

The singing gradually increased in volume. Slow and dirgelike, it seemed far removed from the more lively music one would naturally associate with weddings. But the singers, it was plain, enjoyed it thoroughly. The men particularly seemed to get a certain simple satisfaction from their vocal efforts. High and rather thin in quality, their voices rose in quavering rhythm, with occasionally a shrill falsetto soaring on alone for several bars, then sinking back again to join the general chorus. On a windowsill behind the table Mr. Yoder's red-haired brother and two other men were perched informally, a hymnbook shared among them, as they threw their hearts and souls into the old, familiar tunes. But with the boys and girls the singing was a mere side issue, it appeared. Still eating as they talked and laughed among themselves, they raised their voices with the others' only as the spirit moved them to.

The solemn-sounding concert went on endlessly. But finally the young folks rose once more and went outside to play their games and have a little rough but harmless fun in the tobacco shed. The other tables still were occupied by die-hard groups of hearty eaters, with small children wandering aimlessly about, and indefatigable servers bustling hospitably to and fro. The afternoon was growing late now. Several couples donned their wraps, hitched up their carriages, and started home to do their chores, then hurry back a little later for the evening meal. Some new arrivals came upon the scene—guests at another wedding in the neighborhood, I learned. And hardly had the final tableful been fed than it was five o'clock and time for supper!

It seemed incredible to outland eyes, but once again the eating orgy started. At our table new additions to the bill of fare included dishes of stewed chicken, sweet potatoes, home-canned peaches, caramel pudding, and fruit salad. Meanwhile, for the second time that day, the boys and girls had gone upstairs to pick their partners for this last and most important part of the proceedings.

"This time the boys pick out their steady girl friends!" Mrs. Yoder told me as I joined her where she stood with other parents at the bottom of the stairs. She watched indulgently as, hand in hand, the long parade of couples filed down to their places. "I guess you ain't seen anything like *this* before!" She turned to me with patent pride and pleasure showing on her round flushed face.

I hadn't, certainly. The scene was one I'll probably remember to my dying day. Outside the early autumn dusk had fallen, but the rooms inside were brilliantly illumined by the light from heavy lanterns, fed by gasoline, suspended from the ceiling. Underneath them, like a picture taken from another world, the snowy headgear of the smiling girls, the square, rough haircuts of their callow-visaged partners, the flowing beards and richly colored dresses of the men and women gathering now behind them—all combined in an effect of unreality that left me silent and engrossed.

I noticed four young folks whose slightly different style of clothing made them stand out plainly from the rest. These were Church Amish guests, I gathered, for the boys wore suits of blue and gray, respectively, instead of sombre black like those of their House Amish cousins. One girl was dressed in pink, a color never worn except by tiny children in House Amish circles.

"There's Christy and his girl friend!" Mrs. Yoder pointed out her youngest son. "And that there's Katie's oldest boy!" She indicated a slim youth who looked to be about sixteen—her grandson, evidently.

I asked a question that had bothered me for some time past: "When will the groom be thrown across the fence?" This was a part of Amish weddings about which I'd never been quite clear. The tossing actually took place, I knew—a custom symbolizing that the newlywed no longer had a place among the single men who threw him, but belonged now in the ranks of married men who waited for him on the other side. At times, I'd heard, this rather rough-and-tumble horseplay had been known to end in serious damage for the groom—a broken leg, for instance, or some other injury. My heart went out to poor John Stoltzfus.

But my fears were groundless for the present, it appeared. "*Ach*, not tonight yet!" Mrs. Yoder told me. "He won't get thrown across the fence till the next wedding that he goes to!"

And now a sudden hush fell on the table. A long and silent grace was said, and then the singing started once again. This time a different hymbook was in use, I noted, and the strains that rose above the general clatter were a bit more lively than the music of the *Ausbund* songs. Meanwhile, a steady stream of food was being brought in from the washshed. The Corner took on the appearance of a glorified confectionery shop, with lofty layer cakes and gay fruit baskets and containers of all sorts of candy covering every inch of space. Above the heads of the spectators trays of crisp fried oysters, plates of rich vanilla ice-cream, jars of olives, fancy molds of gelatin—an endless chain of tempting fare—paraded past, while from the sidelines those not favored with these special dainties licked their lips in envy and delight.

The singing went on steadily. A half hour passed, an hour, then two hours. Gradually the volume of the music grew as people at the other tables finished eating and went in to join the group surrounding the main board. Louder and louder rose the voices, more and more freely hearts were thrown into the hymns, until the very rafters seemed to ring with swelling sound. This was the climax of the whole occasion, and the pleasure that it brought was written plain on every face.

Another hour passed. Upstairs half a dozen mothers fed and rocked their babies by the light of flickering coal-oil lamps. Occasionally they took another look at Rachel's gifts, or settled down for pleasant gossip, evidently quite resigned to missing what was going on below. No doubt, I thought, since weddings at this season are so prevalent, with sometimes six or seven in a single day, they felt that there'd be other chances to make up the loss. I tiptoed carefully among them to the place where Mrs. Esch had left my wraps. The night was still young from the Amish viewpoint, but my own endurance wasn't equal to the test. The heat, the food, the noise, the endless panorama of perpetual motion, left me groggy and confused. I had to head for home or cravenly collapse upon the spot!

"We thought you'd stay all night, still!" Mrs. Yoder's voice was frankly disappointed as I sought her out to make my slightly bleary-eyed adieux. My watch said after nine, but she and Mr. Yoder were just sitting down to eat their supper with the last group at the kitchen table.

"You'd better stay—we'll find room for you somewhere!" Mr. Yoder put in hospitably. But I shook my head. With Amos, Stephen, Sarah, Katie, and Elmina Yoder, plus their wives and husbands and small children—not to mention the new bride and groom—all staying overnight, accommodations might be just a trifle strained, I thought.

I took a last look at The Corner as I started out the kitchen door. The vista of square haircuts and white prayer caps alternating down the length of the entire table seemed to end abruptly at the spot where John and Rachel sat. Their faces stood out clearly from behind the towering heaps of food that covered every vestige of the tablecloth. The bridegroom's eyes were somewhat blurry, and the bride's face underneath her snowy headgear looked a little pale, but both were smiling blandly. Even as I watched them, John reached out to take another piece of cake, and Rachel helped herself to fruit from one of the large baskets near her place.

I stepped outside and shut the door behind me. A wave of lusty singing followed me as far as the tobacco shed. Some thirteen hours of the wedding were behind the couple now, with several hours yet to go. But if they still could eat— I sighed relievedly. They'd last the night out, I decided, as I took a long, deep gulp of blessed outdoor air.

—AND STILL FLUTTERED DOWN THE SNOW

The telephone was ringing urgently. I clambered out of bed to answer it, and found that Hildegarde, my niece, was calling me from Lancaster.

"It's snowing!" she informed me blithely.

"I wish it were up here!" I answered. And within an hour or so I had my wish—and more.

All day and all night long the snow came down in fine and furry flakes that swirled and blew and seeped in through the cracks surrounding doors and windows of my little summer cottage. For the house was still unsealed except for one small corner where my driver had held forth not long before, with hammer, nails, and rockwool by the bag. How fervently I wished that all the other corners—not to mention every inch of floor and ceiling, too—were equally protected!

But anyway, I know now what a blizzard must have felt like in the olden days. Those sturdy Pennsylvania German pioneers who settled in these parts two centuries or so ago could really take it! With a demon wind of sixty miles an hour howling down their chimneys, and a heating plant consisting of a fireplace and nothing else, with Indians up to no good lurking in the wilderness, and hungry wildcats snuffling at the door cracks, and the nearest neighbor fifty miles or so away—well, personally, that isn't *my* idea of comfort. Perhaps I'm just a sissy, but I still prefer steam heat to fireplaces in the wintertime. And even though there's not a single Indian or marauding wildcat in my neighborhood, and my brick fireplace is supplemented by a big oil heater in the living-room, a summer cottage in a blizzard isn't all it might be, to my way of thinking.

But still, there's no denying that it has its points. Especially in a spot as beautiful as my particular small piece of real estate. So, just before the storm got really under way, I bundled Patsy in her warmest coat, put on my ski suit, and the two of us went out to view the miracle that silently was taking place. For all around us was a world that suddenly lay hushed and breathless in a float-ing mist of white. And for one long, thrilled moment we stood listening to that loveliest of lovely sounds—a snowfall in the woods.

Our solitude, however—luckily for us—was broken by a visitor. Each year around this time my cleaning woman's little daughter Mary comes to spend the day with me, and just before the blizzard shifted into high she suddenly appeared. Her brother, who escorted her, came in the house just long enough to warm his feet and limber up his numbed and icy hands. The radiator of his Ford, he said, was frozen solid, and he didn't dare to turn the engine off. We watched him disappear into the whiteness all around, then, as a measure of precaution, started dragging logs and kindling from the woodpile just behind the house and heaping them in closer reach outside the door.

The temperature kept falling steadily. A driving wind began to claw and clutch and batter at our little stronghold with a fury almost frightening in its vehemence. In spite of glowing heater and rip-roaring fireplace, a wave of bitter cold crept slowly upward from the floor. The far side of the room was bleak and chilly as an ice floe, and a wintry draft swirled downward from the rafters overhead. At five o'clock a sortie to my pantry on the side porch showed that everything was frozen hard—a jug of cider and a quart of milk, some apples, lettuce, oranges, and vegetables galore. So, feeling gallant and stout-hearted in the face of hardship, we ate our dinner out of cans.

All through the night the snow and wind and cold kept up incessantly. At intervals I called to Mary, on the couch beside the heater, to get up and throw another thick log on the fire. And every time she did, with twelve-year-old facility she went right back to sleep again, while Patsy, curled up in a warm, soft ball beside her, never even stirred. But on the balcony above I lay beneath my foot-deep covers, shivering with the cold and listening grimly to the unabated fierceness of the storm outside.

The morning came at last, however, and we got up to a universe completely buried under snow. The lake was frozen solid. Drifts a good two feet in height were piled up on the tables, couch, and beach chairs of the porch, looking incongruous and rather silly. On the road below a snowplough scraped and snorted lustily. After we'd had our breakfast, we set out with reckless courage for the village, slipping and sliding as we followed in the snowplough's wake and shouting in a wild excess of spirits such as only the first snowfall of the year can bring. Wading above our knees at times through waves of crystal white, we struggled back again at last —and spent the afternoon in digging out.

By sunset every cloud had left the sky. When darkness came, a little yellow slice of moon rose timidly above the snow-clad hills. "It's purty!" Mary said in childish understatement. And I nodded wordlessly.

My promise to return my small guest to her home that evening wasn't kept, it turned out. For the Rat, parked patiently upon the road behind the house, lay swaddled in a downy drift of snow. So for a second night we huddled underneath our weight of blankets, with both fireplace and heater blazing madly and the stealthy cold still creeping in on every side. And when we woke next morning, to discover that the water pipes were frozen and the woodpile down to half a dozen logs or so, I suddenly decided that we'd had enough.

The telephone, of course, was dead by this time—one of the minor casualties accompanying the storm—so once again we trudged down to the village and I sent a message from the store to Mary's father. He came right over after lunch to get her, and I sighed with real relief to see her safely on her way. Next, I arranged by special dispensation from the transit company to have the bus stop at the bottom of the hill. And when I heard the welcome blaring of its horn I slithered down the slope again, with Patsy at my heels, and thankfully embarked.

We settled comfortably inside its cozy warmth, and Patsy's bright brown eyes looked up at me approvingly. We both were thinking the same thought: Good riddance to a summer cottage in the dead of winter!

I guess we're just a pair of tenderfeet at heart.

December

A HOOKED RUG IS BEGUN

Mʀs. Glick was making me a rug.
The Glicks are Amish, and the Amish are particularly strong on "rucking," as the Glicks pronounce it. Until lately, though, I'd never been especially smitten with this type of textile effort. Hunks of pink and orange flowers *rampant* on a mustard-colored background, with a purple heifer standing nonchalantly in a pea-green field beside an azure stream, had always left me just a little cold. But then, of course, I'd never seen the work the Glicks turn out. But when I did—thanks to the Goods, who

have a sample hanging on their parlor wall—I felt a little differ-
ently about the matter. For the Glicks are definitely artists in
their line—especially Mrs. Glick, who does the actual designing.
And ever since I first laid eyes on their particular type of handiwork I'd had a hankering for a rug produced by them—but made,
of course, according to my own directions.

So at last one day I went with Mary Good to call upon the
Glicks. Their household numbers ten, including Mom, Pop, Ab-
ner, Mattie, Elmer, Susie, Nancy, Lena, Benjamin, and Lydia—
not to mention Miriam and Jake who've died. The older four are
married, and Nancy, I learned, will follow in their footsteps soon.
The day we called, the only ones at home were Nancy, Lydia, and
Mrs. Glick. Lydia, about fourteen, hung shyly in the background
while her mother and her sister brought out all the rugs and mats
they had on hand to show me. By way of starting things, I bought
a small one with a little kitten in the center, then I broached the
subject that was really on my mind. Could they—and would they
—make the special kind of rug I'd set my heart on?

"Well, we're pretty busy," Mrs. Glick replied a little doubtfully.
"And there's a couple of other rucks yet that we got to make.
But anyway," she finally relented, "since you ain't in any hurry,
maybe we can make it for you, still!"

Delighted with this promise, I proceeded to describe in great
detail the kind of "ruck" I wanted. It had to be a strictly Pennsylvania Dutch one, I informed her. It must have a Conestoga
wagon on it, with six horses and a big, red barn with several "hex
signs" sprawled across the front. Then, at one side there had to
be a little house with gate and windowblinds of Amish blue, and
two small Amish children playing in the garden—and of course,
the soft, blue hills and earth-brown fields of Pennsylvania Dutchland in the background.

A bit amused by all these strange instructions, Mrs. Glick
assured me that she'd do her best. But how about a picture of a

Conestoga wagon for a model? Could I get her one? I thought I could, so we arranged that I'd drive up again the following week and bring it to her. I said I'd pick her up at market, where she has a stall on Saturdays, and drive her back with me the ten miles to her home.

So off I started on the designated day. I took my driver's car (a point insisted on by him when he discovered that he couldn't go himself), with Patsy as my only passenger. I found my Amish friend behind her wooden counter at the curb, except for a hardy male competitor the sole survivor of the market that began at eight and lasted until noon. While I was there a late arrival bought a dozen eggs, then with no other purchasers in sight Mrs. Glick began to pack her wares for the homeward journey. A neighbor's truck—the one they hired every week, she said, to take their produce back and forth—appeared upon the scene, and Mr. Glick emerged from the front seat. A round, gray-bearded little man, with a fat and roly-poly paunch but rather wizened features, and a high, shrill, cackling chuckle, he reminded me of a fidgety and somewhat absent-minded elf. His job, it seemed, was gathering up the various items still unsold and packing them back in the truck to carry home again. He smiled and nodded at me briefly, then got right to work.

When finally the truck was loaded to the satisfaction of them both, we waved him off and turned back toward my waiting car.

"Have you got room for Lydia?" my plump companion asked.

"Of course," I told her. "Loads of room! But just where *is* she?"

"Down the street, still!" Lydia's mother waved a casual hand in the direction of the town. "She's at the other market."

So, with her as guide, I headed for the spot she indicated. The second market, I discovered, was in progress in a large, low-ceilinged markethouse where business still was going on at a rapid pace. With Christmas just a little more than two weeks off, there was an air of gay festivity on every side. Thick, juicy mince pies, golden pumpkins, shellbark meats in tiny glassfuls, Christmas cakes of every size and shape, besides the usual vast array of gleaming vegetables and shiny fruits, of fat and well-scrubbed chickens, spicy applebutter and smooth, creamy *Schmierkaes*, chow-chow and tall, frosty layer cakes—all seemed to beckon with a special holiday appeal.

But it was none of these familiar foods that caught the roving eye of Mrs. Glick. The stall she stopped at, to stand gazing open-mouthed in whole-souled admiration, held a group of artificial birds—small pheasants made of peanuts, with real feathers glued on top, and paper owls perched solemnly on bits of twig. "Oy, anyhow!" she breathed in fascinated wonder. It took a mighty effort, I could see, for her to tear herself away.

We came on Lydia at last, standing beneath a fringe of paper streamers hanging from the rafters, helping an Amish woman at the stall next to her own. Her mother introduced me, then without apology she left me to my own devices while she had a little visit with a neighbor at the next-door stand. I understood, of course, for market day has other purposes than that of merely selling—it's the week's outstanding opportunity for gathering news as well. So, while she caught up on the latest gossip, I roamed hungrily about the markethouse, as usual falling victim to the charms of shellbark meats and Christmas cookies—two ambrosial items that I never can resist.

At last, however, we both managed to detach ourselves from these engrossing occupations and prepared to leave. Lydia had bundled up in a thick sweater underneath her long, black shawl, put on a big, black bonnet that concealed entirely her crisp, white house cap, and was ready for the street. But even when we finally emerged outside the markethouse, her eagerness to taste the treat of a real auto ride was doomed to a delay. For Mrs. Glick had spied another group of old acquaintances, and once again our progress struck a little snag.

"You'll have a hard time getting me away!" she told me with a chuckle. "There's a lot of people here in town I know!"

Eventually, however, we were really off, with Mrs. Glick beside me on the seat in front and Lydia crouched happily behind. We talked about the topics of the day, including taxes, and my friend informed me that in Lancaster County, where she lives, a farm of some two hundred acres means a tax bill of about five hundred dollars.

"Now, in Delaware," she added, "where my married daughter Mattie lives, the same amount of land brings only forty dollars' taxes." And the same rate, she believed, applied in Maryland—which was the reason why a group of Amish families some time back had left their homes in Pennsylvania for that other state.

I mentioned the historic battle which at one time raged between the Amish and the school authorities in East Lampeter township, when the Amish fathers had opposed the building of a huge consolidated school to take the place of smaller ones. Just what, I asked her, was their real objection? Was it, as some people thought, because their children had to ride in busses to and from the school?

She shook her head. No, it was more than that, she said. The difficulty actually was their objection to the law that boys and girls must go to school till they're sixteen. "They thought onct it was going to be eighteen," she added fairly. "But they made it sixteen, so I think they oughtn't to expect *too* much!"

We passed an Amish carriage, with its neat, gray top and lively-stepping horse both gleaming brightly in the winter sun. I spoke of it admiringly, and Mrs. Glick's black bonnet nodded in complacent pride.

"Now, down in Delaware," she said, "the Amish folks don't take such pride in horses like we do up here. Just any kind of horse will do for them! You don't see such well-cared-for ones like ours. I guess we'uns are sort of horse proud!" And she smiled in frank self-satisfaction.

We drew up finally before the whitewashed picket fence surrounding the Glick homestead.

"Just come in!" she told me hospitably, and preceded me into a spacious kitchen with green-painted walls. The windows, baseboard, sink, and coat-rail were a neat and well-scrubbed gray. Above the sink a square of green and yellow oilcloth struck a cheerful note, reflected in the bright chrome trimmings of a six-plate stove and half a dozen flowering plants in painted tins upon the windowsill. A parlor opened on the right, and into this my hostess led me. Here the walls were papered, and the windows, doors, and baseboard had been painted the inevitable Amish blue. A round, black coal stove glowed invitingly on one side, and a figured red plush sofa occupied the other. In the corner stood a cupboard filled with colored glass and china, with additional potted plants on one wide windowsill, a jar of goldfish on the other. Mathematically centered on a small, high table with a white lace doily stood a coal-oil lamp. A potted fern reposed upon another table, and four rocking chairs completed the room's rather crowded furnishings.

I noticed a large wooden frame upon a sort of easel near the cupboard. A piece of burlap stretched across it, and I stepped up close in sudden interest. This, apparently, was the foundation for my rug, and I was eager to find out how much of it was done. It turned out to be very little, actually. For only penciled lines were visible upon it and the hooked part hadn't even been begun. But Mrs. Glick had lived up to my expectations as an artist. She can draw—there isn't any doubt of that.

We stood a moment looking at the sketch, and then she turned to me expectantly. The model that I'd promised for the Conestoga wagon—had I brought it with me? I shook my head.

"I couldn't get the book I wanted," I explained a trifle sheepishly. "I guess the rug will have to wait until I do."

"Yes, well!" Her voice was disappointed but resigned. She turned away, and changed the subject. "My, but you ought to see them wagons that my cousins, Eph and Eli Lapp, can make! They're twins, you know. They carve such wagons out of wood. It wonders me just how they do it! Why, the last one that they made they sold for twenty dollars!"

I had a sudden thought. "Where do they live?" I asked. "Couldn't we go to see them? Do you think—?" I stopped abruptly. The Amish, I remembered just in time, don't like to have their pictures taken. Graven images, the Bible says, are to be shunned, and photographs as far as they're concerned are graven images as much as any other kind of man-made idol. But perhaps, I thought, a wagon might be different? Anyway, it wouldn't hurt to ask. So: "Would they let me take a picture of their carvings?" I inquired. And added hastily: "As model for the rug, you know."

My hostess smiled indulgently. Why, yes, she thought they wouldn't mind at all, she said. Besides, she hadn't been there lately and she'd kind of like to go herself.

So that's the way we left it. We agreed that in about two weeks or so I'd come again to pick her up. The Lapps live just about ten miles away, she told me—we could drive there easily and take a picture of the wagons then. And if they proved to be as accurate in all details as she remembered—why, we'd have a model for my rug and it could finally get under way.

TWIN WOOD CARVERS

THE last time my Chauffeur and I were at the Goods' we mentioned Mrs. Glick's twin cousins and my contemplated visit to them. The Goods, of course, are Mennonites, the Glicks and

Lapps are Amish, but they're all acquainted and all neighbors, since they live within a radius of a dozen miles or so. Mom Rachel, though, had never seen a sample of the carvings Eph and Eli turn out, and she seemed so interested and full of childlike curiosity about them that we asked her if she wouldn't like to go along and have a look.

"Yes, that I'd like!" she answered promptly. So on the afternoon agreed upon we drove straight to the Goods' to pick her up, then to the Glicks' where Mrs. Glick and Susie joined us, and then headed for the Lapps'. Apparently they'd been informed of our impending visit, for as we turned into their private lane and drove around the corner of a big, white barn, then stopped before a picket fence enclosing a neat lawn with concrete walk that led up to a yellow house, the master of the Lapp ménage came out to greet us.

With a friendly smile, and handshakes all around, he ushered us into a large and comfortable kitchen, where Mrs. Lapp was waiting at the door to welcome us. The Lapps, although House Amish, evidently aren't too strict about it, for I noticed Mr. Lapp was wearing a wrist watch, and Mrs. Lapp's black woolen dress was finished at the neck with a white turn-down collar rather than the usual plain, round, unadorned effect.

The room seemed full of children. There were five of them—all girls and all fair-haired—inside the room itself, plus several others who kept bobbing shyly in and out the doorway leading to the outer kitchen. I asked how many were included in the family circle, and our hostess answered simply: "We had ten to start with, but one died." Then, pointing to a little boy whose blond head happened to be showing at the moment: "*Him* we got a little later on. So now I say—" she smiled with conscious archness—"we got *another* ten!"

By this time we were seated, and our host announced regretfully that it was time for him to go to market. A little girl, bespectacled and solemn, and a little boy of twelve or so, who suddenly appeared from somewhere in the offing, fell in line behind him as he said good-bye and started off. His wife explained that she, too, used to go to market up in Lancaster, but with so many children to take care of she'd decided finally to give it up. She used to sell the homemade chocolates that she specializes in, she told us, and by way of demonstrating them, she went and got a plateful which she passed around.

As we were munching happily, a clatter sounded on the stairway leading to the second floor, and Eph and Eli, the wood-carving twins whose work we'd come to see, made their appearance and were introduced. There wasn't any doubt that they were twins—a single glance was quite enough to prove it. They looked to be about nineteen or so, with round, good-natured faces and short, stocky figures that were perfect replicas of one another. I gave up on the spot all thought of ever being sure of which was which.

Quite naturally, without self-consciousness, the two wood carvers led the way into the ice-cold parlor and proceeded to show off their works of art. They had on hand two Conestoga wagons, a small sleigh with two be-capped and bundled occupants, a fire truck, and two or three *Haus-Segen* (house blessings) painted on thin, crosswise slabs of tree trunks, and on glass rectangles edged with brass. The wagons were by far the most impressive of their efforts. With the horses, each one was about three feet in length, and every tiniest detail of wheels and harness, animals and wagon body, feedbox, linen top, and even the brass bells that arched above the horses' necks, was absolutely perfect. Yet neither of the boys had ever had a bit of training in his life, their mother said.

"Yes, they've been doing work like this since they were nine!" she told us proudly. "Because they wanted toys themselves at first, and later on because they found that they could sell them."

Each twin, she added, worked alone on his respective project, and between them they'd turned out eleven Conestoga wagons, not to mention various other carvings like the ones we saw.

"The only trouble," Eph put in—or was it Eli?—"is to make sure that we get things right. We ain't got any model, and we ain't seen many pictures of such wagons, neither. There's a lot of things about them that a body can get wrong!"

I knew exactly what he meant. Those old-time carriers that used to travel up and down the roadways of this section were quite different in detail from any other vehicle before or since. And suddenly the thought occurred to me that on a shelf at home among my various Pennsylvania German volumes was a book that set forth all those differences in diagram and picture form. It might be helpful.

I mentioned it, suggesting that the next time we drove up that way I'd bring the book along, and Eph and Eli nodded a reserved assent.

"Yes, well!" Eph said—or was it Eli? And: "Yes, well, then!" Eli echoed—or was it Eph? They didn't sound too effervescent, but of course you can't expect unbridled rapture from a Pennsylvania Dutchman. I knew that they were pleased, and so I said I'd bring the book and leave it with them soon.

We left a little latter, but not before I'd taken several pictures of the wagons, to be used by Mrs. Glick as model for my rug. I also ordered two *Haus-Segen*, but because the day was Sunday they wouldn't sell them to me on the spot. Instead, they laid them carefully aside for me to pick up when I came again. The boys went with us to the gate, and after handshakes all around once more, we started homeward. A silver moon was hanging in a pale blue sky and it had turned quite cold. Young Susie, huddled in the back seat with her mother, shivered frankly. "*Ach*, I hope it don't *stay* cold!" she said, and Mrs. Glick explained that Susie would be driving to the singing in Sam Diener's barn that night.*

* See Chapter XIV, *Hex Marks the Spot.*

I didn't envy her. An open, topless Amish buggy isn't my idea of solid comfort in December!

We let the Glicks out at their gate, and drove Mom Rachel home. Katie and Mary Good and both their brothers welcomed us with unaffected pleasure. The girls had supper almost ready, and they all insisted we must stay and share the meal.

"It's only oyster soup and custard pie!" Mom Rachel told us modestly. But when we sat down at the white-spread kitchen table we found cold sliced beef, canned peaches, honey, chow-chow, coffee, bread and butter, crackers, and preserves as well. The chow-chow was among the best I'd ever eaten, so of course I asked Mom Rachel how she made it.

"There ain't no special recipe," she answered. "Just take plenty of celery and string beans, some bread-and-butter pickles that you slice up crosswise, some carrots and a little corn, some lima beans and green soup beans—" She paused at this point. "Not too many, now!" she warned. "They'll get all *sotzich* [mushy] if you do!"

You also take some red and yellow peppers ("Just *schnubbel* them up fine!" our hostess said,) and boil each vegetable alone in salted water till it's tender but still firm. Then drain them all, leaving a little of the water on each one, and mix together. Next, you make a bath of vinegar and season it with celery seed and mustard seed, plus several drops of oil of cinnamon and oil of cloves. You taste the mixture to be sure you've got the proper quantities, then pour it over the mixed vegetables and put it on the stove. When it begins to boil, you take it off again—and presto, there you are!

It sounded somewhat complicated, but I've added it to my collection anyway. Some day I'm going to try it out.

SILENT NIGHT

THERE'S nothing in the world, as far as I'm concerned, more utterly depressing and forlorn than Christmas in the city. Somehow, to attain the ultimate perfection of that lovely holiday it simply must be celebrated in the country, with the bright stars shining overhead and all around the friendly silence of the great outdoors. And so, when my Chauffeur arrived to pick me up and head his laden car in the direction of my little cottage in the hills, I heaved a sigh of deep and heartfelt satisfaction. We were going home for Christmas—all was well!

Of course, since I'm Moravian born and bred, December twenty-fourth is just as full of meaning to me as the day that follows it. For we Moravian children always looked on Christmas Eve as the exciting climax of the festive preparations which for days, and even weeks, before had kept us all agog. For it was then we got our presents, eyed with palpitating curiosity all through the endless afternoon, and it was then we had our first bedazzled glimpse of that Moravian variation of the ordinary Christmas tree—the *Putz.* I've never lost the feeling that it's Christmas Eve which really counts and Christmas Day is just a pleasant aftermath, highlighted by a sumptuous but somewhat overpowering dinner.

So, to get things organized without undue excitement, we'd decided to start off a day ahead of time. The back deck of the car was full of packages as we got under way, and so was every inch of space not occupied by us inside. A Christmas tree was tied securely to the bumper, and a pile of English holly destined for the mantelpiece showed plainly through the window at the rear. As if this blatant advertisement of the season weren't enough, Patricia, dressed up like a Chirstmas tree herself in bright green sweater and a large red bow, sat smugly on the seat between us—just a public proclamation of the holiday ahead.

The day was clear and brittle, with a bright blue sky flecked here and there with softly opalescent clouds. We rolled along at lively speed, and with the homesick eye of one returning from a distant journey, I scanned the countryside about us as we went. The soft blue hills of summertime were somewhat grayer now, I noted, and against the barren meadows bare, white arms of buttonwoods were outlined sharply. In the stubbly fields bedraggled rows of cornstalks still were standing, and the sun shone with such brilliance that the landscape everywhere seemed clothed in white—white barns, white houses, white tin roofs, white buttonwoods. Even the limestone fences took on simulated whiteness, and the glint of sun on hoods and windshields of the cars we passed was almost blinding.

We drove with hurried briskness through the Amish country, passing an occasional wagon from whose depths small, rosy faces framed in blue and green and dark red bonnets peered out seriously. We went through little towns that swarmed with Christmas shoppers, and along wide central streets criss-crossed with strings of vari-colored lights. Here a stout man in leather lumberjacket proudly toted home a brand-new sled for some enraptured child to spy beneath the tree on Christmas morning; there a woman loaded down with shopping bags paused long enough to pinch the plump breast of a turkey hanging in a grocery window, staggering out a moment later with the bird perched carefully atop her other loot. And everywhere throughout the crowds the blue-clad figures of Salvation Army workers with their outstretched tambourines were gathering in their annual harvest of small coins to be translated into Christmas cheer.

We stopped for dinner on our way, and when at last we reached my little house the woods and hills and fields were dark and silent. The weather still seemed fairly mild, so my Chauffeur descended underneath the porch, with flashlight and some patient grunting, to turn on the water, while I lit the heater and got under way a roaring fire on the hearth. Unshipping of our various bags and packages came next, and in the midst of it the florist's man arrived from town with two poinsettia plants, some fresh green wreaths, and other Christmas fixings ordered by my driver. When finally the house was more or less in order and our various chattels weeded out and segregated, it was getting late and both of us were tired. So we said good-night and my Chauffeur departed for his quarters in the village, leaving me to revel in the beatific thought of being home for Christmas.

Before I went to bed, however, I took a look at the thermometer outside. It registered a fairly moderate thirty. But next morning when I got up I discovered that there'd been a sudden change—the mercury was standing at fifteen above. The bath and kitchen drainpipes were completely frozen, and I had to make my rather brief ablutions with the water in the kitchen kettle and a swiftly dwindling trickle from the spigot. My Chauffeur was late in showing up, due to the fact that particles of ice had blocked the radiator of his car, so it was luncheontime before we really got a start on our activities. But just as soon as all the dishes had been cleared away, we set to work.

By dinnertime the house had been transformed. Each window had its holly wreath, embellished with a scarlet ribbon, and from every newel post a slender, red-tipped candle shed its softly lambent light. The warm glow from the fireplace, outlined in holly with a flaming red poinsettia at either side, threw dancing shadows on our gaily decorated gifts and mingled with the rosy radiance from the Herrnhut star—that sacred relic of my younger days—suspended underneath the balcony. And, most impressive sight of all, the *Putz* stood finished in its own important corner!

We viewed our handiwork with modest satisfaction. The *Putz*, though small compared to those magnificent affairs remembered from my childhood, with their half dozen trees or more, their hills and plains and streams of running water that extended sometimes over an entire room, had meant a lot of work. The tree itself was

trimmed with endless balls and dangles, and the platform underneath—about a foot or so in height—had had, first to be built,
then topped with logs and stones and moss and crumpled paper
to supply the necessary hills and valleys. The stable in the foreground with its cows and sheep and tiny wooden manger, its figures of the Virgin Mary holding on her lap the Holy Child, of
Joseph in the background, of the shepherds and the Wise Men
bearing gifts, had come down from my childhood. So, too, had
the flocks of woolly sheep upon the hillside, and the pasteboard
castle in the distant background where King Herod ruled. So
had the fountain, with its round hole at the top in which you
pour the water that a second later gushes upward in a tall and
wavering stream. This last ingenious toy had thrilled my mother
as a little girl, and still remains the best beloved of all my family
treasures.

The Herrnhut star had also taken concentrated effort, for its
more than twenty points, each with an edge of tin around the
bottom, must be fitted into separate grooves—a long and nervous
process that entails a lot of patience and a steady hand. These
stars, from Herrnhut, Germany, are hung in the Moravian church
on Advent Sunday, to remain throughout the Christmas season
as a symbol of the Star of Bethlehem and what it means to all
mankind.

With sighs of weariness, offset by admiration for our work, we
locked the doors at last and sallied forth for dinner. There'd be
no cooking, we'd decided, till tomorrow. Then we'd concentrate
our efforts on a single noble meal. The embers in the fireplace
were glowing cozily when we got back, and in the rosy light cast
by the Herrnhut star and the electric candles, all the house seemed
bathed in Christmas peace. With almost childish eagerness, I
laid aside my coat and hat.

"Come on!" I urged. "It's Christmas Eve! Let's light the *Putz*, and then—" my glance sought out the pile of tissue-wrapped and brightly ribboned presents— "we can have our gifts!"

My hands were trembling slightly with the thrill that even yet this fateful moment always carries with it, as I struck a match and laid it to the beeswax candles standing in their little holders on the fresh, green moss. Those candles in themselves spell memory to me and nostalgia and a gentle tugging at the heartstrings that I never can escape. They're made in Bethlehem at the Christmas season, in the old Moravian drugstore—oldest in the whole United States. Each year they're used for that quaint, lovely candle service which to every true Moravian is the essence and the summing up of Christmas Eve.*

I lit the final candle and we set about the business of untying ribbons and unwrapping parcels. We made a little ceremony of it. Instead of plunging simultaneously into a welter of torn paper, seals, and ribbon, we took turns at choosing from our separate heaps of gifts whatever box or package looked most interesting. Then, while the one whose turn it *wasn't* watched with fascinated interest, that special present was decorously exposed to view, and Patsy from the floor between us added an investigating sniff to the duet of exclamations going on above her head. It made the process once again as long and twice as pleasant.

At last, however, both the towering heaps had dwindled down to nothing. Even Patsy's modest little mound of gifts had been disposed of, and in peaceful silence we sat gazing at the fire. Throughout the room, intangible but definite, the faint perfume of spruce and moss and beeswax hovered like a benediction.

From out the hollow of the great wing chair across from me a sigh of pure contentment sounded. "Christmas in the woods!" The wing chair's occupant spoke softly. Puffs of blue smoke from his cigarette hung lazily between us, floating motionless a moment,

* See Chapter XI, *Hex Marks the Spot.*

then in gentle undulation wafting up the chimney. "It's perfect, isn't it?"

I turned the dial of the radio, and nodded. Suddenly a Christmas carol filled the room:

> Silent Night, Holy Night!
> All is calm, all is bright—

It was the final touch that made our Christmas Eve complete.

The voice sang on. It rose and fell and rose again, swelling in vibrant harmony as if to claim our full attention. For a moment even Patsy, happily dismembering a rubber mouse, stopped gnawing long enough to cock an ear and listen till the last sweet, mellow note had died away. I switched the music off, and my Chauffeur got up to lay another log upon the fire. He stood a moment at the window looking out, then turned and beckoned to me quietly.

I joined him. As my eyes became accustomed to the ghostly glimmer of the night outside, I gave a little gasp. Above us in a pale blue sky alive with stars, a round, full moon was riding high. The brilliance of its shining drowned both woods and hills in incandescent light. The lake, ice-covered since the night before, showed white and spectral, and the bare limbs of the trees about its edge stood out in silver filigree against the sky. As we stood watching, in the distance a lone screech owl hooted eerily. Below us on the road two figures passed, their footsteps sounding sharply on the clear, crisp air—the only human sound to mar the quiet of this perfect night.

We turned away at last—back to our snug oasis of luxurious warmth and comfort. This, we both were thinking—this was Christmas as it ought to be. That loveliest of all the lovely seasons—Christmas! Christmas in the open spaces, with the peaceful beauty of the moonlit woods about, with stout logs blazing on the hearth, and in the hearts of both of us the simple gladness of that first sweet Silent Night so many years ago.

CHRISTMAS DAY

THE Great Repast was over. Another Christmas dinner had become a memory only, with just a turkey carcass, much reduced, and various odds and ends of vegetables reposing in the kitchen cupboard, to tell the story. But what a meal it was!

We'd started preparations rather late, and it was almost dark when finally we finished. The turkey, safely in the oven, sizzled beatifically and the whole house reeked with that delightful fragrance which precedes all Christmas feasts. We'd sat down finally to catch our breath, when suddenly the clatter of approaching feet was heard outside, and the whole Nissley family, seven strong, descended on us.

They came, of course, by invitation. For Mrs. Nissley, staunch and loyal friend of mine as well as an efficient cleaning woman, had heard me speak of the peculiar version of the Christmas tree that we were going to build. She seemed so taken with the whole idea of a Moravian *Putz* that I'd suggested that she come and bring the children for a first-hand glimpse. So, while they stood about in wide-eyed silence, gazing at its sparkling lights and lifelike figurines and splashing fountain, I started for their benefit the little German chimes that run by lighted candle power, and my fellow-host began distributing our various Christmas treats. The youngsters' mouths and hands were full when finally they left, still rapt and speechless at the wonders of this different kind of Christmas tree from any they had ever seen before.

Our sumptuous repast was ready by this time, so, fairly drooling with anticipation, we began to dish it up. The table, spread with my most cherished cloth—a cloth whose brown and orange tulip pattern was adapted by a gifted friend of mine from an old Penn-

sylvania German dower chest—was laid before the fireplace, and
we sat down to eat in blissful leisure. The turkey, succulent and
golden, finished to a perfect toothsome turn, oozed temptingly
the special stuffing made by my Chauffeur. A ring of round, fat,
juicy mushrooms rimmed the platter, with a rich conserve of
guavas and some hot and spicy mango chutney—both included in
a Christmas box sent by my brother from the Virgin Islands—
as accompanying features. The meal concluded in a blaze of glory
with plum pudding, topped by my own specialty, rum-flavored
hardsauce, and a mincepie for my driver's benefit. Then, happily
replete and thoroughly at peace with all the world, we cleared
away the table and sat down before the fireplace, the Herrnhut
star aglow above us and small, flickering points of light a-twinkle
on the *Putz*.

Patricia, too, had had her share of turkey meat and gravy. But
her appetite, like that of every normal dog, is never satisfied for
very long. Her rubber mouse engaged her efforts for a little while,
but suddenly with some strange canine sense, she sniffed the air
and made straight for a plate of Christmas cookies in the offing.
Her smooth, black head turned from my driver to myself and
back again as she sat up before it coaxingly.

He took a cake and tossed it to her, then appropriated one
himself. "Did anyone," he queried innocently, "mention cider?"

I took the hint and disappeared in the direction of the kitchen.
I was back a moment later with a foaming pitcherful of amber
liquid in my hand. He poured us each a glassful, and we settled
down once more, to crunch our cakes and sip our cider in the
warm and ruddy brightness of the fire.

"Of course," I spoke at last, a trifle thoughtfully, "you know
we really should be drinking wine instead of cider, don't you?"

"Wine?" The man across from me looked up.

I nodded solemnly. "It's Christmas, isn't it? And Christmas

is the one time in the year when everybody can have all the wine he wants without its costing him a penny!"

The gentleman seemed strangely interested. "How come?" he asked.

"An old-time Pennsylvania German superstition! Every Christmas night the water in all wells is turned to wine for three whole minutes. All you have to do is go and dip it up."

"For three whole minutes, eh?" He pondered deeply. "And *which* three minutes, may I ask?"

I shrugged. "That's just the trouble—no one seems to know!"

"Oh." Disappointedly he sank back in his chair. "You couldn't dig up anything a bit more definite, perhaps?"

I thought a moment. Here was a chance to launch forth on my favorite subject, Pennsylvania German superstitions. I turned a searching glance in his direction. "Are you by any chance susceptible to fevers?"

"Fevers? Me?" He looked at me suspiciously.

"Well—old-time Pennsylvania Dutch believed that if you caught a fever, all you had to do was put three different kinds of food out on the windowsill on Christmas Eve, then in the morning eat a little bit of each, and presto, you'd be safe for the remainder of the year! So, just in case you're apt to catch a fever—"

"But I'm not!" With grim finality he bit into another Christmas cake.

I sighed and tried again. "Well, there's another old belief that if you take a bath or change your clothing between Christmas and the New Year you'll be sick. You wouldn't like that, would you?" And I waited hopefully.

There was a pause. My driver poured himself another glass of cider. "I'll be sick!" he said.

"All right—go on and *be* sick if you want to!" I looked at him reproachfully. "But still, you might at least protect your livestock! All you have to do, you know, is put some hay outside on Christmas Eve and let it freeze, then in the morning bring it in and feed it to your cattle. They'll be safe from any sort of illness after that all through the year."

"I don't own any cattle!"

"Well, you *should* own some!" My patience by this time was wearing rather thin. "Especially at this season of the year!"

"Why?"

"Because," I told him, "every Christmas Eve all cattle suddenly receive the gift of speech. And anybody born on Christmas Day can understand just what they're saying. Only sometimes—" and I shook my head—"it's better if you *don't* know!"

"Why?" my listener asked again.

"Because," I said, "you might hear something bad about yourself. Like one old farmer that I know of who listened in on Christmas Eve to what his yoke of oxen were discussing."

"And what happened?"

"Well, he got an awful shock. One ox was saying to the other: 'We're going to have a new experience Sunday!' 'Yes, I know!' the second ox replied. 'We're going to pull the cart that takes our master's body to the graveyard!' And the farmer got so worried and wrought up about this dire prophecy that pretty soon he came down with a serious illness, and within a day or two he died. And sure enough—" my voice was very solemn—"on the following Sunday his two oxen drew the cart that took his body to the cemetery!"

"Well, it served him right!" my audience said unfeelingly.

"You mean eavesdroppers always hear the worst about themselves?" I nodded slowly. "Yes, I guess that's true. Perhaps it's better *not* to know what lies ahead of us. Except, of course, in certain cases."

"Such as what?"

"Well, just suppose I want to know the occupation of my future husband. It's quite all right to set a pan of water out-of-doors

on Christmas Eve and let it freeze, then in the morning read the
answer in the crystals formed on top. I should have tried it out
last night," I added. "And of course, *you* should be out this very
minute looking for a crossroads."

"Crossroads?" My companion seemed a bit confused. "Just
why a crossroads?"

"Why, because it's Christmas!" I reminded him. "On Christmas night, between eleven and twelve, you've got a splendid
chance to get rid of your direst enemy. You simply cast a bullet
right there at the crossroads, load it in your gun, and pull the
trigger—and no matter where your enemy may be, the shot will
find him out!"

"And if I haven't any enemy?"

I threw my hands up in despair. "Well, all I've got to say is
that you're mighty hard to please!"

He grinned. "Oh, don't give up so easily! I'm really getting
interested. But how about some less bloodthirsty superstitions?"

Obediently I racked my brain once more. "Well, could I interest you in knowing how to counteract the spells of witches?"

"Possibly." He waited.

"Don't clean your stables during Christmas week!"

"All right, I promise—you can count on me for that, at least!"

A gentle hissing from the fire emphasized his words. As the
last log broke in two and turned to glowing embers we sat watching it in fascinated silence. Overhead the naked branches of a
swaying oak tree scratched across the roof—and suddenly I cocked
an ear to listen.

"You don't by any chance," I asked, "hear anything that sounds
like baying hounds?"

My driver shook his head.

"Or maybe the far-distant tooting of a hunter's horn?"

"Nope!"

"I don't either!" And I sighed regretfully. "Which merely goes to show that neither one of us was born on Christmas night!"

The man across from me stretched out his long legs toward the fire and arranged himself more comfortably. "Another Christmas superstition, I suppose?"

"The best one of them all!" I told him. "It's the legend of *Der Ewich Yaeger.*"

"What does that mean?"

" 'The Eternal Huntsman,' " I translated. "Want to hear it?" And without a pause to hear his answer, I was off.

"Long, long ago there lived a man named Jacob Brewster. For miles around his name was known to everyone as that of a terrific braggart, always boasting of his feats of strength and skill. One afternoon as he and several of his friends were sitting underneath an ancient oak tree just outside the public house, the conversation turned to horses, and at once, as usual, Jacob took the center of the stage. Why, when it came to riding, he informed them, he and his gray hunter could outdistance any of them!

" 'Oh, you can, eh?' his companions jeered. 'Then show us, man! Let's see you prove it this time. Prove it—or forever hold your peace!'

"And finally poor Brewster, forced into a corner, had to face the situation that he'd brought about. With a tremendous oath, he leaped upon his feet. 'Show you I will!' he bellowed furiously. And calling to his pack of hounds, he jumped astride his dappled hunter, tethered to a post near by, and galloped off. 'I'll ride,' he shouted back across his shoulder, 'to New Amsterdam within five days—or ride through all eternity!' And as his figure with its tall, peaked hat and long, dark cloak that billowed out behind him melted in the gathering dusk, they heard the melancholy baying of his hounds and the weird music of his silver hunter's horn."

I paused impressively. The room was growing darker. On the *Putz* the last sweet-smelling beeswax taper long ago had guttered and gone out. Inside the fireplace the rosy embers gradually were fading to an ashen gray. "For three days Jacob rode unceasingly," I went on. "And at last, toward evening of the third day, a small band of Indians on the warpath happened on his trail. With shouts of glee they started after him, while Brewster galloped madly on, his poor hounds streaming wearily behind him with lolling tongues and heaving sides, his horse's laboring gait more halting and uncertain with every mile that passed. Then suddenly a volley of blood-curdling whoops rang out. A feathered arrow whizzed past Jacob's head, and with a yell he sank his spurs still deeper in his horse's sides. The faithful hounds closed in behind their master and his gallant mount dashed forward in one final burst of speed—but it was useless. A second flight of arrows rained about them, and horse and rider toppled to the ground. The dogs fought bravely on a little while, but soon they, too, were overcome, and in the blood-soaked woodland glade the shades of night began to fall."

My voice sank lower as I reached the climax of my little tale. My listener didn't stir. In something not much louder than a whisper I continued: "And to this very day, the legend goes, if you were born on Christmas night, sometimes at evening, far off in the distance, you will see a tall, straight figure riding on a dappled hunter, with a long cloak blowing out behind him and a silver hunter's horn clutched tightly in his hand. And as you watch, there'll float out from the shadows a shrill blast of ghostly music and the deep-toned baying of a pack of hounds that cast no shadow as they run. And Pennsylvania German housewives, hearing that uncanny sound, will shake their heads and mutter knowingly: 'It's *Der Ewich Yaeger*—riding—riding still!'"

Deep silence greeted the conclusion of my narrative. Unconsciously we both were listening to the sighing of the wind that moaned and sobbed in fitful cadence through the trees above. It wasn't hard to fancy in its dreary sound a thread of silver music weaving in and out. We started as Patricia suddenly emerged from underneath my rocking chair. She yawned prodigiously and looked up at my driver with a meaning glance.

He rose reluctantly. "All right!" he said. "I guess I know when I'm supposed to take a hint. Come on, young lady!" With a long-armed swoop, he picked her up and swung her to his shoulder. From that dizzy eminence of six feet three she looked down on the world below with smug delight. "It's getting late," he added. "When she's had her little run, I'll say good-night."

The crispness of the out-of-doors exuded from them both as they came bursting in a short while later. Patricia, ready to begin the evening over, made a beeline for the cooky plate and looked up at her escort with imploring eyes. Unable to resist, he took a cake and tossed it to her, then consumed another one himself.

"You know—" he turned to me—"I like those Pennsylvania German Christmas superstitions!" He munched a moment silently, then grinned. "I like your Christmas cookies, too!" he added.

"You and Patsy!" I remarked, and stuffed a generous handful in his pocket.

He stepped out in the starry stillness and a blast of cold, clean air swept through the opened door and stirred the dying embers to a final, fitful glow. Patricia, finally convinced that no more cookies were forthcoming, stretched out on the warm bricks of the hearth and drifted off to sleep.

The door closed sharply and I heard my driver's footsteps thump across the porch.

"Good-night!" he called back softly. "Merry Christmas!" And a moment later as he clattered down the steps: "Be sure to save some cookies for me, won't you?"

January

MORE OF MRS. RICHARDS

$\mathcal{M}$Y OHIO correspondent, Mrs. Richards—the good lady whose misguided spouse believed that woman's place was in the home and not the voting booth—turned out to be a most prolific letter writer. That first epistle telling how she'd matched her wits against her husband's to make good her right to vote was merely the beginning of a long succession of fat missives—ten or twelve typewritten pages each—in which she told me all about herself, her husband, and her Pennsylvania Dutch in-laws, until I felt as if I'd known the whole amusing *Freindschaft* all my life.

Her husband, she informed me, grew up speaking only Pennsylvania Dutch. When he was eight and started going to school he knew no English whatsoever. Both his mother's and his father's people—blue-eyed, fair-haired Saxons all of them—had come from Germany and settled here in Pennsylvania. On his father's side, his great-grandfather was a butcher, and this gentleman, it seemed, had never had his clothes cleaned from the day he got them till he wore them out. My letter-writing friend had often heard her husband say they were so stiff with grease and dirt that when he took them off they stood up by themselves!

Apparently my correspondent's somewhat arbitrary better half had been brought up on various old-time Pennsylvania German superstitions that he clung to stubbornly in spite of all his wife could do to disabuse him of his quaint beliefs. A piece of red silk woven in a horse's tail, he told her, would prevent the animal from being scared and bolting off. Burnt matches stuck in flowerbeds would keep the lice away. An owl inside the barn insured the cows' well-being. And a toad that made its home inside the springhouse was the perfect guarantee that milk would never sour.

But Mrs. Richards had no faith in any of these superstitions. And what's more, she never lost a chance to tell her husband so in no uncertain terms. But one day—and I thought I noticed in her narrative a certain bafflement at this point—Mr. Richards had the final laugh.

It came about like this, she wrote: The Richards' son and heir, a little boy named Jake, had for a long time suffered from a crop of warts on both his hands. He'd tried all sorts of remedies, his mother said, but nothing helped until one day his father undertook a cure. "Go get some beans!" he told the boy. "Just ordinary soup beans—one for every wart you've got." His son obeyed.

"Now rub a bean on every wart!" the father ordered. "When you've used the last bean, take them to the flowerbed and bury them beneath the droppings from the eaves. As soon as they begin to rot, your warts will go away!"

The youngster's mother scoffed and jeered, but little Jake did as his father told him to. And much to the surprise of everyone but Mr. Richards, when a week had passed there wasn't one remaining wart on either of his hands!

Another superstition that annoyed my Pennsylvania-Dutch-by-marriage friend, she told me, was the childlike faith with which her relatives regarded all chain letters. These mysterious and occult communications, she believed, are specially prevalent among the Pennsylvania Dutch.

"My husband and his relatives were champions of the whole chain letter system," she informed me scornfully. "I took my stand against them, and because I did they all accused me of encouraging misfortune for my family and myself. They were forever sending me such letters, but I always threw them in the fire without even mentioning that I'd gotten them—which made them good and mad!"

But one day, Mrs. Richards went on, for some strange and unintelligible reason, she departed from her usual custom—with results that even yet she can't quite understand. A letter with the customary glowing promises had come that morning, and as usual she was getting ready to destroy it, when a sudden thought of Jessie crossed her mind.

Now Jessie, as it happened, was a childhood friend whom Mrs. Richards hadn't seen for many years. She'd never married, even though in girlhood she'd had more than one devoted suitor pining for her heart and hand. There'd been one obstacle that none of them had been quite bold enough to hurdle: Jessie was too firmly anchored to the family apron strings. For instance, Mrs. Richards cited, when a young man came to call on Jessie, Jessie's father, or perhaps her brother, always stayed around to take an active part in entertaining him. And if the youth got up sufficient courage to invite his lady for a buggyride—why, Mamma promptly donned her wraps and went along. So, courting Jessie under such a handicap proved too discouraging, and one by one the boys began to drift away. The years went by. Both Jessie's mother and her father died, and Jessie, left alone became a shy and tittery old maid who flushed up painfully whenever any man addressed her, and hid her sterling qualities beneath a drab and unattractive front.

But Mrs. Richards never gave up wishing better fortune for her girlhood friend, she said. And so that morning, as she carelessly began to tear in pieces the chain letter she'd received, a new and daring thought occurred to her. On impulse she began to act at once. Erasing all the usual promises of riches and good luck the letter held, she substituted something more appropriate to Jessie's case. It went like this:

> Dear friend: If you will copy this letter five times and send it to your friends, you will be blessed with a very fine husband and lots of good luck. Just a little effort on your part will cause the fates to seek you out a fine man for a husband. Why be lonely when a fine companion is ready for you, selected by the hand of Fate?

Next, Mrs. Richards added the original list of names and sent the missive off, accompanied by a fervent prayer that Jessie's old credulity was still intact. And sure enough, her little scheme bore fruit. A few weeks later what should she receive from Jessie but a notice of her sudden marriage! The whole thing dated back, the happy bride informed her, to a marvelous chain letter sent her by an unknown friend. Somehow, she said, the letter had instilled in her a new and easy confidence, and when a handsome stranger shortly afterward came knocking at her door to ask for lodging, she'd been able to receive him with her old-time naturalness and charm. And lo, Romance had entered with him and her lonely life was once more filled with joy!

So Mrs. Richards' plunge into the mystic province of chain letter writing was a great success, it seems. But even so, it failed completely to convert her to the side of her in-laws. Although poor Jessie's problem had been solved by such a missive, everything that smacked of superstition still was nothing but a childish joke to Jessie's girlhood friend. In fact, I feel quite certain it would take a miracle at least to win her over to her husband's people and their way of life!

BAKER-GENERAL OF THE ARMY

ON MY personal schedule week-ends stood for just one thing—a chance to carry on my favorite sport of getting educated on the Pennsylvania Dutch. And my Chauffeur, of course, had always been my aider and abettor in this strange pursuit. So, when he called up with his usual question: "Where do we go today?" I had my answer all prepared.

"We're going to a graveyard," I informed him.

"Oh—a graveyard." Unsurprised, for long ago he's learned to put up with the curious character of some of our objectives, he inquired: "*Which* graveyard?"

"Oh, a very nice one!" I assured him. "Right here in the city, too!"

He sighed relievedly. "Well, that's a break, at least! You may not know it, but the temperature outside is five above!"

"Oh, well!" My voice was carefree. "You've got a heater in your car, so let's not worry. I'll be looking for you around one o'clock!"

He came, as usual, punctual to the minute. "It's getting colder!" was his first remark.

With cheerful nonchalance I stepped into the car. Patricia,

muffled in a bright green sweater whose engulfing turtle neck gave her a totally misleading air of toughness, hopped in after me. She settled down accustomedly between us and laid her velvet head across my driver's knee.

"I'm *glad* it's cold!" I said complacently. "It makes the whole thing seem more realistic, don't you think? Valley Forge—the Continental soldiers' bloody footprints in the snow—the frozen Delaware—and old man Ludwig turning out his endless loaves of bread!"

The man beside me grunted. "You've been delving in the past again!" he said.

I nodded. "Aren't you glad? Just think of all the painless education that you get from me. *I* do the digging—all *you* have to do is listen to the gems of wisdom I impart!"

He stepped on the accelerator and we oozed out in the traffic. "Well, I'm listening!" he observed. "Go on—impart some wisdom. Who was this Ludwig character, anyway?"

"He was a baker," I began. "And incidentally, he's the man we're on our way to see right now. That is, we're on our way to see his *grave!*"

"You pick such fascinating places!" my Chauffeur commented. "All right—go ahead. What did he do, and why should we or anyone know anything about him, to begin with?"

I looked at him in pained surprise. "Why, Ludwig," I informed him, "was the man who did far more to win the Revolution than the whole rest of the Continental forces put together! I suppose you've heard about an army's fighting on its stomach?"

"Certainly. So what?"

"So Christopher Ludwig filled the Continental Army's stomach!"

"Oh." A slow light seemed to dawn on my companion. "By baking bread, you mean!"

I nodded. "He was Baker-General of the Revolutionary forces."

" 'Baker-General'? But I never heard of such a rank!"

I shrugged. "Well, that was his official title—'Baker-General of the Continental Army.' Washington himself approved it. Only when *he* spoke to Ludwig, he addressed him as 'My honest friend'."

"Why 'honest' friend?"

"Because that's what he was—an honest Pennsylvania Dutchman who believed in playing fair. You see—" I settled back more comfortably—"it happened this way: Back in 1777, when the resolution naming Christopher as Baker-General had been passed by Congress, the committee chosen to confer the honor made a slight mistake. They told him they'd expect him to turn out a pound of bread for every pound of flour that they gave him—not realizing that the yeast and water which he'd have to add would naturally increase the flour's weight. But Christopher knew all about it. 'No, gentlemen!' he told them with his funny accent. 'I will not accept your commission on such terms! Old Ludwig doesn't want to get rich by the war—he *has* enough money. But I will furnish you one hundred and thirty-five loaves of bread for every hundredweight of flour that you give me!' And," I finished, "that's the reason for the title given him by Washington—'my honest friend'."

"Well, good for Christopher!" My driver seemed impressed. "Know any other tales about him?"

I nodded. Secretly delighted with this golden opportunity to air my recently acquired facts, I launched forth on the story of the Baker-General's life. "Old Ludwig," I began, "was born in Germany—in the Palatinate, to be exact. That's on the Upper Rhine, you know, where thousands of the early Pennsylvania Germans came from. His father was a baker, and young Christopher, of course, was taught the secrets of the trade. He had a leaning toward adventure, though, and at the age of seventeen enlisted in the army of the Holy Roman Emperor and fought for three years on the side of Austria against the Turks.

"When finally the war was over," I went on, "he started back from Turkey to Vienna, walking all the way, through bitter cold that killed off more than half his comrades right before his eyes. He spent some months then in Vienna, and one day he saw the public execution of an officer who'd stolen money that was meant for food and clothing for the common troops. And to his dying day he never did forget that lesson!"

"Which probably accounted for his own strict honesty," the man beside me said.

Again I nodded, and picked up my little tale. "He did a lot of fighting after that, and ended up eventually as baker on a ship that plied the India seas. Then one day he decided suddenly he'd like to pay a visit to his father. So he started home. But when he got there he discovered that old Ludwig, senior, was no longer living—he'd passed on while Christopher was sailing merrily around the seven seas. He'd left his son his whole estate, however, so the young man promptly sold it, and with pockets full of money hied himself to London, where he started spending it so recklessly that soon there wasn't any left. So—back to sea he went again, with pockets just as empty as they'd been before." I paused for breath.

"And then what happened?" my Chauffeur demanded.

"Well, he'd learned his lesson, evidently, for he saved some money after that. And finally, when he'd accumulated several thousand dollars, he went back to London, bought a stock of clothing and set sail for Philadelphia. There he sold it for three times the sum he'd paid for it, and then went back to London once again—"

"To buy more clothing, I suppose."

I shook my head. "You'll never guess! To learn to bake—of all things—gingerbread!"

The man behind the wheel looked frankly skeptical. "Don't tell me that he fed the Continental soldiers *ginger*bread!"

"Of course not!" I assured him. "Just plain, ordinary bread

was what he baked for Washington. But that was later on, of course. Before he settled down here in America for good, he spent nine months in London learning everything there was to know about the art of making gingerbread. And then at last, when he'd become an expert, back he came to Philadelphia. In Letitia Court, the place where William Penn once lived, you know, he started business, and it wasn't long before he'd built up quite a thriving trade. In fact, he got quite rich eventually. He owned nine houses and a farm in Germantown, and had a lot of money in the bank besides. What's more, he used it for all sorts of patriotic purposes."

"For instance?"

"Well, for one thing," I explained, "he was a member of the various groups that handled Revolutionary matters at the time. And he was always ready to contribute to the various causes, too. At one convention General Mifflin tried to start a private fund for buying firearms, but all the members hemmed and hawed and hesitated till at last it looked as though they'd have to call the whole thing off. But suddenly old Christopher spoke up. '*Ach*, Mr. President,' he said in broken English but a loud, determined voice, 'I'm just a poor old baker, but I want that you should put my name down for two hundred pounds!' And after that the motion was unanimously passed."

"Well, good for Christopher again!" my listener said.

"And he was patriotic in a lot of other ways besides," I went on. "Back in 1776 he joined the 'flying camp' and served there without pay or rations, preaching liberty and holding up to others as a horrible example the condition of his native land. One day he heard a number of militia were about to leave the camp because they didn't like the food. So, without losing any time, he went to them and fell down on his knees. 'Oh, brother soldiers,' he implored dramatically, 'listen for one moment to old Christopher! In Philadelphia when we hear the cry of fire, we all fly there with our buckets and attempt to keep the blaze from spreading to our homes. So let us keep the great fire of the British Army from our town! In just a few days you shall have good bread and plenty of it!"

"Did it work?"

"Of course it did!" I answered. "It made them feel ashamed, I guess. At any rate, they all decided that they'd stay and see it through. And Christopher went on with other missionary work, as well. One day when several Hessian prisoners had been caught and brought to camp, and everyone was wondering what to do with them, he had a bright idea. 'Suppose we take them all to Philadelphia?' he suggested. 'Show them our fine German churches, let them see our tradesmen eating beef and drinking out of silver cups and riding comfortably in chairs each afternoon. Then send them back to tell their countrymen, and soon they all will run away, to settle in our city and be Whigs as good as any one of us!'

"Another time he asked to be allowed to pay a visit to the Hessian camp on Staten Island, posing as an enemy deserter. When he got permission he began to circulate among the British mercenaries, telling them the most enticing tales about their countrymen in Pennsylvania German counties—how they lived in ease and comfort, without owing loyalty to any greedy ruler overseas. '*You're* merely slaves!' he said—or words to that effect. 'Why don't you come to Philadelphia, where you'll live in peace and freedom?' And a lot of them deserted—several hundred, I believe —and Christopher, with Congress' permission, took full charge of them himself. He got some money voted for a little scheme to settle them out in the country districts, where they lived and flourished happily from that day on."

My audience of one was silent for a moment as we glided swiftly through the week-end traffic of the city streets. "I wonder why," he said at last, "I've never heard of Christopher before? I'll bet a lot of other people haven't, either! Yet the old boy was a patriot, all right—he certainly deserved the honor that he got. And incidentally—was that *all* he got?"

"You mean the honor of his title—Baker-General of the Army? No, he got a salary, too."

"He did? How much?"

"Oh—seventy-five a month, plus rations twice a day," I told him.

"Hm. Munificent!" The tone was scornful.

"Well, it wasn't much, of course," I said. "But after all, he had a lot of fun besides. He dined with Washington quite often, and his reputation as a storyteller, plus his sense of humor and his funny German accent, made him welcome as an honored guest. He always took along with him, whenever he was dining out, a china bowl he'd bought in Canton many years before. It had a silver rim, and on it was the date on which he'd bought it, and his name. Each time he used it he'd propose a certain toast that went like this:

> "Health and long life
> To Christopher Ludwig and his wife."

"You shouldn't toast yourself," my listener objected. "It's supposed to bring bad luck!"

"I know," I said. "Perhaps that's why old Christopher's good fortune didn't last. Because when finally the war was over and he went back to his farm in Germantown, he found the place had been completely looted by the British troops. His clothing, all his silver plate, and every solitary piece of furniture had disappeared. He hadn't any ready cash to mention, and the thought of borrowing or buying things on credit horrified him, since he'd never in his life run into debt. So, rather than begin at that late date, he swore he'd get along the way things were. Instead of ordering badly needed sheets, for instance, and then paying for them later on, he slept without them for six weeks, between a pair of ragged blankets. And at last, by selling off some real estate, he got together enough cash to re-equip his house and go on living in it as it was.

"Through all the years that followed," I continued solemnly, "he kept one precious relic of his former life—a statement of appreciation from the man he'd loved and served so many years. He hung it in the place of honor on his parlor wall, and every day he'd look at it and think back to the years gone by. Look—this is it." I drew a piece of paper from my my pocketbook. "I brought a copy of it with me. Listen:

> "I have known Christopher Ludwig from an early period in the war, and have every reason to believe, as well from observation as information, that he has been a true and faithful servant to the public; that he has detected and exposed many impositions, which were attempted to be exercised by others in his department; that he has been the cause of much saving in many respects; and that his deportment in public life, has afforded unquestionable proofs of his integrity and worth.
>
> "With respect to his losses, I have no personal knowledge, but have often heard that he has suffered from his zeal in the cause of his country.
>
> GEORGE WASHINGTON."

A sound that hardly could be called enthusiastic issued from behind the wheel. " 'I have no personal knowledge'—'I have every reason to believe'— Just full of practical assistance, isn't it?"

I shrugged. "Well, Ludwig liked it, anyway. He kept it with his dearest treasures till the day he died."

"And when was that?"

"In 1801—in Philadelphia, where he'd moved from Germantown six years before. He boarded with a former journeyman of his, and when the yellow fever epidemic struck the city, he went back to baking—at the age of seventy-five!"

"That's pretty old to be an active baker, isn't it?"

I nodded. "Yes, but Christopher was just as tall and straight and active as he'd ever been before. He outlived Washington by several years, you know. But when at last death did approach, he seemed to have a premonition that his time had come. One day somebody asked him if he wouldn't buy a copy of the General's life. 'Indeed I won't,' he answered, 'for I'm traveling fast to meet him. I'll hear about it from his own brave lips!'"

The car had glided to a stop as I was speaking. With an air of grim finality, my driver turned the key in the ignition. "And thus ends the story of the Baker-General's life!"

I shook my head. "Oh, no it doesn't! Don't forget we came here for a purpose! Where's the cemetery?"

"Over there!" He waved a hand across the snowy street. I peered in the direction indicated. Sure enough, behind an iron fence stretched row on row of ghostly graves, each covered with a sheet of gleaming white. I laid my hand upon the door.

"You'd better button up!" the gentleman beside me said paternally. "It must be five below by this time—at the very least!"

The warning went unheeded. Waiting only long enough to see that Patsy was locked safely in the cozy warmth we left behind, I hurried through the traffic to the other side. I'd reached the gate when my Chauffeur caught up with me.

"What do you think you're going to find?" he asked.

I didn't answer for a moment. In the icy air that swept across the open cemetery there was something dreary and forlorn, I thought. Here on this busy thoroughfare, unnoticed by the crowds that surged obliviously past, the city of the dead lay silent and alone. I shivered as I turned to my companion. "Will you promise not to laugh?" I asked.

He nodded.

"Well, you see, I read somewhere that Christopher had only one eye—he had lost the other in an accident."

"What kind of accident?"

"That's just it—I don't know!" My voice was plaintive. "In all the books I've read about him—every one of them—they simply say 'an accident' and let it go at that. They don't tell how, or why, or when, or where it happened. So I thought perhaps—just possibly, you know—I *might* find something on his gravestone that would clear it up."

My driver nobly hid a smile. "Of all the optimists!" he muttered. But obligingly he followed as I made my way along the path that led between the graves.

"Look!" Suddenly I stopped. A huge, flat slab of marble raised on four square columns from the frozen ground loomed several yards ahead of us. "That must be it!" I said, and hastened on. My driver's long legs brought him up with me in half a dozen strides. We reached the grave together and with simultaneous vigor started brushing at the snow-encrusted stone. Our hands were stiff and numb with cold when finally we had the surface cleared. In eager silence we stood peering at the graven words before us. This is what we read:

IN MEMORY OF
CHRISTOPHER LUDWICK
and of his wife CATHARINE

She died at Germantown the 21st of September
1796 aged eighty years and five months

He died at Philadelphia the 17th June
1801 aged eighty years and nine months

* * * * *

He was born at Giessen in Hessen D'Armstadt
In Germany
And learndt the baker's trade and business
In his early life he was a soldier and sailor
And visited the East and West Indies.

In the year 1775 he came to and settled at
 Philadelphia and by his industry at his
Trade and business acquired a handsome
 Competency, part of which he devoted to
The service of his adopted country in the contest
 FOR THE INDEPENDENCE OF AMERICA:
 Was appointed Baker General to the Army
And for his faithful service received a written
 Testimony from the Commander-in-Chief
 GENERAL WASHINGTON
On every occasion his zeal for the relief of the
 Oppressed was manifest and by his last will
He bequeathed the greater part of his estate
 For the education of the children of the poor
 Of all denominations gratis.
He lived and died respected for his integrity
 And public spirit by all who knew him.

Reader, such was LUDWICK.

 Art thou poor:
 Venerate his character.

 Art thou rich:
 Imitate his example.

Quaking and shivering in the wintry wind that chilled us to
the very bone, we read the final words aloud. Then, with an air of
grim reproach, my comrade of the arctic turned and looked at me.
"So *this* is what we nearly freeze to death to find! A long account
of everything we know already—and not a word about his missing
eye!"

I nodded sadly. Somewhat conscience-stricken, if the truth be
told, I turned and headed for our waiting car. It *was*, I thought,

a bitter day on which to drag a man out in the great, wide, open spaces on a fruitless quest!

The atmosphere was heavy with unspoken disapproval as we plodded slowly through the hard-packed snow. "Well," I observed at last, defensively, "at least you got a *little* something from it, didn't you?"

The man beside me halted. "What?" he asked.

"An education!" I suggested brightly.

"Oh." The word was eloquent. "An education—*plus* a pair of frozen feet!"

WHAT PRICE ANTIQUES?

THE morning mail had brought a note from Katie Good, in which she told me of a sale that Levi King, an Amish neighbor of the Goods', was going to hold. Levi, she said, was moving to his daughter's home and all his household chattels would be auctioned off. He had some nice old things, she added—it would probably be worth my while to come and look at them.

My driver, as it happened, had to work that morning, so when finally we reached the sale we found that it was almost over. A line of Amish buggies and "top wagons" heading in the opposite direction told us so before we turned the corner of the road that leads to Levi King's abode.

We parked our car among the other vehicles drawn up before the fence—some Amish wagons and a scattering of autos, with the usual dealer's truck nosed in among the rest. The lawn that spread out on the left was filled with furniture—chairs, tables, bureaus, chests—pathetic relics of a home that soon would be a home no more. An old spool bed was being loaded on the dealer's truck, we noted, and some Mennonites were cramming odds and ends of household gear into a well-scrubbed car.

Beside the barn the final sales were still going on. We stopped and listened curiously. A knot of men and boys were grouped around the auctioneer, bidding on articles of farm equipment. It was bitter cold, and all the Amishmen were hunched up in their long, caped overcoats, with flat-crowned hats pulled well down over ears, and ruddy, bearded faces peering out from underneath. The little boys were muffled in bright-colored scarfs that streamed behind in gay abandon as they romped about, unmindful of the frosty nip that bit at bare, red hands and little purple noses. The womenfolks, it seemed, were all inside the house.

We stood and watched a moment from the outer fringes of the group of bidders. A cultivator of the hand variety was knocked down for the startling sum of twenty-seven cents. Apparently the buyer's credit wasn't all it should be, for the tally man pushed forward and collected on the spot. The penny man—none other than the brand-new owner of the place himself, we learned a little later—kept an avid eye on every purchase. Up to now he'd bid in, for a penny each, an oil lamp and reflector, a dilapidated sofa, and a colander that visibly had seen much better days.

We moved on to the barn. An enterprising vendor had set up a stand inside, where hot dogs, sauerkraut, cup cakes and coffee, candy, oranges, hamburgers, oyster soup, cigars, and cigarettes were laid out on a wooden table. They didn't tempt me, but my driver, hardier than I, decided to remain outside and bought a cup of coffee to sustain him.

"I'm going inside to get warmed up," I told him shiveringly, and headed for the house near by. The front door opened at that moment and the smiling face of Katie Good appeared.

"Just come on in!" she called. "We been expecting youse!"

I didn't need a second invitation. The room I entered seemed to be the kitchen, empty now of everything except a glowing stove, some chairs, and a tall painted dresser. The place was filled with women—women everywhere—and all of them, I saw, still wore their shawls and bonnets. The bonnets for the most part were the large, full-skirted, deep-brimmed Amish kind, with only an occasional smaller, skirtless one like Katie's showing that some Mennonites were also present. Their sombreness contrasted sharply with the reds and blues and greens and purples of the little girls' headpieces, framing rosy faces smeared with licorice and lollypop, all blissfully agog with the excitement of this holiday event.

Through an open doorway to the left I glimpsed another group of women more informally attired. Invited guests and relatives, apparently, they'd laid aside their outer wraps, and with their white-capped heads grouped close about their hostess, Mrs. Levi King, were deep in a discussion of the day's events.

I spied Mom Rachel seated by the kitchen window, with Mary standing near her, and I joined them gratefully. My teeth were chattering as I sank into a vacant chair beside them and stretched my frozen fingers toward the stove.

"It's pretty cold out, ain't?" Mom Rachel greeted me. I nodded an emphatic "Yes."

"You should of got here sooner—things went pretty good!"

I wished we had myself—especially when I found we'd missed some really fine antiques. I glanced about me ruefully. A cake pan filled with odds and ends lay on the kitchen dresser, and two articles it held immediately intrigued me—a meat fork and a pancake turner made of solid tin. The shape and workmanship were excellent, and suddenly I craved them desperately.

I turned to Mary. "Do you know who bought them?" I nodded covetously toward the implements of my desire. She pointed to an Amish woman standing near me. With bated breath I took my courage in both hands and spoke to her.

"You wouldn't want to sell me those two pieces, would you?"

The woman hesitated. "Well," she said. "I wouldn't mind so much the fork. The pancake turner, now—"

"I'll gladly pay a dollar for them," I put in. And with a little gasp she turned to stare at me, her eyes quite round with wonder.

"*Ach*," she said, her hesitation suddenly evaporated, "for *that* I sell them to you!" And with mutual satisfaction the deal was closed.

Word of my reckless purchase spread about the room like wildfire. There was some whispering, and I heard a woman murmur eagerly: "Sell her some more!"

A group of men now entered from the lean-to kitchen. They included my Chauffeur, the auctioneer, and Levi King himself. The bearded Mr. King, a tall and ruddy Amishman, made straight in my direction. Apparently he'd heard the news of my astounding purchase and came to add his blessing to the sale. "My wife and I," he told me sociably, "got them two pieces when we first got married—forty-five years back. They've worn real good!"

I thought so, too. With frank proprietary pride I held them up for my Chauffeur's inspection. But that gentleman, it seemed, was far more interested in something else. The vendor of refreshments in the barn, he told me with a grin, had just informed him that a second vendor in the lean-to kitchen had come out and priced his wares, then gone back to the kitchen and deliberately begun to undersell him. Hot dogs and sauerkraut five cents instead of ten, and oyster soup ten cents instead of the legitimate fifteen! It wasn't right!

We were discussing this appalling lack of business ethics, when I felt a gentle tugging at my elbow. A voice behind me spoke. "I got some awful pretty cups!" it murmured timidly. "Perhaps you'd like to buy them, still?"

I turned to find a plump and eager-visaged Amish woman standing at my elbow. "They got such flowers on the front," she told me earnestly. "And handles yet, and rings around the edge! Just come out on the porch onct and I'll show them to you."

I had no thought of buying any cups, but to be sociable I followed her outside. There from the tin depths of a bucket she unearthed a cup and held it up to view. I'm not a connoisseur of china and its decoration, but I know bronze lustre when I see it, and the rings and flowers that she'd mentioned were indubitably that. The cup was old—just *how* old I don't know—but something in its shape and general outline took my fancy.

"How many have you?" I inquired.

"Six of them—and saucers, too!" She brought forth from the pail five other cups with matching saucers. Except for several surface cracks they were in good condition—and at once I knew that I must have them.

"What do you want for them?" I asked.

She looked at me uncertainly. The crucial moment had arrived! Just how much would I pay, I saw her wondering silently?

"Yes, well—" She took the fatal plunge at last—"I'll give them to you for—a dollar!"

To my driver's undisguised amusement, I agreed. He didn't think so much of my bronze lustre cups. But I was more than satisfied—and so, I gathered, was their erstwhile owner. I learned why when I showed my purchases to Mary Good a little later and she told me their original price had been—six cents apiece!

With this transaction finished, we went back into the house, and hardly had we entered when I felt a second tugging at my arm. The little game, it seemed, was spreading, for a second woman now held out enticingly a cup and saucer *she* had purchased—one of half a dozen, she informed me, that she'd gladly sell. These second cups were even nicer than the first, it turned out. For they had no handles, and around the edge of cup and saucer both there was a wreath of green leaves and gold wheat heads outlined boldly in bronze lustre—and in none of them a crack or nick of any kind.

However, I was getting just a little weary of the whole affair by this time. After all, I couldn't buy up everything! So I declined with thanks, and my Chauffeur and I decided it was time to leave. The Goods had asked us to stop off for supper with them, as it happened, so we rounded up the sisters and departed without further purchases. Mom Rachel, busy visiting with neighbors, was to follow later with the boys.

Our talk as we drove swiftly toward the big, white house that crowned a near-by hill was naturally about the incidents occurring at the sale. "I have two larger plates like those that second woman tried to sell you," Mary mentioned as we rolled along. "I'll show them to you when we get back home!" And just as soon as we alighted she proceeded to unearth from out the depths of her big dower chest upstairs the plates in question. I looked them over carefully—and suddenly I knew that I'd been mighty foolish not to buy those cups and saucers when I'd had the chance!

But luckily the Goods knew where their owner lived. Her name was King, they said, and she was married to a son of Levi King, the man whose sale we'd just attended. So after supper, on our way home, we stopped off to see them. My driver waited for me in the car while I went in to buy the cups and saucers that by now I'd set my heart on.

I found the family in the kitchen getting supper—Mrs. King, the oldest daughter, and three smaller children. Seth, the youngest, aged a scanty two or three, had evidently fallen recently and skinned his face. His big, brown eyes, still full of tears, regarded me in solemn wonder as I entered.

"I've changed my mind," I came right to the point. "I'd like to buy those cups and saucers that you showed me, after all."

My hostess hesitated. Could it be, I thought, that she as well as I had had a change of heart? I waited anxiously. "Well," she replied at last, "I'll have to ask my husband first." And little

Sadie of the blond pigtails wound tightly in a big bun at the rear, was sent out to the barn to fetch her father.

He came in, brisk and blowing, with the odor of the barnyard clinging to his heavy boots, and listened curiously while Mrs. King repeated what I'd said. Then: "What will you give for them?" he asked.

I based my answer on the price I'd paid the other woman for her set of cups, and said a dollar. He shook his head. "They're all we got belonging to my Mom and Pop," he told me. "I ain't so anxious to get rid of them."

I said I understood—I wouldn't want to take them if they meant so much to him. But, as I turned to go, he called me back abruptly. "Well—you can have them for a dollar and a half!" he said. And, thoroughly delighted with my new possessions, I went forth to flaunt them in the mildly disapproving face of my Chauffeur.

"What are you going to do with all this china?" he demanded practically as we started on the last lap of our homeward way.

I looked at him in sudden blankness. Actually, I hadn't thought of that!

"You'll probably be buying a Dutch cupboard next, to put it in!" He sighed resignedly and stepped on the accelerator.

I didn't answer. But it wasn't such a bad idea, at that. Not bad at all, in fact! I made a mental note to think it over.

HEXEREI

MY OHIO correspondent, Mrs. Richards, has regaled me with an-other batch of recipes and superstitions. How she ever finds the time to write such lavish letters is more than I can understand! But still, they're interesting, and though she evidently has no use at all for anything or anybody Pennsylvania Dutch, I've found her anecdotes about her husband and his people most amusing.

In her latest missive she recited a long list of favorite charms and bugaboos that her in-laws believe in. For example, if you want to harm an enemy, they told her, all you have to do is make a likeness of him with potatoes, stick some pins into the head and heart, then take it to the woods and bury it beneath the leaf mold. Just as soon as the potatoes rot, your enemy will promptly die.

If lice or vermin trouble you, they further told her, a piece of coffin dug up from a grave will solve the problem without fail. A coal-black rooster, lame at birth, is good luck of the most effective kind, they went on. And the feathers of a black hen placed inside the bed of anyone you wish to harm will cause his death. To kill a snake and hang it in the sun insures a rainfall by the following day. A rooster's crow at midnight means the passage overhead of the Death Angel. And, they added darkly, to avoid a violent death, be sure to get a splinter from a gallows, or perhaps a strand of rope with which somebody has been hung, suspend it from your neck, and presto, you'll be safe from harm!

I gathered there'd been others, too, besides her family, who had offered Mrs. Richards bits of equally naïve advice. Last summer she was troubled with a blister on one eye, she told me. It would fill with water, break, and fill again alternately—the aftermath of an old injury she'd suffered several years before. A Pennsylvania German neighbor, noting her discomfort, gave her what my correspondent called, quite simply, "That Priest's magic book." (She didn't bother to explain the reference, but it sounded very much like my old friend, Albertus Magnus, with his weird *Egyptian Secrets*.) Anyway, to be polite, she took the book, she said, and she and her two children had a good laugh as they read it.

Now it happened that among the various remedies included there was one that bore this title: "How to Cure a Wheal in the

Eye." Its aptness caught the fancy of the children, and they urged
their mother eagerly to try it. So, following the book's directions,
she picked up an unwashed dinner plate and held it to her face,
about four inches from her nose.

> "Dirty plate I press thee,
> Wheal in the eye, do flee!"

her small son quoted from the book, as both his mother and his
sister scoffed amusedly to think that anyone should credit such a
foolish charm with actual power.

"Next morning," Mrs. Richards finished her engaging tale, "my
children asked me how I felt—and suddenly I realized that the
pain was gone! The blister on my eye was still there, but it didn't
hurt again and soon I clean forgot about it. And today it's disappeared!"

Another time, my letter-writing friend related, she and her
family were out walking, when her little girl was smitten with a
sharp pain in her side. At once her father pointed to a smooth,
round stone embedded in the grass and told the child to pick it
up. The youngster did as she was bidden. Mr. Richards looked
it over carefully, then shook his head.

"Try that one!" he commanded, pointing to another stone.
Again the little girl obeyed. Once more her father scrutinized it
closely. The second stone was flat on one side, Mrs. Richards said.
Her husband nodded in pleased satisfaction. "Spit in the hole
you took it from," he told his daughter, "and then put it back
exactly as you found it!"

And sure enough, my friend continued, by the time her little
daughter had replaced the stone the pain was gone completely—
and it never did come back!

The recipes that Mrs. Richards sent me this time were for tur-
nip kraut, potato cakes, and bean kraut. The two krauts don't

appeal to me, but the potato cakes (her husband's favorite dish, she said) are really good, and I agree with Mr. Richards' taste! They're made like this:

First, grate an onion and 8 medium-sized potatoes (raw); add pepper, salt, 1 teaspoonful of baking powder, 2 well-beaten eggs, and 1 tablespoonful of flour. Drop by spoonfuls on a good hot frying pan or griddle, and turn over on the other side when brown.

February

THE LAST OF THE OLD-TIME POTTERS

FOR QUITE awhile my conscience had been troubling me. It had begun, a bit belatedly, when I unearthed a red clay pieplate from a box of odds and ends I'd brought down from the country. Why I'd brought it in the first place still remains a mystery, for there surely wasn't any chance that I'd be doing any baking in the city. But there it was, its smooth, glazed, convex surface, ornamented with three rows of wavy lines, looking at me

[189]

reproachfully and daring me to keep the promise that I'd made when first I'd added it to my collection.

At that time I'd assured my driver recklessly that no pies in the world were quite so good as those baked in an old-time Pennsylvania German pieplate—and what's more, I'd *prove* it to him! What kind would he like, I asked? The question was a foolish one, of course. For is there any man alive who doesn't think of apple pie as the *ne plus ultra* of all pastries? So—I promised that I'd bake him one in my old brown and yellow pieplate and establish once for all how utterly delectable an apple pie could be.

But that was more than a year ago. And, to my shame let it be said, I'd never kept that promise. So, as I looked guiltily at my old pieplate I contritely promised once again that when I moved up to the cottage in the spring the first thing that I'd do would be to bake that pie for my Chauffeur! And as a sort of challenging reminder, I stood the plate atop the bookcase where I'd have to look at it each time I passed.

I'd looked at it quite often, too. Somehow, its crude yet skillful craftsmanship, the homely grace of its uncomplicated pattern took me back a year or so ago to one warm summer day when Eleanor and I went calling on two quaint old brothers up in Lehigh County—sole survivors of those old-time Pennsylvania German potters who turned out such traditional pieces as this old plate of mine.

We'd heard of the Stahl brothers often. Several times a year we knew, the small green cranny in the hills that's known as Powder Valley, where their homemake kiln and workship are located, suddenly became a scene of brisk activity. For then the gaping opening of the kiln was crammed with carefully selected lengths of cherry, poplar, oak, and chestnut wood and the huge pile was lit into a roaring blaze. All day the logs burned brightly and all through the night as well, while gradually the heat in creased, till finally it concentrated in a white and steady flame that thundered from the chimney in a droning roar.

Then people gathered from the near-by hills, and from the distant places, too, and both the gnomelike little brothers—high-priests of the oven and its treasures—would test and analyze with patient skill, then wait until the heat had died, the oven cooled, and they could take out from its sandstone depths another batch of carefully designed and molded objects such as they, and only they, still knew the secret of creating.

Both Eleanor and I were full of keen anticipation as we bounced along the stony way that led us to the Stahl abode. A small gray signpost farther down the hill had mentioned casually: "Stahl Pottery," and somewhat hesitantly we'd embarked upon the road it indicated. The sharp, clear shadows of late summer lay serenely on the green-clad hills and peaceful valleys as we rattled past a country church with tiny graveyard at the rear, past the inevitable big, red barn and golden cornfields swaying in the breeze, and turned at last to jounce spasmodically upward on a winding trail that ended just outside the barn which formed the brothers' workshop.

Completely unsurprised, for they were used to visitors, of course, the two old potters looked up as we entered. Isaac, the younger brother, round-faced and assured, with small, bright eyes that peered out shrewdly from behind a pair of gold-rimmed spectacles, was standing at a table with an urnlike object cradled gently in his hands. We watched him, fascinated, as with sure, deft stroke he sliced the object through the middle, laid one piece aside and started to evolve a candleholder from the other. Just behind him Tom, the less aggressive member of the partnership, was seated at another table, leisurely engaged in finishing a batch of tiny, handled casseroles of fresh, gray clay.

Impassively they went on working as we introduced ourselves. But underneath that Pennsylvania Dutch exterior there lay, I knew, the usual friendliness that needed only to be sure of answering friendliness to be released. We asked the usual questions. Matter-of-factly Isaac answered them. Quite evidently he, and not the older brother, was the guiding spirit of the firm—a spirit, incidentally, with opinions and convictions of his own. For unlike Tom, who stuck to old designs and decorations used by ancient masters, Ike believed in making up his motives as he went along.

"This here's an art that's been in history long already!" he informed us learnedly, as with uncanny skill his stubby fingers shaped a piecrust edge. "But I ain't *so* for duplication! When I leave this world, I want some of my own ideas to stay behind!"

I looked up at the shelves that lined the little workshop. Row on row of ghostly shapes—some small, some large, some fancy, some quite plain, some with the glaze applied, and some still moist and dark—stood waiting for the firing of the round, stone kiln. With such variety, I thought, there didn't seem much doubt that Isaac's wish would be fulfilled.

Behind me Thomas got up slowly from his workbench and approached an old-time kick-wheel standing in the corner. I looked about for Eleanor, but she had gone outside to sketch the oven that stood opposite the barn. Absorbedly I watched as Tom sat down before the wheel and gave the wooden treadle a determined kick. The round disc started into whirring motion—and unconsciously I glanced across at Isaac's wheel, electrically run. I was about to comment when the younger man forestalled me.

"What's the difference?" he demanded, evidently reading in my mind the question there. "The work I turn out's just the same, no matter what kind of a wheel I use! Now, ain't it?" And he peered at me, a trifle testily, above his spectacles.

I nodded hastily. Perhaps, I thought, I'd better change the subject. How about the oven, I inquired? And the clay they used —where did it come from?

Pacified, he took the bait. "A potter," he informed me with didactic relish, "has got to be a mason, too!" He went on to explain how he and Tom had hauled the stone and built the kiln themselves. "He's got to be a chemist, yet, and make his own tools also," he continued. "And he's got to know just what he's doing if he wants to turn out work that's any good!"

As for himself, it seemed, he had a little laboratory and a small kiln of his own where he experimented and wrote down his formulas with painful care. And what he learned—he slapped another lump of clay upon the whirring wheel as emphasis—that there belonged to him! "Nobody give *me* anything for nothing!" he remarked. "And so I say, just let the other fellow worry for himself!"

The two old brothers dug the clay themselves, right in Montgomery County—four or five tons at a time, he told me further. Five tons made about three kilnfuls of three thousand pieces or a little over. They fired it as high at 2,250 degrees, he said. And added proudly: "And we get as high as ninety-five per cent perfection to a kiln!"

It all went back a hundred years or so ago, I further learned. At that time, there in Powder Valley, just a short way down the hillside from the present kiln, there stood another pottery that bore the name of Stahl. Its owner, Carl Stahl, was the father of old Tom and Isaac, and the trade he'd learned right in that very valley as a potter's hired boy, he'd passed on to his sons. Before young Ike was born the older brother had already mastered the first stages, and the younger boy was quick to follow in his elder's footsteps. Taught by the other workers, and especially by those hobo craftsmen who in wander years went back and forth between the various potteries and left at each a little of their individual skills, they learned to kick a wheel and turn out pots and pieplates with the best of them. And when at sixty-eight Carl Stahl laid down his mold and quill box for the last time, his two sons were ready to step in and take his place.

For four years Ike and Tom had run the pottery, they told me. But the times kept changing and the trend toward substituting chinaware for earthen pottery increased, until at last the output of the kiln had dwindled to a small commercial stock of objects made according to a uniform design. That wasn't what the brothers wanted, so, reluctantly, they'd closed the pottery and gone their separate ways. For thirty-seven years they'd followed other occupations, while the ranks of Pennsylvania German potters everywhere grew slowly thinner and it seemed as though an ancient craft were destined to be lost.

And then one day in 1929 a country sale set Isaac's business instincts palpitating. For there among the various pieces auctioned off he recognized some pieplates he himself had fashioned many years before. Instead of selling for the trifling price of six or seven cents apiece, however, they now brought the same amount in dollars, and at once the thought of going back to the trade he'd left so long ago took root in Isaac's mind. He talked it over with his brother, and a few years later both of them were back in Powder Valley, partners once again and sole remaining craftsmen of an old-time art.

At first, Ike told me, Tom had done most of the glazing, leaving his brother to manipulate the wheel. But nowadays Tom's work was chiefly modeling, and the glazing, painting, and *Sgraffito* operations all had fallen to the younger man. He pointed to a row of pieplates on the shelf above. Their crude yet cunning decoration of uneven lettering and improbable-appearing birds and trees and flowers were his handiwork, I gathered. Some were just plain slipware, others were *Sgraffito*—and he didn't need to tell me that the pastries baked in either would be viands fit to offer to a king!

I picked up one and turned it over. On the under side was

this inscription: "This plate is made and decorated by I. S. Stahl —The 19 day of September, 1940—Clear and Warm." I looked at Ike inquiringly. He smiled, A year ago, he said, he'd started adding to his signature a weather statement. Now his brother Tom did, too, and everyone demanded that the custom be retained. That wasn't all, though, he went on. For often as he stood before his turning wheel a bit of verse would start to go round in his head. Sometimes it might be English, sometimes Pennsylvania Dutch, and sometimes German, he explained. But always it reflected what was foremost in his thoughts. And, as the soft, damp clay took form beneath his fingers, he'd proceed to trace on it the sentences that came to mind.

He handed me plate after plate. Engraved on each one was a naïve rhyme, and though the spelling and the metre were, to say the least, original, the sentiment was clear. *"Mench, hab Verstand, geh nicht so weit, trink nicht so viel, und bleib gesheit"* ("Man, be wise, be moderate, don't drink too much, and stay sensible") read one; *"Wer nicht leibt sein Gott und Weib, der hat kein ruh in Ewigkeit"* ("Who doesn't love his God and wife, won't have any rest in eternity") another. And, in the nature of an epitaph, a third: *"War noch lebt wann ich bin dot, Seit so gut un nem den rot, Wann er schwetz von mer, Sagt es gut un sieberich Loss unnich dem Hut."* ("Let him who lives when I am dead take this advice: Speak only that which is good of me, and leave the rest under your hat.")

Sometimes, it seemed, Ike's mind was occupied with patriotic themes. Then the inscriptions on his plates would go like this: "Dictators, please take notice. We Americans trust in God. In politics we are divided, but in time of war we are unided [united]." Or, bursting into rhyme once more: "If we love Peace we can Live In Ease—If we Hate Peace—well For An Example Look Beyond The Seas."

It was late when Eleanor and I went trundling down the hillside on our homeward way. We didn't talk much, but we both were well content. For safely tucked away inside the storage space behind us lay a painting of the kiln that Eleanor had almost finished, while in my memory, stowed away for future reference, lay a picture of a different but quite satisfying kind. Perhaps *my* picture wasn't quite as clear and vivid to the outward eye as Eleanor's, but still it pleased me. For I knew that from now on, whenever I discovered an old pieplate anywhere, or when at last I baked within my own slip-decorated dish that apple pie I'd promised my Chauffeur, I'd conjure up a mental image of two quaint and friendly white-haired potters bent above their whirling wheels—the last surviving members of a proud and ancient craft.

OLD BETHLEHEM DAYS

IF THERE's one place in the world completely tangled in my memory with the joys of food it's Bethlehem, the town where I grew up. I often pity all those poor unfortunates who never had the luck to spend their childhood in that quaint and lovely old Moravian setting. For there if anywhere, it seems to me, the rich traditions clinging to good eating found their true expression. There we favored souls who never knew the pinch of shortages consumed unthinkingly those beatific foods whose memory, even at this distant date, can fill me with a homesick longing such as nothing else in all the world of culinary thrills can conjure up.

I'd just come back from Bethlehem after three days spent among familiar scenes that brought back vividly a host of such nostalgic memories. And suddenly I found myself a drooling gourmet, totally possessed by visions of ambrosial food! Of course, the fare that figured with such yearning in my recollections was almost all Moravian food. For Bethlehem was founded by Moravians, and together with the customs and traditions that they brought along with them, those early settlers also brought a wealth of ancient recipes—for fluffy *Buttersemmeln* and Moravian sugarcake, for *Leckerli* and round, flat love-feast buns, for rich Moravian Christmas cakes and spicy applebutter, gleaming souse and large, fat, sugar-sprinkled *Fassnachts*, and an endless list of other specialties too numerous and too appetite-tormenting to recount. And, with allowance for such changes as a new and different land made necessary, those old recipes were handed down intact through all the intervening generations.

I think if I were forced to choose the one outstanding specialty which more than any other brings back poignant memories of my childhood, it would have to be Moravian sugarcake. The choice would be a pretty hard one, though, for such a welter of mouth-watering dishes mingles in my mind with places and events and people of those bygone days that choosing only one from out the number hardly seems the sporting thing to do. And yet no other favorite, probably, appeared with more persistence—or disappeared with more consistence—than that rich and tawny coffee-cake-de-luxe whose generous thumbholes brimmed enticingly with sugar, cinnamon, and butter melted to a luscious, crunchy crust. Always, I think, Moravian sugarcake will be connected in my mind with Saturdays. For on that day, as regular as clockwork, lavish platefuls cut in long and narrow slabs appeared upon the luncheon table of the ancient Seminary where I lived, and hungry schoolgirls—eighty-some of them or more—who never tired of its goodness, reached for it with eager hands. And when in later years I went back to revisit Bethlehem and my thoughts immediately reverted to the old-time thrill this favorite treat had brought me, I discovered that the sweet-faced sister who produced the kind I liked the best turned out her tempting masterpieces only on a Saturday!

There are a number of old recipes for sugarcake, with minor variations that depend entirely upon the housewife's individual

taste. But here's the one which seems to me most closely linked
to that delightful pastry of my sybaritic past:

MORAVIAN SUGARCAKE

1 cup hot mashed potatoes	1 cup granulated sugar
2 yeast cakes	1 cup melted butter
1 cup lukewarm water	2 eggs
1 teaspoon salt	7 cups flour (about)

Topping: 2 cups brown sugar, ½ cup butter, 5 teaspoons cinnamon.
Dissolve yeast in lukewarm water, mix ingredients and let rise
overnight. In morning place in pans, spreading dough about ¾
inch thick. Let rise again about 1½ hours, or until dough looks
quite puffy. With thumb make holes in rows about 2 inches
apart and fill with butter and brown sugar, sprinkling cinnamon
over top. Bake 20 to 25 minutes in medium oven.

Next, I believe, to sugarcake in bringing back the greedy rap-
tures of my early days come *Buttersemmeln*—those delicious, melt-
ing-in-the-mouth concoctions that appeared at parties given in the
afternoon. The parties centered usually about my mother's fat,
brass teapot swinging from a twisted crane above the lamp that
flickered eerily beneath it. The teapot stood in what was always
known as the "school parlor"—differentiated from our "private
parlor" just across the way. The latter, for some reason, seldom
was in use, as I remember, and its leather-covered davenport and
elegant upholstered chairs—one done in pale blue plush, another
in rich, coppery brocade—its Chinese table with the fearsome
dragon candlestick on top, the walnut what-not in one corner and
the jar of spiced rose petals into whose uncovered mouth my
childish nose was poked ecstatically every time I entered—all were
left to bloom in lonely splendor while we took ourselves across
the hall to more familiar scenes. For our "school parlor" was
much larger than the other, and the groups that gathered there

were seldom known to number less than ten or fifteen at the very least.

At each end of this parlor was a mammoth mural painting with protruding plaster frame that actually was part and parcel of the wall itself. The pictures were intended to depict a festive outing on the Lehigh River. Rowboatloads of buxom ladies, shawled and bonneted decorously, were heading toward Calypso Island—scene of many a lively picnic of my simple past. The inference, of course, was plain to see—a gay and happy time was being had by all. But somehow, due no doubt to a peculiar, nauseous shade of green the artist had employed with lavish ardor, the whole effect was thoroughly depressing. All the ladies looked a trifle bilious, and as far as eye could reach a plague of verdigris seemed just about to settle on the land.

Despite this slightly gruesome atmosphere, however, no one seemed to mind the paintings in the least—there were too many other fascinating features of the room to hold our fancy. The full-length, gilt-edged mirrors on the other walls, for instance, and the heavy sliding doors that could be closed to make two separate parlors where there'd been but one before. And even more enchanting, the soft, deep-pile carpet which miraculously acted as a dynamo to feet dragged slowly on its surface, starting an electric current that made possible the lighting of a big gas chandelier by the mere contact of an outstretched finger.

On party afternoons, however, all these extra charms took second place before the steaming invitation of my mother's teapot. Underneath it was a fat, brass lamp whose alcoholic flame, invisible at times, lent an excitingly uncertain element to my important job as teapot-tender. With my fascinated eyes glued to the spectral point of light, I'd wait impatiently until a gentle hissing from the teapot's spout announced the boiling of the water. Then, with the gleeful gusto that all children bring to little matters, I'd proceed to exercise my special right of putting out the flame with the brass snuffer hanging from a hook beside the crane. And, thoroughly delighted with my role of mother's helper, I'd pick up the plate of warm, soft *Buttersemmeln* that our faithful Laura in the kitchen had passed in to us and circulate with it among our waiting guests.

I have that fat, brass teapot to this very day, complete with lamp and crane and snuffer. And I have as well the recipe for those ineffable fold-over puffs of melting goodness known as *Butter-semmeln*. This is how they're made:

BUTTERSEMMELN

At 6 P.M. set to rise ½ cup mashed potatoes, ½ cup sugar, ½ cake yeast dissolved in ¼ cup warm water. At 10 P.M. add 2 cups milk, 2 eggs, ½ cup sugar, ½ cup butter and lard mixed, ¼ teaspoon salt, and about 6 cups flour sifted twice.
Knead until dough blisters and drops clean from the palm of hand, then set in warm place to rise overnight. In morning, roll out ¼-inch thick, brush with butter, cut into 2-inch squares. Lap the four corners of each square, set 2 inches apart on greased baking sheets, let rise *very* lightly, and bake 15 to 20 minutes in a quick oven. Remove from oven, brush with melted butter, and sprinkle with granulated sugar. Makes 5 dozen.

Occasionally instead of just an ordinary party round the teapot Mamma would be moved to hold a real Moravian "vesper." Then, in keeping with the spirit of the quaint occasion, she'd unearth from the Dark Closet—that mysterious little storeroom off our private quarters, from whose depths the most amazing articles were wont to issue forth—a large box of white aprons, shawls, and caps of the peculiar cut affected by Moravian sisters in the years gone by. Choosing a headpiece with blue ribbon tiestrings for herself (blue was for married women, pink for single ones, and white for widows), she'd hand out the others to her helpers, and thus picturesquely dressed they'd pass around the simple vesper fare. It never varied. Dried beef, applebutter and rye bread, small chunks of cheese, and the inevitable sugarcake and coffee—such were the odd components of this old-time meal.

There was another type of vesper also that occurred with pleasant frequency in Bethlehem. When a minister of the Moravian church observed his birthday, it was customary to invite his fellow ministers around for what was called a "birthday vesper." Once again the ever-relished sugarcake and coffee would appear in generous doses, and the reverend brethren, seated at small tables in the study, would relax in cheerful informality, to smoke and reminisce the afternoon away. I know of only one exception to the rule on these occasions. Up the street from us lived Brother Paul deSchweinitz, who preferred *Strumpfbänder* to the usual sugarcake. So when his birthday rolled around, this specially toothsome form of cruller, knotted like a ribbon (hence the name) and puffed up to a lovely golden brown, appeared on the deSchweinitz board instead of sugarcake. This is the recipe Mrs. deSchweinitz used:

STRUMPFBÄNDER (*Garters*)

½ pound butter	6 eggs
¾ pound powdered sugar	½ teaspoon cinnamon
4 to 5 cups sifted flour	

Roll out dough into a thin sheet. Cut with jagging iron into 1 by 5 inch strips. Tie each strip once, like a loose knot, leaving small hole in middle of knot. Fry in *hot* fat (they should rise almost instantly to the surface). Sprinkle with powdered sugar. *Strumpfbänder* are better on second day than on first.

I think my father was the only minister in town whose birthday *wasn't* celebrated by a vesper. For inside the school itself so many other gay events were taking place that day that outside functions had to be foregone. First, bright and early on his birthday morning (and I don't remember any June the fourth that *wasn't* bright) the girls would gather underneath my father's window for a serenade to start things rolling smoothly. They'd appear by groups, or "room companies" as they were called, and each would vie with all the others in selecting songs they knew my father loved the best. "My Old Kentucky Home," "Old Folks at Home," "Old Black Joe"—the warm June air would fairly reek with Stephen Foster as we lay luxuriously abed upstairs and listened to the strains that floated through our open windows.

At chapeltime my father's favorite in the line of sacred music, the Crusaders' Hymn—"Fairest Lord Jesus, Ruler of All Nature" —would be sung with zest by the entire school, and afterward as many of the girls as possible would crowd in Papa's private office to present their birthday wishes. He was dearly loved by all of them, and many, not content with wholesale greetings, brought him individual birthday presents—candy for the most part, and red roses which they knew were his particular delight. Obligingly, our own bush of "Jack" roses in the yard below would bloom in time for the occasion, and my mother would arrange a generous cluster in a pressed-glass rosebowl on my father's desk.

The morning classes in the Seminary dragged along as usual, but the afternoon was always a half-holiday that reached its climax in a festive birthday supper on the lawn. The actual meal I don't remember, but the fresh strawberry ice-cream that invariably concluded it will linger in my memory till my dying day. All smoothly pink and creamy, with the year's first berries frozen in its luscious depths, it conjures up for me the whole nostalgic fragrance of those lovely, long-past holidays in June.

And speaking of ice-cream, there was also "Rauch's." Rauch's was a wonderful confectionery shop on Main Street—happy hunting-ground of every girl or boy in Bethlehem who possessed a nickel to his name. For back in those Elysian days a nickel really went somewhere, and to the owner of such wealth the only problem was the desperately important one of knowing which among the ravishing variety of sweets to choose. Should it perhaps be half a dozen of those colored sticks arranged in jars upon the highest shelf above—clove, lemon, orange, cinnamon, and winter-green, plus various other flavors each more tempting than the rest? Or maybe some of those ineffably delicious chocolate cara-mels that beckoned from the glass case underneath, their melting middle layer of soft, creamy white a miracle of culinary skill? Or should the choice fall on a handful of those tangy spearmint sticks that came in three enticing colors—the pink and green ones rather slender, with a slight twist in the middle, and the white ones flat and shiny like a ribbon band?

Perhaps it might be cake instead of candy that the buyer ogled with such greedy joy. Then from another case upon the left he'd have the painful task of making his selection. Little cakes no larger than a silver dollar, some with lemon icing, some with chocolate on the top; crumbly cakes with fluted edges and a drift of powdered sugar where it tasted best; delicious half-moon cakes with brown and yellow frosting evenly distributed; enticing yellow creampuffs, light and fluffy as a summer cloud—the list of palate-tickling goodies to be chosen from would fill a book. And ice-cream—! Never anywhere, I think, has anyone evolved a more celestial treat than Rauch's incomparable ice-cream! The memory of its lingering flavor, delicate as roseleaves, and its texture, soft and smooth as finest silk, will even now induce a tearful sigh from old-time Bethlehemites familiar with those dear, dead days long buried in the past—buried, unfortunately, forever. For the recipes for all those rare concoctions that made Rauch's so famous never have passed on to other hands. Hidden away, no doubt, in some snug drawer or closet of the Rauch ménage they may be still preserved. But no outsider ever has been favored with them, and the whole delightful panorama of ambrosial offerings must be laid away in mournful recollection.

There were, of course, still other seasons of the year that brought their special treats for the entire Seminary family. *Fass-nacht* Day (Shrove Tuesday), for example, when throughout the school the last girl in each group to reach the studyroom before the breakfast bell was rung became a "Lazy Doughnut." At the noon meal, in addition to the heaping plates of ordinary *Fassnachts* on the table, she'd discover at her special place a doughnut of gigantic size to advertise her slothful dawdling to the whole wide world. The "lazy" *Fassnachts* always followed out the usual doughnut shape, but the less showy ones that filled the high-piled plates would be of two varieties—the usual round kind and a fat, square species with a dab of jelly in the middle. Both were made as follows:

FASSNACHTS

About 5 P.M. boil 3 potatoes in enough water to cover. When soft, remove potatoes and mash. With potato water scald 2 cups flour, add mashed potatoes. When cool, add 1 yeast cake dissolved in a little lukewarm water. At about 10 o'clock mix 2 cups flour with 2 cups lukewarm milk, making a batter that will drop easily from spoon. Add first mixture and let rise over night. In the morning add 4 beaten eggs, ½ cup melted butter (or butter and lard), and 1 cup sugar. Knead stiff enough to roll and let rise till dough has doubled in size. Roll, cut out in doughnut shape, or in squares with jelly in center, and let rise again. When light, fry in hot fat, drain on absorbent paper, and sprinkle with powdered sugar.

Still another Seminary custom that was highly popular occurred at Christmas time. The day before vacation started, an additional festive note was added to the general air of cheer by the appearance on the luncheon table of a bulging paper bag at every place. Each bag contained a generous portion of Moravian Christmas cakes—the brown and white varieties especially typical of Bethlehem. And, since this entailed about a hundred bags with, say a dozen cakes in each, the baking orgy in the kitchen on the day before can easily be pictured. The brown cakes, dark and thin and very spicy, represented men and birds and animals; the white ones, rich and even thinner, were cut out in star- and heart- and diamond-shapes, according to an ancient practice followed to this very day. Each girl could do whatever pleased her with her special bag of cookies. She could eat them on the spot, or "swap" the brown ones for the white ones with her next-door neighbor, or take them home with her to give her parents an idea of what Moravian Christmas cakes were really like. But I have still to hear of any parents ever fortunate enough to get a taste of them.

Of course, each year at Christmas there'd be several girls who didn't go home for the holidays, and these my mother always made a special effort to include in our own private celebration. For each of them there'd be a heaping soup-plateful of goodies standing side by side with ours upon a certain white-clothed table in our sitting-room, accompanied by a box of candy garnished with a sprig of holly, and a pack of *Leckerli*, our own inimitable family brand of Christmas cake. Each plate would hold a generous handful of assorted nuts, a cluster of dark raisins on the stem, a slab of dried figs and a square of sticky dates, an orange and a tangerine, a bunch of grapes, and, sprinkled over all, the pink and white deliciousness of sugared popcorn. Each was labeled with a slip of paper written in my father's flowing hand, and every slip was carefully retained as plateloads started to diminish and the question of who owned the smaller and the larger portions cropped up with surprising frequency.

These soup-plates and their contents served to while away the endless hours of the afternoon preceding Christmas Eve. For Christmas Eve, not Christmas Day, was then and still is now to every true Moravian the outstanding climax of the Christmas season. Then the lovely and beloved candle service, famous now throughout the land, is always held. And then the viewing of the *Putz*, that stirring and unique Moravian version of the Christmas tree, takes place in all its thrilling glory.

The week that followed Christmas also was a busy and exciting one for all of us. For nearly every Bethlehem family had its individual *Putz*, and visiting the homes that held the most elaborate ones was something that we wouldn't think of missing for the world—especially as each visit usually resulted in the sampling of that household's special brand of Christmas cakes. The evenings not devoted to the sport of "putzing" would be whiled away with games and other pastimes, punctuated by more Christmas cakes, in the inevitable "parlor," with the whole vacation family, not excepting any teachers who might possibly have stayed in Bethlehem for the holidays, uniting in the fun. "Black Art," a game that never failed to mystify the uninitiated, "Coffee pot," "Up Jenkins," and charades were always favorites, but the one that led in popularity was "Run, Sheep, Run!" This somewhat rowdy game consisted in dividing up the players into two opposing companies that took turns hiding in the most remote and unexpected places they could find. The members of the searching party prowled in stealthy silence up and down the dim-lit corridors and in and out the spooky rooms adjoining, till at last some hiding member of the other company was found. Then with a lusty shriek of "Run, Sheep, Run!," discovered and discoverer—as well as all the other members of both parties—sprinted for the designated base as fast as legs could take them, while the din and clatter in the ancient hallways of the Seminary could be heard for miles around!

On New Year's Eve a specially gala air pervaded the "school parlor," and the spirits of us youngsters soared to dizzy heights. For, first of all, instead of being shooed off to our beds at some untimely hour, it was understood that we, like all the grownups, would attend the midnight services across the street. To us these services contained a secret and delightful thrill that came our way but once a year—the thrill of hearing the Moravian pastor rudely interrupted in the middle of his sermon, promptly on the stroke of midnight, by the blaring of the trombones from the belfry tower!

The Watch Night service was preceded by another meeting

known to all Moravians as the "Memorabilia," when events throughout the year just past were carefully reviewed in some detail. We youngsters were excused from this first meeting, but the midnight one we wouldn't have passed by for anything that anyone could offer. In between the services we gathered in the "parlor" for a sort of extra supper—meant, no doubt, to help us weather out the unaccustomed lateness of the hour. Generous soup-platefuls of steaming oyster stew were passed around, with bowlfuls of round crackers, fat and dry and very hard, to break up in it, followed by the usual aftermath of sugarcake and coffee, topped off by a plateful of my mother's cherished fruitcake, rich and black and heavy with the weight of its ingredients.

And even when the holidays were over, there were other taste thrills interspersed throughout the humdrum round of schooldays to make life exciting for us sweet-toothed children. One particular bright spot was occupied by candy—candy in a quite astonishing variety of shapes and forms, it seems to me in looking back. To start with, every Monday evening Sister Schultz, a tenant of the old *Gemeinhaus* * up the street, would suddenly appear with basket on her arm and set up shop in what was known as the "back office." There, behind a little table, she'd dole out to us her fascinating wares—dark, chewy "blackies," made of sugar, peanuts, and molasses, and Moravian mints of five distinctive kinds. The pink ones would, of course, be wintergreen or rose, the brown ones spice or chocolate, and the white ones peppermint, according to an ancient and accepted custom. And today when I go back to Bethlehem and, as usual, stop at the *Gemeinhaus* for a box of mints to take me back across the years, I still feel personally affronted when I find no spice or chocolate discs

* "Congregation House," as differentiated from the "Brethren's House" and "Sisters' House." In the early days of Bethlehem, when its Moravian settlers lived a communal life, the single women lived in the Sisters' House, the single men in the Brethren's House, and the married couples in the Congregation House.

among the rest, and—still more brazen flouting of tradition—mingled with the pink and white, the alien green and yellow of fresh lime and orange flavors!

The recipe for those Moravian mints is still in use by various persons, but the one for "blackies" must have disappeared somehow among the shadows of the past. Perhaps Miss Schultz, long since gone on, invented it herself and took the secret with her when she died—at least, nobody ever has been able to supply it. But here's the other one:

MORAVIAN MINTS

2 cups granulated sugar   ½ cup hot water
14 drops oil of peppermint

Stir water into sugar, boil just 8 minutes, and add oil of peppermint or other flavoring. Beat till slightly cloudy, then pour into small, round tins one and three-quarter inches in diameter.

Another candy treat appearing at quite frequent intervals throughout the school year was concocted by my mother in our private kitchen. "Mosies" and molasses candy, made in patty pans and sold for five cents each (the gross receipts contributed to missions), were the two varieties she turned out by the dozen. On me fell the pleasant job of peddling them, ranged temptingly upon a wooden tray, among the Seminary girls—a job whose rich reward was one whole patty for my very own. This is my mother's recipe for Mosies:

MOSIES

4 cups brown sugar   1 cup water
1 tablespoon butter   walnuts (black or English)

Boil till it forms a ball in cold water, beat till thick and creamy and starting to harden, then pour into buttered gem pans into which nuts have been scattered.

Occasionally, at more or less uncertain intervals, exciting word would pass around the school: "The old cough-candy man is here!" And then from every "side room" hungry girls would start converging on the spot outside my father's office where a mild old gentleman with basket full of oblong objects wrapped in brown waxed paper would be waiting. We never knew just who he was or where he came from, and we never thought to ask him. After all, it wasn't he but what he sold that really held our interest. For the objects in his basket were long, shiny slabs of brown and golden candy marked off carefully in one-inch squares. Twelve squares comprised a five-cent slab, and though the purpose of the candy was supposedly medicinal, none of us so much as gave that end of it a thought—the tantalizing flavor of the sweet was all *we* cared about. I don't remember when the old cough-candy man slid gently from the Seminary scene, or who if anyone succeeded him. But probably, like old Miss Schultz, he took the key to his particular prescription with him—and the world of childhood is the poorer for his going.

Two other sweets stand out among my memories of those wholesome, happy years spent in an ancient school. Both, once again, were Mamma's specialties—but specialties reserved this time for our immediate family. Crisp, dark brown peanut brittle, made according to the simplest formula, was one of them. She merely put two cups of granulated sugar in a heavy frying pan and let it melt above a low-turned flame, stirring continually. Then, adding two cupfuls of peanuts, coarsely ground, she spread it out quite thinly on a well-greased baking sheet or marble slab. When cold she picked it up and, holding it in one hand, broke it into bite-size pieces with a single blow from the hard handle of a silver knife.

The other specialty was popcorn cake, a bit more complicated and requiring several pairs of hands to bring it to its luscious consummation. A dishpanful of popcorn sprinkled lavishly with various kinds of nut meats was the basis for this rapturous confection. Over it was poured a syrup made of four cups of molasses and two tablespoons of butter, boiled until it spun a thread. The whole delightful sticky mass was then mixed thoroughly and pounded with a wooden mallet till it formed a hard, firm cake that could be cut or broken into pieces.

Heart-warming days those were in old-time Bethlehem, with a quality of artless gaiety and innocence that gradually has faded with the passing years. Yes, most decidedly I pity all those poor unfortunates who never had the luck to spend their childhood in that quaint and lovely old Moravian setting!

NEMESIS ON THE TRAIL

I NEVER cease to be surprised at the unending wealth of fascinating lore about the Pennsylvania Dutch that I keep stumbling on. Of course, the winter months spent in the city, within reach of every kind of book that touches on the subject, give me lots of chance to dig up picturesque and thrilling stories of the kind in which I specially delight. And chief among them is the legend of Tom Quick.

I'd thought I was familiar with the various figures who went stalking through the Pennsylvania wilderness around the period of the French and Indian War, but Tom Quick's name was new to me. And for sheer, brutal cruelty and ruthless vengefulness, the tale of his amazing exploits definitely tops them all!

My first acquaintance with this gentle soul was brief but stimulating—merely a casual reference to his name and what it stood for in a book I chanced to come across one day. It sent me scurrying, though, to other sources for additional harrowing details about his scandalous behavior. And, believable or not, here are the facts I managed to unearth:

Tom's father, Tom Quick, Senior, I discovered, was a Holland Dutchman who came over here as part of that great wave of eighteenth century immigration which flowed chiefly from the

region of the Upper Rhine. He settled in the wilderness along
the Delaware, among the lofty cliffs and shady glens and water-
falls of what is now Pike County, and there built the first home
occupied by whites within that wild and lonely section of the
Indian country.

The Indians roundabout proved peaceable and friendly, though,
and young Tom junior, born the following year, mixed freely with
them in their woodland haunts. They taught him how to hunt
and fish and catch wild animals, and like the natural savage that
he evidently was, he took to their untrammeled way of living like
a fish to water. So much so that when a little later on a school
was built, to keep pace with the growth of the community, he
balked completely at attending it, and never in the years that followed could be bribed or beaten into giving up the kind of life
he loved.

The years went by, and steadily more white men penetrated to
the Indians' favorite hunting grounds. The tribe of Delawares,
resentful of this slow but sure encroachment, gradually became
less peaceful, and the young man who had grown up in their midst
and proved so apt a pupil of their ways now found himself deserted by his former friends. When finally the French and Indian
War broke out, the Indians had withdrawn completely from that
section of the river, and the Quicks, no longer looked upon as
brothers, now were forced to carry weapons with them everywhere
they went. However, life flowed smoothly for a little while, and
not till one day when the elder Quick, his son, and son-in-law,
becoming careless, started out unarmed to cross the frozen river
to the gristmill on the other side did tragedy occur.

The trio were just skirting round a jutting point of rock along
the bank when they were startled by a sharp report, and with a
groan the father crumpled to the ground. In frantic haste the
young men lifted him and started to return the way they'd come.
But once again a bullet whistled through the air and this time

struck Tom's foot. In sudden headlong panic they laid down their burden and took swiftly to their heels. They reached the safety of the farther bank at last and glanced back fearfully across their shoulders. A knot of savages had gathered round the dead man on the ice, and even as they watched, one redskin with a yelp of horrid triumph held aloft a raw and bleeding scalp.

Abruptly Tom went berserk. With a frightful oath he swore that from that moment on his life would be devoted to revenge. "I'll not go to my grave," he shouted, brandishing a pair of brawny fists, "until I've slain a hundred of those devils!"

And he kept his word. Thenceforth, his days were dedicated to one single purpose. Cruel and ruthless as an Indian on the warpath, he skulked the woods where once he'd roamed in friendly comradeship with those he now tracked down. Man, woman, child—there wasn't any member of the redskin race he didn't look on as fair quarry.

Once he met a worthless Indian by the name of Muskwink in a tavern on the Neversink. Made fearless by the white men's fire-water, Muskwink tipsily invited Tom to have a drink. Tom cursed him loudly, and immediately a quarrel was under way. Insulting words flew back and forth, and finally the Indian, drunk and garrulous, began to boast. He'd been a member of the little band that killed Tom's father, he declared—and what was more, he was the one who'd done the actual scalping! With brutal glee he even acted out the tragic scene and cruelly mimicked the grimaces of the dying man. Then finally, to clinch his tale, he brought forth from his pouch two small, dark objects—buttons that Tom recognized as having once been sewn upon his father's coat.

With a wild shout of rage, the white man seized a rifle hanging near the bar. "Get out!" he yelled. "Get out of here before I kill you!"

Slowly the Indian rose. With drunken dignity he started for the door. Close at his heels Tom followed, and the murderous spark that glinted in his eyes struck terror suddenly to Musk-wink's drink-befuddled brain. He bolted for the forest—and the chase was on. It lasted just a mile. Muskwink had boasted once too often, and the death Tom meted out to him was swift and sure.

It wasn't long before the fame of "Tom Quick, Indian Killer," as he soon came to be known, had spread abroad and he became a sort of hero in the land. With chuckles of delight, men would recount his latest exploit, and the savages for miles around walked warily in fear of sudden, unexpected death. For in Tom's pleasant little game of Indian hunting there was neither sportsmanship nor quarter. He took his quarry where he found it, without warning, without mercy, and from one day to the next nobody knew just where he might be found. Clad in a tattered buckskin shirt and breeches, with a tomahawk and knife stuck in his belt, his trusty rifle cradled lovingly beneath his arm, he popped up here and there at unexpected places. The forest was his home—he had no special dwelling—and all his time and efforts went to stalking his despised and hated prey.

One day, the story goes, Tom spied an Indian family—father, mother, and three children—drifting down the river in a bark canoe. With stealthy tread he sneaked up through the tall grass on the bank and shot the unsuspecting figure sitting in the stern; then, wading out from shore, he seized the little craft and plunged his tomahawk into the woman's head and those of her three children. With businesslike despatch he sank the bodies and destroyed the boat, and many years elapsed before he told the story of this noble deed.

"Why did you kill the brats, Tom?" someone asked him then.

In arrogant disdain, Tom spat and answered tersely: "Nits make lice!"

But wholesale vengeance wasn't always quite that easy. Once there was a time, they say, when Tom's cold-blooded killing nearly reached a sudden end. Deep in the woods one day, his efforts focused on the job of splitting rails, his gun propped carelessly against a near-by tree, he looked up to discover several redskins grouped about him threateningly. In gruff command, their leader ordered Tom to drop his axe and come along. It looked as though at last the tables had been turned and Tom's nefarious career would be concluded then and there.

But the Indians hadn't reckoned with their crafty victim. Tom made a gesture of assent. "All right," he answered meekly. "Only first, just help me split this final rail."

Childlike and credulous, the little group agreed. They grasped the wood and pulled with all their strength. But at the same time Tom dislodged the wedge that held the log apart—and suddenly his captors had become his captives! Grinning, he stood and looked at them a moment. Then with a shout of fiendish glee, he fell upon them and despatched them one by one.

The years rolled by, while more and still more redskins bit the dust to gratify Tom's cruel obsession. At times he'd hobnob with his prey in seeming friendliness to gain his deadly ends. Once on a hunting expedition he approached the summit of a towering cliff and beckoned to the Indian brave accompanying him to follow. The Indian joined him, and Tom pointed urgently to something far below. The Indian looked, and as he gazed intently downward Tom's strong right arm shot out—and one more red man's life had gone to swell the white avenger's toll.

Another time Tom and his Indian comrade of the hunt had brought down seven deer. "I'll take the meat," Tom offered generously, "and you can keep the skins to sell." Accordingly the Indian started on ahead, his back bent underneath the load of precious pelts—and suddenly Tom raised his gun. There was a shot, and his companion fell. Then, stopping only long enough to raise the dead man's load to his own shoulders, Tom made off.

"I killed a buck with seven skins!" was his facetious boast in telling of this little escapade.

At last, when forty years or so had passed and Tom's misdeeds had mounted to a shocking high, he suddenly fell sick one day while visiting a friend. And here the different stories vary. Some say that at the point of death he boasted of a score of ninety-nine dead Indians and insisted that one more be brought him to complete his horrid toll. "An old man lives not far from here," he pleaded. "He's an Indian—bring him to me! I can't die until my job is done!" But with a most annoying lack of sympathy, his friend refused. According to another tale, however, Tom's unceasing prayers for health and strength were answered, and he left his sickbed finally to go back to his pleasant little game of butchery. And when at last he died, a smile of placid triumph on his face, he'd killed his hundredth Indian and fulfilled the unbelievably appalling task he'd set himself so many years before.

March

FIVE-FOOT BOOKSHELF OF THE PAST

MY EDUCATION on the Pennsylvania Dutch was coming on apace. My newest interest—one that I had cultivated with the greatest zeal—was old-time Pennsylvania German almanacs. Of course, my knowledge of the subject still can stand a lot of broadening, but I certainly succeeded in accumulating an amazing list of facts I'd never known before.

To start with, I discovered that the earliest known almanac was

[217]

published in the fifteenth century. Back in Nuremberg, Bavaria, in 1476, a certain Johann Miller brought it out, in Latin, and forecast the future for the following thirty years. However, not till somewhat later—1546—did the first annual publication of the kind appear, at Hamburg on the Elbe. And a century or more had passed before the earliest *Calénder* published in the German language made its bow in Pennsylvania. Later on, the famous printer, Christopher Sauer of Germantown, got out an almanac he printed every year for forty years, while other issues of these treasured gems of literature—the five-foot bookshelf of the past— appeared in various towns and cities of the middle east to keep up with the growing Pennsylvania German population.

For generations John Baer's almanac—or *Johann Baer's Neuer Gemeinnutziger Pennsylvanische Calénder*, if you want the actual title—hung in practically every home of eastern Pennsylvania, and today its English replica is still in use in Pennsylvania Dutch farmhouses up and down the State.

The uses of the old-time almanac, of course, were endless. If a farmer wanted to find out the proper time to plant potatoes, or set up new fenceposts, or prepare for a sharp change of weather, all he had to do was read the careful rulings set forth in the illustrated calendar upon his kitchen wall. If his good *Fraa* were anxious to discover what her children's virtues or infirmities might reasonably turn out to be, or what she ought to do if any of them ran to freckles or developed warts, or how to make a batch of sugar cookies, all *she* had to do was turn the pages of the almanac and somewhere in its contents she'd be sure to find the information she desired. If anyone should suddenly become athirst for general knowledge, whether scientific or historical, concerning phases of the moon or "Golden Rules of Conduct"—once again the never-failing oracle that hung near by would answer every need. It held a calculating system and a list of holidays, short stories with decorous morals, mensuration tables and the dates of all court sessions, weather prophecies and tales of high adventure, astronomical details and interest tabulations—everything, in short, that people living in the sparsely settled country sections possibly could use.

To me, however, the most interesting of all the various odds and ends of knowledge crammed inside the pages of these ancient calendars were, first, the homemade remedies supposed to cure all sorts of ills, and second, the delicious-sounding recipes whose very reading set my mouth to watering and my hands to reaching for the mixing bowl.

For instance, as a sample of the remedies, one almanac suggested for the ague a concoction made of "brandywine," gunpowder, soap, and strong tobacco, mixed in equal parts and rubbed into the patient's wrists. Another offered as a cure for yellow jaundice two raw eggs in water, drunk upon an empty stomach in the morning, then repeated every four hours through the day. For those who suffered from insomnia, a panacea in the form of counting endlessly the figures 1 and 2 was given. You exhaled when counting 1, it seemed, and inhaled on the count of 2, while picturing clearly in your mind each figure in its turn.

Then, if you burned yourself, the thing to do was to apply some water made by melting snow that fell in March, and, presto! all the pain would disappear—provided, that is, that you'd set the water in the sun before you used it. For earache, it was wise to stick a piece of bacon half an inch long in the ear that hurt. To ease a cough, you drank tea brewed from dried leaves of a black-cherry tree. To stop the nosebleed, you were told to hold a cork above an oil lamp's flame until the cork was black, then scrape away the clinging ashes and inhale the fumes.

To guard against infection from a snakebite, one old almanac insisted that you drink a spoonful of the sap of hoarhound tea well-mixed with water. To cure a felon all you did was heat fresh ox-gall to the boiling point, then plunge the ailing finger in the liquid and the throbbing torture would immediately depart. In case you had a wart, the powder made from burning willow bark and mixing it with vinegar would cure it. And a little garlic fried in red-hot ashes and applied beneath a linen bandage would remove a corn.

They didn't sound too appetizing, some of those old nostrums, but the recipes for food were calculated to make even the most sated gourmet drool. Of course, it's true that most of them were pretty reckless with the butter, eggs, and sugar, not to mention the poor housewife's energy and time ("Stir for an hour"—"Beat for thirty minutes"). But I rather think the end attained was apt to justify the means. Take "Eggless Cakes," for instance. This is how it goes:

EGGLESS CAKES

1 cup of butter, 1 large cup of buttermilk, 2 cups of sugar, 1 cup cold black coffee, 4 cups flour, 2 teaspoonfuls of baking soda, 1 small teaspoonful of cinnamon, a small amount of cloves, allspice, and nutmeg, and a tablespoon of vinegar. Beat well, and add a cup of raisins and a cup of nuts.

"Cream Cookies," too, sound temptingly delicious, and they're made like this:

CREAM COOKIES

Mix 1 pound flour, 1 half-pint of sour cream, 1 quarter-pound of butter and 4 tablespoons of sugar. Roll the dough out to the thickness of a knifeblade, spread it with 1 beaten egg, and sprinkle sugar on the top. Bake in a medium oven.

And then, to add the final titillating touch, there's "King's Cake" and its partner, "Queen's Cake," each more rich and palate-tickling than the other. You make them thus:

KING'S CAKE

Mix 16 egg yolks in a pound of whipped cream. Stir one hour, then add gradually a pound of finest flour. Stir a half hour more and add a pound of raisins and a pound of currants, plus 3 ounces citron, finely chopped, and the beaten whites of 9 eggs. Bake one hour.

QUEEN'S CAKE

1 pound sugar, 1 pound flour, 1 pound butter, 8 eggs. Beat egg whites for 20 minutes, yolks for half an hour. Add a half pound currants, 1 ground nutmeg, and an equal quantity of cinnamon.

LITTLE RED SCHOOLHOUSE

FOR several years, each time we'd driven to or from the country by a certain route, we'd passed a small red schoolhouse standing at a lonely crossroads. Often at recess time there'd be bright-colored knots of children in the schoolyard—little girls with red and blue and purple dresses, boys with shirts of brilliant green or lavender and long, tight trousers reaching almost to the shoetops. It was an Amish school, of course, and many times I'd had the urge to stop and find out what went on inside those neat, red-painted walls. And so at last that's just exactly what I did. It was a strange and fascinating experience. It made me feel as though I'd stepped right into another day and age and out again —and all within the space of several hours and some fifty miles or so from the big city.

For once my driver didn't need his car that morning—or said he didn't, knowing that my faithful Rat was stored up in the country for the winter months and transportation therefore something of a problem in my life. He couldn't go with me himself, it happened, so I started off with only Patsy sitting in the seat beside me. The day was raw and chilly, and the drab snow patches of the suburbs that we drove through had a badly shopworn look. Cities, I thought in passing, are no proper place for snow. The endless trampling of unheeding feet is far too harsh a despoiler of its virgin beauty.

I thought so doubly when I reached the open country. For those same snow patches, snuggling cozily in little pockets of the wind-swept fields or clinging stubbornly to wooded slopes, lay white and spotless here. Funny, I marveled, with what careless ease the city-dweller can forget the glory of the land that lies beyond his own immediate ken! With a hunger that I hadn't been aware of until now, my eyes took in the barren loveliness that stretched ahead. There was no trace in sun or wind or landscape of the springtime that the calendar had said was on its way. Completely bare, the trees stood huddled close in bristly groups as if for warmth, and in the distance—always in the distance—rose the ever-present blue of rolling hills. Were they, I wondered for the thousandth time, more blue on cloudy days or sunny ones? I never can decide.

I turned off from the concrete highway to the Conestoga Road —that old-time trail on which in days gone by great fleets of white-topped inland ships had sailed, drawn by their four and six and eight stout horses, to the music of the sweet-toned bells that arched above the patient creatures' necks. It zigzagged crazily, this ancient thoroughfare, for time and mileage were no object when it came to easing long, hard pulls of wagons loaded to the brim with shifting freight. With a sigh of deep content I settled down to follow where it led.

It led, I found, beside a slender, tinkling brook, between the posts and rails of stark, gray fences, under trees whose branches traced a swaying fretwork on the background of the sky. It wound along a low wall built in country fashion of flat stones piled one atop the other, past a lonely church and graveyard with a carriage shed at one side, and a pair of old stone barns with high ramps leading to the second floor.

And now it curved more steeply upward. As I climbed, the casual spots of white that punctuated field and woodland turned to actual snow piles bordering my way. I reached the mountaintop at last and started down the other side—across a stone bridge, through a quiet town, and out into the open country once again. A red barn loomed up on the left with three round painted symbols on its front—familiar symbols, for I'd copied them when first I'd started my collection of those gaily-colored earmarks of this countryside I love. I passed another barn, adorned this time with simple five-point emblems, and I sniffed disdainfully. Such crude and unimaginative designs! Perhaps the wealth of complicated art I've found on other barns has spoiled me, for I'm just a little supercilious nowadays about my decorations.

I glided smoothly on. This was a weekday and the highway which on Saturdays and Sundays teems with Amish buggies and "top wagons" was deserted now. It seemed to me I should be getting to my destination, and I looked about for someone to direct me. But the road spread out in lonely blankness straight ahead. At last a square-topped wagon hove in sight, however, and an Amish woman, prim but friendly, peered at me beneath her wide-brimmed bonnet as I stopped to ask my way. With firm and practised hand she reined her well-groomed chestnut to a halt.

Oh, yes, she said in answer to my question, the red schoolhouse I was looking for was on this very road. "You passed it just a piece-ways back," she added smilingly. "Just follow the road down half a mile or so—you can't help missing it!" And with a nod of thanks for these well-meant but slightly upside-down directions, I turned back.

She was correct, I learned. For just a "piece-ways" back—the half a mile or so she'd specified—the little schoolhouse stood as plain as day. I parked the car along a whitewashed fence, wrapped Patsy snugly in a blanket, and switched off the engine. Mournfully she watched me as I slammed the door and locked her in the safety of the car.

I crossed the road and reached the gate just as a whooping avalanche of youngsters burst out from the schoolhouse door—

small boys emitting lusty yells and waving broad-brimmed hats, and little girls with sleek hair parted in the middle and drawn smoothly back in braided knots above the neck. With only casual interest they regarded my approach. There were two other cars drawn up before the door, I noticed, and a barking dog in one of them had focused the attention of the boys.

"*Setzen!*" (Sit down) a round-faced youngster in green shirt-sleeves shouted through the windowpane. The dog paid no attention. "*Setzen!*" the other boys took up the chorus. In the general hubbub that ensued I passed unchallenged through the open door.

I found myself inside a large, square room completely filled with desks—four rows of them, each seven deep, on both sides of a central aisle. A tall, round stove sent out a pleasant warmth from halfway down the room, and by it stood a slender, blond young woman with a self-contained but unassuming air. She wore a tiny cap of sheer, white net, and I surmised correctly that this must be Teacher.

I introduced myself, and with a certain quiet dignity she made me welcome. Then, as tactfully as possible, I launched the questions that were buzzing in my head. She answered them quite simply. Yes, she told me, there were forty-four small pupils in the school, and all but four of them were Amish. Of these forty, thirty-eight all answered to the name of Stoltzfus. "And," she added with a little smile, "*my* name is Stoltzfus, too!"

As we were talking, gradually a little group of boys surrounded us. The smallest, wearing a bright purple shirt beneath an opened vest, was looking at me solemnly through gold-rimmed spectacles. Another, nearly twice his size, stood frankly staring at the red camellia I was wearing on my coat lapel—while others goggled with deep interest at the leopard skin that made the collar of my coat. The teacher turned away a moment and the leader of the group spoke up.

"Can you talk Dutch?" he asked abruptly.

I hesitated. "Well—*glee wennich* [just a little]!" I replied. Then, seized with sudden inspiration: "But I know some poetry in Pennsylvania Dutch!"

"Let's hear it!" The command was uttered in the tone of one suspending judgment till he knew the worst.

Obediently I launched forth on my favorite verse:

> "D iss fer Deitsch,
> Es is aw ken Zweiwel,
> Sie glawve an Gott
> Un sie hasse der Deiwel;
> Sie glawve an Arwet
> Un yeder soll schaffe,
> Fer selle Weg ehrlich
> Sei Leewe zu mache;
> Sie glawve an's Schpawre,
> Doch blendi zu esse,
> Un duhne bei allem
> Die Gschpass net fergesse." *

There was a little silence as I finished. Anxiously I looked from one face to another. Finally the big boy spoke. "She can talk Dutch, all right!" he said, and I relaxed. Apparently I'd passed the acid test.

---

* By the late John Birmelin. English translation, by the same author, as follows:

> D is for Dutch
> And we cannot deny
> That they worship their God
> And the devil defy,
> Believing that labor
> For man is ordained,
> And that labor's reward
> Is rightfully gained;
> With a bountiful table,
> Yet thrifty beside,
> The rarest of humor
> And hearts open wide.

At this point Teacher's voice was heard above the general babel and our budding friendship came to an untimely end. "Recess is over!" she announced, and from all sides the pupils started to converge upon their desks. Where would I like to sit, Miss Stoltzfus asked politely? At the back, perhaps? Or maybe here? She motioned to the row beside us.

I chose the latter. With a shy but friendly glance, my deskmate moved aside to give me room, and suddenly the place was overflowing with the droning hum of lessons mumbled underneath the breath.

Again the voice of Teacher rose in urgent summons. Obediently four boys and half a dozen girls—all Amish but the chubby one in figured dress and pigtails—shuffled to the platform at the front. Like little soldiers standing at attention, they lined up. The girls' heads, bound by narrow velvet bands, were bent above their open books. Their dresses, plainly made but bright in color, with dark aprons covering them from neck to hem, reached almost to the tops of stubby, high, laced shoes. The boys, with hair cropped straight across the front and back, and homemade black suspenders showing under open vests, were mouthing earnestly the words they were about to read.

Protected by the whispers floating all about us, I turned to my companion. "What's your name?" I asked.

She blushed a rosy red. "It's Fanny Stoltzfus."

"And how old are you?"

"Why—nine!" Shy Fanny hung her head in painful bashfulness.

I tried again. "What grade do you belong in?"

"Second." Then, with worried glance in the direction of the platform: "We come next!"

I looked across her shoulder. She was reading one of those bucolic tales where creatures of the barnyard talk together endlessly in quite exhausting fashion. One small finger traveled slowly underneath the printed lines as she forlornly wrestled with the unfamiliar words.

The finger halted suddenly. "What's this here word?" Her shyness overcome by grim necessity, she shoved her book beneath my nose and pointed to the letters that had tripped her.

"It's 'whinny,'" I informed her, and she nodded silently.

And now a clatter sounded from the platform, and we both looked up to see the first class streaming down to take their places at their desks once more. Again the teacher's voice was heard in fateful summons: "Second grade!"

A little sigh left Fanny's lips as she got up. Three other second graders joined her, and again a reading class began to struggle through its lines. In treble monotone, completely void of all expression, each one read in turn: "'I will!' said the cat." "'I will!' said the dog." "'I will!' said the horse." And so on endlessly.

The story failed to grip me, somehow, and I glanced about the room. Its walls, I saw, were lined with highly educational pictures —of Washington and Lincoln, of "The Boy in Blue," of "Jesus and the Rich Young Man"—besides the usual maps and calendars and crayon drawings by the youthful pupils. One corner held a flag, its stars and stripes depending limply from a gold-tipped staff. A clock ticked leisurely above a row of blackboards at the front, and near the entrance door behind us, neatly ranged on wooden pegs, hung flat-crowned hats and tin lunch baskets, blue and black and purple bonnets, long, fringed shawls, and one small bright blue cape.

The older girls, I noticed, occupied the last two rows of seats. They were about fourteen or so, the age when Amish girls begin to think of "joining church," and so, of course, their heads were covered with white caps instead of velvet ribbons like the younger children wore, and plain, straight pins instead of buttons closed their dresses.

I looked about still further, and my glance fell on a pair of bright blue eyes that peered inquisitively from the row behind me. Their owner, evidently dying to converse, was leaning sociably upon the desk that lay between. I smiled at her, and she slid nearer.

"Who are *you?*" I asked.

She answered readily: "Lavina Stoltzfus!" and immediately launched forth upon a flow of rapid information. The members of the first grade, she informed me, were all Stoltzfuses except three. Rebecca, Rachel, Paul, Elmina, Katie, Stephen, Samuel— these seven answered to that Amish name. Besides, there were Rebecca Zook, her brother Ivan, and another little girl named Florence Enck. Florence, it seemed, was only six—the baby of the school. She sat now at the desk in front of me, turned sideways in her seat so nothing that I said or did could possibly escape her soft, brown stare.

"She's English!" my informant told me with a quaintly condescending air. (I knew from past experience that this meant she wasn't Amish.) "That's her sister over there," she added, pointing to an older child upon our right. "They've got two brothers, Charles and Melvin. That there's Charles up on the platform now!"

I found our little game of "Who's who?" quite as pleasant as Lavina evidently did herself, and egged her on quite shamelessly. "Who else is on the platform?" I inquired.

Well, there was Fanny, she replied. And also Lydia and Freddy Stoltzfus.

"And the third grade—who's in that?"

Lavina smiled self-consciously. "Why, me!" she said. And added as a minor afterthought the names of Sadie, Sarah, Amos, and Naomi Stoltzfus, plus two Marys of the same surname, and Melvin Enck.

"My goodness!" I exclaimed, a bit confusedly. "Two Marys in one class, and both named Stoltzfus! Doesn't Teacher get them all mixed up?"

Lavina shook her head. "She calls them Mary B. and Mary K.," she stated simply. "And the same with Amos, too—he's Amos L."

"You mean that there are other Amoses?" The plot was thickening by the minute, it appeared.

"Why, sure!" Lavina nodded briefly. "In the fourth grade there's an Amos, too—he's Amos J. And in the seventh grade there's Amos M."

"And are there any other boys and girls with names alike?" I asked.

Lavina grinned. The fourth grade had its Johnny B., she said, the fifth its Johnny D., and in the sixth were Johnny Y. and Johnny L. "We've got two Stephens and two Katies, too—and two Rebeccas! Only one," she added in a tone of conscious anticlimax, "is a Zook!"

I glanced at poor Miss Stoltzfus. What a life, I thought! One dizzy round of Amoses and Marys, Johnnys, Stephens, and Rebeccas! How on earth could she or anybody cope with such a list?

I thought I might as well complete the catalogue, however, so I asked Lavina for the other names. She reeled them off with brisk familiarity: Leona, Omar, Richard, Abraham and Emma, Benual, Suvilla, Anna, Barbara, Nasey, Ammon, Nancy—I was breathless as she reached the end at last. In some relief I turned to Fanny as that little student took her place beside me once again. The second grade had finished, evidently, and the members of the third grade started for the platform now. With carefree nonchalance Lavina joined them, while my little neighbor, shy and diffident as ever, wordlessly got out a jigsaw puzzle from beneath her desk and set to work. She kept her small head carefully averted, and the hands that held the brightly-colored pieces shook.

I couldn't bear to see her suffer. Something must be done, I thought—and suddenly a bright thought struck me.

"Look!" I whispered. With the cunning of a none-too-subtle

fox I indicated the camellia on my coat. The timid eyes rose slowly and I saw a tiny sparkle kindle in their depths. "I'm going to give you this!" I said.

My little seatmate held her breath in rapture as I pinned the flower on her gingham dress. "*Ach*—thanks!" she murmured in a voice so low I barely heard it. But the smile she gave me—natural and spontaneous for the first time since I'd met her—was my real reward.

Lavina came back from her recitation. Frankly envious, she glanced at Fanny's floral decoration and ensconced herself once more upon the desk behind. Some other little girls, grown used to an outsider's presence now, began to gather round us, and our whisperings took on a general tone. Did they, I asked, like going to school? They nodded quickly. Was the schoolhouse very far from where they lived? A casual: "Not so far!" was all I gathered. I tried again.

"What church does Teacher go to?"

"That there one!" Lavina pointed out the window up the road. "It ain't *our* church!" she added. "She's a Mennonite!"

The lessons droned their weary course above our heads as we conversed, while all around a steady buzz of whispers mingled with our own. The biggest boys and girls stayed in their places to recite, I noted, with the teacher standing in the aisle beside them as they answered her in turn. Two boys whose horseplay threatened to become too serious earned a mild reproof at one point, but the recitation went off smoothly for the most part as the afternoon wore slowly to its close.

At last the clock above the blackboards pointed to dismissal time. Miss Stoltzfus shut her book. "Grade One may get their wraps!" she said, and with a minimum of noise the smallest pupils streamed back to retrieve their hats and "wammuses" and broad-brimmed bonnets from the pegs beside the door. Grade Two came next, followed in quick succession by the others, till at last

the final little girl was shawled and buttoned carefully and ready
for the homeward trek. There was no loitering or hanging back.
At home the chores were waiting to be done—and woe betide the
boy or girl who didn't get there at the stipulated time!

When finally I said good-bye and thanked Miss Stoltzfus for
my visit, just one solitary figure lingered in the yard outside. John
D., with smoke-gray eyes behind their fringe of sooty lashes fastened on my car, was waiting for me hopefully. I couldn't disap-
point him.

"How about a lift?" I asked.

The gray eyes brightened. "I don't care!" he said.

It didn't *sound* enthusiastic, but I know my Pennsylvania
Dutch. That casual phrase, translated, means: "I'd love to!" So,
with studied nonchalance that couldn't quite conceal a little
swagger as he climbed aboard, John took his seat beside me and
we started off.

Some distance up the road ahead of us a little blue-caped figure
shuffled stolidly. "That's Rachel!" John observed. And, just in
case I didn't get the hint: "My sister!"

"Shall we take her, too?" I offered.

Silently John nodded. Then in brotherly authority he raised his
voice. "Rachel! Wait onct!" he shouted.

Rachel waited, and we picked her up. Without a word she
crowded in beside us. A little farther on we overtook the Zooks,
and they, too, joined us for a brief but blissful ride. Already all
the other pupils, scattered over rough, uneven fields and rutty
by-roads leading to their various homes, were nearly out of sight.

A half mile down the road a gray barn loomed up on the right,
beside a neat, white house surrounded by a picket fence.

"That there's where we get off!" John pointed out.

I stopped beside the gate, and both small Stoltzfuses alighted.
"Thanks!" they muttered briefly, and without a backward glance
they disappeared inside the whitewashed fence.

The Zooks got out a little farther on. With tin lunch basket swinging free between them, they trotted down a narrow lane, Rebecca's small blue bonnet bobbing side by side with Ivan's broad-brimmed hat.

I smiled in satisfaction as I watched them out of sight. The Zooks and the Stoltzfuses! Of such staunch and sturdy farmer folk, I thought, the backbone of this land of ours is made!

SORROW SONGS AND SUCH

I'D been carrying on a lively correspondence with my favorite expert on things Pennsylvania Dutch. It started back in January, when I'd come across an old-time ballad written in the early 1800's, setting forth the lamentable tale of one Susanna Cox, who killed her baby and was executed for the crime in Reading. The poem, I discovered, had been set to music, and like many another rather gruesome narrative of actual happenings, had become a popular and much-sung ditty of the day.

The subject caught my fancy and I did a little digging. These *Trauer-Liede* (Sorrow Songs), I found, were rather common formerly, and wandering peddlers sold them up and down the countryside from door to door. They told of murders, hangings, suicides, and other choice events with avid gusto, rambling on and on through endless stanzas set to some familiar tune. With morbid relish, men and women hummed and sang and whistled them on all occasions, and the printed broadsides that described each weird detail remain today a fascinating part of Pennsylvania German lore.

My personal delvings, though, uncovered only one or two such songs, so naturally my thoughts turned toward my favorite expert. He if anyone could tell me more about them, I felt certain. So a few weeks later off I went to see him, and sure enough, he had a lot of things along that line to offer.

In his childhood, he remembered, an old peddler with a little cart drawn by a pair of huge, black dogs would stop off at his house each spring and fall, with an assortment of all kinds of fascinating wares. The peddler's pack in those days held a wide variety of household objects for the most part, but in former times, my expert said, these traveling vendors also hawked about the country every sort of broadside and small printed pamphlet that contained long, harrowing accounts of current crimes.

Of course, he added, there were other leaflets, too—like *Himmelsbriefe, Haus-Segen*, rhymed New Year's wishes, prayers, and other pious offerings. He had a folder holding several lurid samples of these last, and we leafed through them with delighted interest. One showed a picture of two roads that led, respectively, to Heaven and Hell. The buildings of the New Jerusalem stood invitingly beyond the straight and narrow path that headed upward, while a red-eyed Satan with a pair of evil-looking horns and wings and shiny pitchfork waited at the bottom of the winding one that pointed to the space below. Beneath, arranged like prose but rhyming in a crude and limping fashion, was this execrable doggerel:

Here is the entrance great and wide, Open to all from each side: Pass on ye with sack and pack, Be unconcerned, be not exact: Walk gentle ahead, not a word will be said; If you seek honor and gain, hastily appear and record thy name: Thousands with a similar design, have traveled this road in proper line; ye that lust after splendor, luxury and pride, pass on, the path is fully wide; The frolicksome in great numbers with music full of sound, Are marching to the place to which they are bound; The rich, poor, the tall and small, In Abraham's lap hope to be taken up, yea withal.

Another sheet, unillustrated, set forth what was meant to be, apparently, a pledge of total abstinence. It went like this:

"A pledge we make
No wine to take;
No brandy red,
To turn the head;
No whiskey hot,
That makes the sot;
No fiery rum,
That ruins home.
Nor will we sin,
By drinking gin.
Hard cider too
Will never do,
Nor brewer's beer,
Our hearts to cheer.

To quench our thirst, we'll always bring
Cold water from the well or spring.
We here do pledge perpetual hate
To all that can intoxicate."

A third, entitled "The Blind Man's Appeal," by Charles Fessler, "who lost his sight through an explosion of dynamite," consisted of eight verses which began this way:

"Dear friends, I cannot labor
I must try and get along;
Dear friends, I cannot labor,
I will try and sell my song.
I trust that you will buy it,
And do not prove unkind;
May kind heaven preserve you
From ever becoming blind!"

"A Miner's Prayer," which showed the picture of a miner at the top, complete with lamp and spade and other underground equipment, read like this:

"Oh, Lord, after I have worked my last shift and come out of the earth and have placed my feet on Thy footstool, let me use the lamp of prudence, faith, hope and charity. From now on till I be called to sign my last pay roll, make all the cables in the machinery strong with Thy love. Supply all the gangways, slopes and chambers with the pure air of Thy grace and let the light of hope be my guidance, and when the last picking and shoveling is done, may the last car be full of Thy grace and give the Holy Bible for my last shift, so that Thou, the General Superintendent of all the collieries, can say: 'Well done, thou good and faithful Miner, come and sign the pay roll and receive the check of eternal happiness.' Amen."

Then, there was "Dr. Wilhelm Stoy's Remedy for the Bite of a Dog," printed in German. The Reverend Stoy, my expert told me, was a clergyman and doctor who came over here from Germany about two hundred years ago—one of the earliest ministers of the Reformed Church in this country. As a physician he was noted for two special things—he was the first to introduce inoculation against smallpox (almost everyone at that time looked on it as a rash attempt to thwart the will of God), and he evolved a remedy for hydrophobia which became quite popular. In fact, when Washington was President of the United States, he sent a messenger to Lebanon, where Stoy was living then, to get a sample of the famous medicine. In Washington's diary it's referred to thus:

October 18, 1797—Gave my servant Christopher, to bear expenses to a person at Lebanon in Pennsylvania celebrated for curing persons bit by wild animals, $25.00.

The formula consisted of a handful of dried pimpernel boiled in two quarts of beer, then drained and tinctured with "two drams of theriaca." There were certain rules that Dr. Stoy laid down for those who took the remedy. For "a strong man" or a horse, the dose was one pint taken at short intervals. A child was given two large tablespoonfuls, while a woman took three gills. The human patient was instructed to avoid all "pig's meat," cabbage, peas, and beans, as well as "any creature that swims on the water." His old clothing must be thrown away as well, while the straw on which a bitten animal had lain was to be burned.

But the leaflets that intrigued me most of all were those which had to do with local tragedies like that of poor Susanna Cox. Written in German mostly, with some traces here and there of Pennsylvania Dutch, many had English versions also, so that everyone could share their morbid thrills. Newspapers and commercial printing houses—even individuals sometimes—published in booklet form long, rambling, melancholy histories of the various crimes and what led up to them, together usually with a confession by the criminal that ended with a solemn warning to the public to avoid temptation and beware of similar offense.

The story of Susanna Cox apparently was one that struck the public fancy—probably because Susanna was among the earliest women to be executed in this country—and the song that celebrated it continued to be sold for many years. Although, according to my expert, no one knows for sure who wrote it, it's believed John Philip Gomber was the author. Gomber, born in Germany in 1764, was a professional rhymester who eked out a living peddling his poetic efforts through the country sections. A professional penman also, he filled in the names on birth and baptism certificates and decorated them with crude, bright-colored hearts and birds and flowers and the like, according to the fashion of the day. His opus on Susanna Cox and her heart-rending fate consisted of a trifling thirty-two fantastic stanzas. Here, in part, is one of the English versions:

> "Come listen now, ye people all,
>   And to my words give heed!
> A maiden's fate I will relate—
>   A mournful tale indeed.

"At Jacob Gehr's in Oley, she
Had been a servant good;
Her name it was Susanna Cox,
As I have understood.

"Instructions she had ne'er received
In her neglected youth;
She had not learned the will of God,
And did not love the truth.

*   *   *   *   *

"The second month and fourteenth day
Of eighteen hundred nine,
A child was born at half past four,
Ere yet the sun did shine.

"Then blinded sorely by her sin,
And in her sorrow wild,
This wicked mother raised her hand
And slew her new born child.

"Soon as the dreadful crime was known
They placed her in arrest;
And that she did this awful deed
She speedily confessed.

*   *   *   *

"Her agony, ah! who can tell?
She knew the end was nigh,
And that upon the scaffold she
A shameful death must die.

*   *   *   *   *

"Forth from the prison she was brought
At eleven o'clock one day

And to the scaffold she was led
A pitiable way.

"A solemn warning she addressed
Unto the people all:
'Take an example now,' she said,
'By this my dreadful fall.'

* * * * *

"And now, alas! the dreadful hour
Of death had come at last;
In seventeen minutes, we are told,
The agony was past.

* * * * *

"The man who wrote this little song
And set it all in rhyme,
And who described the awful scene,
Was present at the time.

* * * * *

"Ye people that on earth do dwell
Unto my words give heed,
And think how far the ways of sin
And ignorance may lead.

"The fleeting pleasures of her life
Were blotted out with tears,
And all the time she spent on earth
Was four and twenty years."

My visit to my favorite expert wasn't long enough to gather
half the information that I wanted, so at various times since then
he's sent me odds and ends of other data, and my knowledge of
these fascinating Sorrow Songs has grown apace. It seems that

most of them were modeled on a certain forty-two-verse *Trauer-geschichte* (mournful tale) about a murder which occurred in Germany—the Meyer-Hof affair. For some strange reason, it became quite popular in Pennsylvania, too, and was reprinted many times, to serve as an example for the balladmongers over here.

One of the bards who turned out dreary doggerel in large doses was a woman, Polly Schropp by name, whose works, in German, treated of such subjects as "A Sad Story of Much Illness," "A Prayer to Redeem the Rich," "A Song of the City of Jerusalem and the Morning Star," and others. Although she published many of her songs herself, apparently she failed to make a living from them, for she died in 1836 at the age of sixty-four in the Schuylkill County Almshouse.

One broadside of the day that had wide circulation was the story of the Böhmische Bauer (The Bohemian Farmer)—Adam Lenke, of Dorf Stockum in the town of Eger. Lenke was a man who recklessly persisted in refusing to observe the Sabbath day. And finally one Sunday, after he'd chopped down a tree within the forest near his home, he suddenly was rooted to the stump on which he sat and doomed to stay there from then on, throughout eternity.

A well-known peddler of these various broadsides—not to mention charms and cures of every kind—was John George Hohman, author of that famous bible of the superstitious, "Pow-Wows or Long Lost Friend; a Collection of Mysterious and Invaluable Arts and Remedies for Man as Well as Animals—With Many Proofs." Hohman himself laid claim to writing many of the ballads that he sold, including one depressing narrative concerning Thomas Siegfried, of Berks County, who committed suicide in 1836. But experts seem to take these claims of Hohman's with a grain of salt.

Among the pamphlets setting forth this type of shocking tale was one about the crime of John M. Wilson, who was hanged for murder in Montgomery County Prison. The paper cover of the

booklet, with a picture of the criminal himself upon it, offered this
complete and dolorous description:

A Full History of the Eventful
LIFE, CRIMES,
CONFESSIONS, REPENTANCE,
and
Death on the Gallows
of
JOHN M. WILSON,
Hanged Jan. 13th, 1887, for the Murder of Anthony
W. Dealy, Jan. 26th, 1884, whose body,
cut up and in bags, was found
March, 1884, in the Wissahickon.
Written by Himself
And Edited, Revised and Published by
REV. W. A. LEOPOLD,
Spiritual Adviser and Pastor of the Cherry
Street Church of the Evangelical Association.
(News Dealers and Agents can get reasonable terms by
applying to the publisher)

Another, "How a Wife's Heart Was Broken: Mrs. Bissinger's
Sad Suicide," presented on the cover page a picture of the victim
in a long, full, ruffled dress of the Victorian era, clutching in her
arms three good-sized children, plus a large and heavy basket, as
she leaped into the water at her feet to end her life. The title
page read this way:

The
BISSINGER SUICIDE
History of that Sad Tragedy
In which Mrs. Bissinger (as alleged), made desperate
by neglect and ill treatment, drowned her-

self and three children in the Union
Canal, at Reading, Penna.
Statement of her Brother in Reply to her Husband.

But of all the ballads and grim histories of such dire events, the
one that specially interested me took place in my own home
county, just a dozen miles or so away. It was the haunting tale
of Joseph Miller, a young Polish teacher, and the high-born German maiden who became his wife. This was the chilling introduc-
tion:

> "Listen now, and I will tell you
> Of a fearful murder case,
> Such as no one ever heard of
> Heretofore to've taken place.
>
> "And whoever hears this story
> Must, if truth be in his bosom,
> Say that in our country's annals
> None is found more weird and gruesome."

Then at great length (thirty-three verses) it went on to tell
how Miller left his home in southern Poland, after Russia had
invaded that unlucky land, and found employment with the
family of a German count. As tutor to the nobleman's small son,
the handsome Polish youth was thrown in frequent contact with
his pupil's sister, and it wasn't long before the two young people
fell in love. They knew from the beginning that their case was
hopeless, for the count had planned to marry off his daughter to
a man of her own noble rank. So, with the meagre store of money
that they had between them, they set sail for Philadelphia on a
summer day in 1817.

> "Came they then to Lebanon county,
> To a spot near Myerstown—

> Paupers here, in Prussia wealthy,
> Suffering now ill fortune's frown.

> "Spent and gone was all their money,
> Who were used to live in state;
> Indigence and want before them—
> Dark and fearful seemed their fate.

> "Far from friends, without employment,
> Just escaped from tyrant's rule,
> Miller formed the plan of teaching,
> And ere long was keeping school."

But keeping school in those days was no occupation by which anyone grew rich. Two cents a day was the enormous sum each pupil paid—and on the days they didn't come to school they didn't pay at all. So things kept going from bad to worse for the poor Millers, and the delicately nurtured German girl, with two small children now to care for and a third one on the way, grew more depressed and homesick every day.

> "And at times, her heart near breaking
> With a longing, homesick pain,
> 'Take me,' she would cry in anguish,
> 'Take me, Joseph, home again.' "

And the ill-fated husband, helpless to restore the luxury and comfort that she yearned for, grew more sad and melancholy in his turn. At last, his mind affected by regret and self-reproach—

> "Flames of fire and fiends of darkness
> Seemed to numb his sense and will,
> Plunged him in a hell of madness,
> Urged him on to strike and kill!"

And next morning when his pupils gathered at the school as usual, they discovered that the door was locked and not a sign of life or movement anywhere about the place. At last one youngster, bolder than the rest, peered through a window and in horrified surprise let out a lusty yell. With gloating zest the ballad dwelt on each detail of the blood-curdling scene:

> "By a rope there hung the master,
> Joseph Miller, cold and dead;—
> Many turned in fear and terror,
> Weeping as they homeward fled!
>
> "On her lowly couch the mother
> Weltering in her lifeblood lay,
> Once a happy German maiden
> Now a lifeless lump of clay.
>
> "Many red-lipped wounds were gaping,
> Whence had ebbed away her life;
> Crushed her skull by hands that often
> Had caressed her as a wife.
>
> "Nearby lay her first born, murdered
> By the self-same ruthless hand,—
> Broken head and cruel knife stabs—
> Work that maniac brain had planned.
>
> "And the infant in its cradle,
> Darling of its mother's heart—
> Also butchered like the others—
> Of this tragedy a part!
>
> "Pity we this wretched woman!
> Pity with her babes abide!
> Pity with the unborn child that
> With its martyred mother died!"

The whole countryside attended the burial rites of the mothei and her children, but—

> "Miller's body to a corner
> Of a verdant field was borne,
> Left to lie unblest, unprayed for,
> Till the resurrection morn."

For in those days churchyards everywhere were barred to suicides, and the young schoolmaster's corpse was dumped into a rough and lonely grave, uncoffined and unsung. But recently I came across an eerie sequel to the dismal story. Back in those days also, it appears, the bodies thus disposed of were in great demand among the medical profession. And on a certain gloomy night a doctor came on horseback to the field where Miller lay, dug up the corpse, and galloped home with it across his saddle. As he bore his ghastly burden down a flight of stairs, however, suddenly his foot slipped and he tumbled headlong to the bottom, with the body falling down on top. For many years thereafter Miller's skeleton served as an object lesson to the surgeon and his students—which provides a rather fitting ending to a grim and gruesome tale!

April

CAVE DIEM!

I T'S ALWAYS been my fond belief, with no regard whatever for accepted theories, that with the first of April spring has actually arrived. Of course, there *was* an April first of my not-too-far-distant recollection that was ushered in by an uproarious blizzard. But that, I still insist, was one of those exceptions which just go to prove the rule. So, with a childlike faith in my conviction, I proceeded to move bag and baggage to my little cottage in the hills.

By way of April Fooling me, however, it blew up cold—so cold, in fact, that I unearthed the ski suit which I'd trustingly retired for the season, put on my long-legged underwear and extra sweater, and turned up the heater to its highest point.

"So you're here for the summer!" various people at the village greeted me.

"That *was* my thought!" I answered, somewhat snappishly. "But it looks as though I've come to spend the winter!"

Of course, I *should* have known much better than to start out anywhere on April first. For that day, if you put your faith in old-time Pennsylvania German superstitions, is one of the three unluckiest in all the year. The reason is that Judas Iscariot was born on April first. The other members of this baneful trio of unlucky days are August first, when Satan was expelled from heaven, and December first, when Sodom and Gomorrah were destroyed. If you should shed as little as a drop of blood on any of the three, you'd die within the week. And any child born April first, or August first, or December first, is just about the most unfortunate person you can find. He'll live to be disgraced before the world, to start with, and he'll die an evil death besides— completely hopeless any way you take it.

And there are other days, as well, that should be treated with respect. Each month has several of them—days on which you never should be born, to start with, and on which you never, never should begin a new activity of any kind. Perhaps the worst month of the year is January, which has seven days to be avoided at all costs—the first, second, third, fourth, sixth, eleventh, and twelfth. Next on the list come April and December, each with four un- lucky days—the first, tenth, seventeenth, and eighteenth of April, and the first, sixth, eleventh, and sixteenth of December. The bad days in the other months include the first, seventeenth, and eighteenth of February; the fourteenth and sixteenth of March; the seventh and eighth of May; the seventeenth of June; the seventeenth and twenty-first of July; the twentieth and twenty-first of August; the tenth and eighteenth of September; the sixth of October; and the sixth and tenth of November.

But that's not all. There are still other days that need a lot of circumspection if you're going to weather them. Shrove Tuesday, for example, when you mustn't sew unless you want your chickens to stop laying. And Ash Wednesday, when you must be sure to sprinkle ashes from the day before on all your poultry and your cattle so that they'll be free from lice all year.

Then, too, there's Maundy Thursday—better known to Pennsylvania Germans as Green Thursday—when each person must eat something green, like spinach, dandelion, or the like, in order to avoid a fever. And Good Friday, when you musn't sweep for fear of being plagued with flies, mustn't clean your stables if you want to keep away the witches, and must be sure to eat no meat but fish for fear your cattle won't survive the year.

No doubt the trickiest day of all, however, is Ascension Day. For then you positively mustn't sew for fear a bolt of lightning will descend upon your barn; you mustn't go out driving or you'll have an accident; you mustn't plough, or raise a barn, or turn out work of any kind at all. About the only thing you *can* do on Ascension Day, it seems, is drink a lot of tea—the more the better, evidently, since seven different kinds insure protection from contagious ailments all year long.

Life must have been quite complicated in the good old days, it seems to me. With all those dates to keep in mind, and all those things you must and mustn't do—well, personally, I'll take our modern calendar. Of course, it *does* have some peculiarities— like National Pickle Week and Let's Play Ball Week, Get More Sleep Week, and a couple of hundred other fascinating features of the kind. But even so, it's better to have indigestion and a charley-horse and not much night life, isn't it, than to be disgraced

before the world because you happened to be born on April first?
Or is it?

MIDNIGHT ALARM

THE weather still continued cold. On every side the woods looked
drab and bare and wintry, but along the streams and in the swamp
where that first unromantic harbinger of spring, skunk cabbage,
was already halfway up, a touch of lush and lovely green gave
promise of the warmer days ahead.

I'd found a few buds of wild pussywillow recently. And on the
back road, walking toward the village, I'd met a tiny chipmunk—
that same flibberty-gibbet little fellow, I could swear, who always
dashed out helter-skelter in the path of cars and narrowly escaped
a sudden death at least a hundred times last summer. From the
marsh I'd heard occasionally the thin, clear shrilling of a hyla,
and I'd thought again of the old Greek legend about Hylas, favorite of the hero Hercules and member of the Argonautic expedition.

Hylas, so the story went, was sent ashore at Kios to get water
for his party and was captured by the nymphs whose spring he
chose to tap. In vain his comrade Hercules sought for him, and
at last in grief and rage swore loudly that he'd ravage all the land
for miles around if Hylas weren't brought back. But all to no
avail—the youth was seen no more of mortal man. And ever
after on a certain day, in memory of that dreadful threat of Hercules, the Kios natives roamed the woods and mountains shouting
lustily for Hylas. And "the cry of Hylas" has become a phrase
that to this very day connotes complete futility.

I don't know that I've ever heard just how the little pipers known
as hylas got their curious title, or if any tie exists between them
and Hylas of the old Greek tale. But as I listened to their liquid
notes come whistling from the fringes of the marsh the other
evening, I wondered if perhaps they might be calling for that lost

youth who had answered to the name so strangely like their own.

Their piping died abrupty even as I wondered. It was getting colder, and I turned to go indoors. The woods were dark and silent now, and the prospect of a crackling fire on the hearth seemed most inviting. A high wind, gusty, violent, had sprung up. It kept belaboring the house, knocking the objects on the porch against the wall, upsetting chairs and vases, and in general keeping Patsy in a nervous dither. At last, to calm her fears, I stepped outside with her again before we went to bed. The moon was full and overhead a hundred twinkling stars shone diamond-bright. Against the cold, clear sky the branches of the trees, still stark and bare, swayed back and forth in wind-swept majesty. And suddenly the Pennsylvania German version of a childish jingle popped into my head. I said the words aloud:

> "Blinzel, blinzel, gleener Schtaern!
> Oh, wie sehn ich dich so gaern!
> Hoch am Himmel, in die Heh,
> So wie'n Deimand, bischt du schee." *

But the little poem didn't seem to soothe Patricia. She remained completely jittery and ill at ease. When finally we went inside once more and I prepared to settle her as usual on the couch beside the heater, she looked at me with such despondent pleading in her eyes that I relented in my purpose. Instead, I took her bed upstairs with me and laid it on the floor beside by own. And, satisfied at last, my little dog curled up immediately and went to sleep.

But in the middle of the night her growling wakened me. I listened, and a little tingle crept along my spine. For on the cold air, stilled at last, the sound of footsteps echoed eerily outside! Slowly and stealthily I raised the windowshade above my bed, then, rising to my knees, I peered into the brilliant moonlight

* "Twinkle, twinkle, little star," etc.

bathing woods and hill. There, plain as day and twice as terrifying, stood the figure of a large and shaggy animal. A wolf, was my first thought! But a closer look revealed it as a big, fat, coffee-colored collie nosing at my garbage pail, and with a breath of deep relief I went back to my interrupted slumbers.

Next morning I attempted to find out the name and owner of my midnight visitor. But all I learned was that the Ellingers had had just such a collie killed three days ago. Perhaps, who knows, I'd seen the collie's ghost? But if I had, at least it was a rather hefty ghost, one not too unsubstantial to upset a garbage pail.

Which brought to mind another ghost, of quite a different kind, however, that I'd heard of for the first time not so very long before. The story went back to the eighteenth century, when the tide of German immigrants from the Palatinate was breaking on these shores in constantly increasing waves. Crowded like cattle in the holds of filthy ships, half starved and ravaged by disease of every kind, abused and cheated by unscrupulous sea captains, the Palatines still flocked with dogged purpose toward the land of their desire. Sometimes the trip across the sea took months instead of weeks, and vessels beaten off their course by storms would have the added menace of fierce pirates to encounter. Sometimes a ship reached port with less than half its passengers—and sometimes it would fail to reach the port at all.

The good ship *Palatine*, it seemed, was one of the unlucky ones. Laden with immigrants, her blazing hulk was sighted off the shore of a small island of Rhode Island one dark night about the middle of the eighteenth century. While the horror-stricken natives watched in helpless awe, the burning vessel drifted to her doom upon the rocky coast, and many of the poor unfortunates aboard her perished in the sea.

For years thereafter, so the legend goes, a phantom ship ablaze from stem to stern was seen by night in eerie silhouette against the northwest sky, and fathers handed down to sons the ghostly

tale of the ill-fated *Palatine*. The story reached the ears at last
of Whittier, the poet, and his poem called "The Tent on the
Beach" sets forth his version of the sombre tale.

It goes like this:

> Old wives spinning their webs of tow,
> Or rocking weirdly to and fro
> In and out of the peat's dull glow,
>
> And old men mending their nets of twine,
> Talk together of dream and sign,
> Talk of the lost ship *Palatine*,—
>
> The ship that, a hundred years before,
> Freighted deep with its goodly store,
> In the gales of the equinox went ashore.

And later on:

> But the year went round, and when once more
> Along their foam-white curves of shore
> They heard the line-storm rave and roar,
>
> Behold! again, with shimmer and shine,
> Over the rocks and the seething brine,
> The flaming wreck of the *Palatine!*

And it ends this way:

> For still, on many a moonless night,
> From Kingston Head and from Montauk Light
> The spectre kindles and burns in sight.
>
> Now low and dim, now clear and higher,
> Leaps up the terrible Ghost of Fire,
> Then, slowly sinking, the flames expire,

And the wise Sound skippers, though skies be fine,
Reef their sails when they see the sign
Of the blazing wreck of the *Palatine!*

Strange, isn't it, that a group of German immigrants bound for Pennsylvania should unwittingly have left their mark on a New England island in this haunting legend that once took the fancy of a famous poet!

MOUNTAIN MARY

For the first time in two weeks or more the sun was shining with whole-hearted fervor. The hills and woods, just waiting for some slight encouragement to burst forth into gauzy green, had perked up in immediate answer. A haze of misty red showed on the mountainside—the swelling buds of oak and birch and maple— and the brilliant gleam of marigold lent sudden radiance to the marshland. Spring at last, it seemed, was actually upon its way.

Perhaps it was the rising temperature—or maybe just a masculine desire to show off what his latest toy, a brand-new car of super-elegance, could do—but anyway, my driver, getting restless, offered urgently, "Let's go somewhere! It's going to be a perfect day!"

I rose in prompt obedience. Going somewhere, today or any day, is something that I'm ready for at any time. We're just a pair of motor tramps—at least, that's what the gentleman himself once called us—and the title seemed to fit as neatly as a glove. So, pausing only long enough to snatch up hats and coats and Patsy's small brown blanket, we were off.

In smoothly rolling luxury we sped along the highway—we and several thousand other motorists lured out by the ingratiating sun. The new toy proved its mettle nobly. Miles flew by as easily as in a pleasant dream. Wrapped in the silence of complete content, we watched the checkerboard of hills and meadows gliding swiftly past. Stone houses standing neat and trim in spaded gardens, with small, toiling figures bent above the fresh-turned ground. Huge barns adorned with painted symbols underneath the eaves— a cow's head here, a horse's there, a baffling star or cross or flower on another. And beyond the meadows, where the brown of new-ploughed earth met clear, fresh blue of April sky, a farmer following his plodding team.

As if endowed with second sight, my driver voiced what I was thinking. "Everywhere you look," he said, "a picture!"

I nodded as the patchwork landscape flowed in steady rhythm past our car. "Where are we going?" I queried conversationally.

He shrugged and grunted. Destination evidently didn't mean a thing. I sighed serenely and leaned back in carefree ease.

A white church with a tall and slender spire loomed ahead of us. A short way back, my memory told me lazily, a signpost had announced in modest lettering: "Hill Church"—and suddenly a bell rang in my memory.

"Look!" I sat up in excitement. "It's Hill Church we're coming to—the place where Mountain Mary's funeral services were held!"

The car slowed down. My driver looked at me. "And who," he asked a trifle warily, "was Mountain Mary?"

"A legend in these parts!" I told him with enthusiasm. "In Berks County, where we are right now, they call her *Barricke Mariche*—that's Pennsylvania Dutch for Mountain Mary. And she's buried somewhere in these very hills!"

"She is?" A sudden gleam of interest lit my driver's eyes. "Let's see if we can't find her grave!" he said.

I nodded in agreement. "Let's!" A visit to that lonely mountain grave that I'd been reading of just recently seemed very much in order. My Chauffeur began to swing the car about, and in a moment we were headed in the opposite direction.

"Of course," I mentioned casually, "I haven't got the least idea

of how you get there. But probably we'll find a marker somewhere on the way."

The gentleman behind the wheel seemed unconcerned. "Don't
worry!" he instructed. "Give me time, that's all—I'll get us there!"
And so, with childlike faith in that unerring faculty of his which
always landed us exactly where we started for, I leaned back and
relaxed once more.

We rolled along in silence for a little while. The sun was dropping slowly toward the mountaintop, and hazily I wondered which
of us would reach it first—that brilliant ball of blood-red glory or
the car in which we sped so smoothly on our unknown way?

"Well, how about it?" From my peaceful lethargy the question
brought me back to earth. "This Mountain Mary person," my
Chauffeur reminded. "Aren't you going to tell me what you know
about her?"

"Oh—of course!" In sudden haste I searched my memory for
the rather meagre facts I'd gathered here and there. "Well," I
began obligingly, "away back in the days before the Revolution
a small German family by the name of Jung, or Young, arrived in
Philadelphia. At their former home in Germany, near Frankfort-
on-the-Main, they'd heard a lot of glowing tales about this province that some people called 'Penn's Wilderness,' and they'd
decided that they'd like to come and see it for themselves. There
were a mother, father, and three daughters in the family—cotton
spinners all of them by trade—and over here, in Germantown,
they settled down to earn a living in this new land of their choice.
Things went real well with them at first. But then the father died,
and then the war broke out, and suddenly they found themselves
right in the middle of the conflict. The Battle of Germantown
was fought right on their doorstep, almost. So at last the four
lone women gathered up their few belongings, said good-bye to
all their friends, and set out for the peaceful Oley Hills—"

"Where *we* are at this very minute!" my Chauffeur put in. His glance swept once again across the shyly budding loveliness of hill and field and roadside all about us. "Personally, I think their choice was pretty good!"

I nodded. "And the special mountaintop we're heading for," I added, "is the one the refugees picked out on which to build their home. They farmed the land themselves, you know, and somehow as the years went by they managed to eke out a meagre living. But the going was pretty tough at times, and none of them was used to such a life, of course, so gradually the heavy labor got them down. The mother and both sisters died at last, and Mary, forty-five by then, was left alone."

"And then what?" my Chauffeur demanded.

"Well," I told him, "Mary lived there on her mountaintop all by herself for thirty years. She had a small log house, an orchard, and a garden where she raised her fruits and vegetables. She also had some cows to give her milk, some hives of bees that kept her well supplied with honey, and a field of grass she cut and dried herself. Each week or so she'd pack a bundle of her produce, set it firmly on her head, and start out for her nearest neighbor's house. The three-mile road that wound along the mountainside was rough and rocky, though, so one day she decided she was going to make it easier. All by herself she cleared away the stumps and stones and saplings, till at last she'd made a trail a whole mile shorter than the one she'd always used before."

"But why?" the gentleman behind the wheel inquired curiously. "Why drag that stuff 'way down the mountain to begin with?"

"She had to earn a living, didn't she? You see, a neighbor, Isaac Lee, would take it all the way to Philadelphia for her, where he'd sell it at the market. And besides, he also saw that part of it was handed out among the poor. Because old Mountain Mary was a real philanthropist. Whenever other people were in need she'd lend a helping hand, and as the years went by her fame kept spreading through the neighborhood. When anyone was sick, or in distress, or wanted some advice, they'd send for Mountain Mary and she'd share with them whatever goods she had.

"She loved all animals as well as people," I continued. "They were friends, according to her way of thinking, and she always treated them with kindness and respect. One day she found some little marmots had been tunneling underneath her garden, chewing up her roots and vegetables and working havoc with her neatly tended plants. And so that night she set a trap and caught a lot of them. But then, instead of simply killing them, she took them to a neighboring hill and turned them loose."

"Soft-hearted, eh?" my driver said.

I nodded once again, and picked up my little tale. "The people in the village at the mountain's foot would often ask her if she weren't afraid to live there on her hilltop all alone. But Mary'd simply shake her head and smile. 'Why should I be?' she'd ask. 'I haven't anything to fear—the good Lord will take care of me!' And sure enough—He did!"

The car had slithered to a sudden stop as I was talking, and my charioteer was pointing toward the far side of the road. "Look —there it is!" he said.

With something of a jolt, I brought my thoughts back to the present. "What?" I asked.

"A marker. Over there across the way!"

I looked where he directed and my eyes lit on a small bronze tablet standing in an angle where a rocky mountain trail debouched upon the road. In eager haste I left the car and crossed to read it. Just as eagerly my driver followed. This is what we read:

> To the memory of Mary Young,
> Mountain Mary
> Barricke Mariche
> who lived to the north in these hills from **early** womanhood
> until her death, November 16, 1819, at **the age** of 70 years.

A pioneer nurse, comforter of body and soul, benevolent, pious, brave and charitable.

She hath done what she could.

"Hm—brief and to the point!" was my companion's comment. We sauntered back across the road, a trifle thoughtfully, and stepped into the waiting car. "Here's where we start to climb!" he said, and turned the wheel so that the auto's nose was pointing upward. "Apparently we take that rocky-looking trail ahead."

We left the open highway for the rough and bumpy surface of the narrow road. Precariously we wound between bare, rugged fields on either side, amidst a drab and barren landscape broken only by the green of garlic and the sprawling, wind-racked fronds of last year's ferns.

"How did she die?" my Jehu at the weel asked suddenly, his thoughts still occupied with Mountain Mary in her lonely hilltop home.

I went back to my interrupted story. "That's the strangest part of the whole tale!" I told him. "Because, you see, one night a friend of Mary's back in Germantown had a particularly clear and vivid dream. She saw the white-haired hermitess alone and in distress, and everything about the dream was so convincing that she made her mind up then and there to start off for the Oley Hills the first thing in the morning. Her family tried their best to stop her, but she wouldn't listen to them, so at last her grandson volunteered to go along. It was November, as it happened, and the rain-washed roads were hardly passable in many spots, but Mary's faithful friend refused to be persuaded to turn back. In dogged perseverance she and her companion kept on going, and finally that night they reached the little hut where Mountain Mary lived."

"And did the lady's dream come true?" My driver's tone was doubtful.

"Yes, it did!" I said impressively. "They found poor Mary lying sick in bed, all by herself, her cattle lowing pitifully from the cowshed, and the whole place upside-down for want of care. For two whole weeks she lingered on, while all that time her friend took care of her. And when at last she died, the neighbors from the hills and valleys all about came flocking to the funeral—held in that little church we passed awhile ago."

The road we followed had been getting steeper as I talked. Bare fields had given place to sombre woods, with dead trees leaning drunkenly against their upright neighbors. As I brought my tale to its conclusion we came out upon the mountaintop. A tumble-down, neglected farm lay sprawled upon our left—a gray stone house, a group of small, ramshackle sheds, a barn with jagged, gaping cracks across its side. From somewhere on the place a mongrel dog appeared and barked at us half-heartedly. Patricia, from her seat between us, answered in exuberant disdain.

Our engine throbbed to a reluctant stop and we alighted. From the lowering shadows of the barn a man as gray and weather-beaten as the building shuffled toward us. Worn and faded overalls were stuffed inside a pair of clumsy boots, and on his furrowed face there was a growth of scraggly beard.

"Can you," my driver asked politely, "tell us where the grave of Mountain Mary is located?"

The old man spoke in halting tones. His voice was rusty, and the words came out in short and broken sentences—the words of one not used to frequent speech. "It lies," he told us creakily, "across the meadow—over there!" He pointed to a clump of woodland in the distance. "Come—I show you!" And he started off abruptly.

With Patsy at our heels, we followed him across a meadow watered by a clear, fresh stream that trickled from a little spring. In timid friendliness he spoke to us across his shoulder: "*Kannst du Deitsch schwetze?*" (Can you speak Dutch?) he asked.

I gave my usual answer: "*Glee wennich* (Just a little)," and he sighed regretfully.

"I don't speak English very good," he said, and lapsed back into silence.

We skirted round a cornfield with its shocks all flailed and flattened by the winter's storms, along a snake fence and a wall of loose gray stones pried up, I gathered, from the bleak and stubborn soil, around the corner of another field, and came at last upon a circular enclosure in the woods. Another wall of stones surrounded it, and at one side a pair of slender cedar trees stood sentinel above the lonely spot. This was our destination.

We stood regarding it a moment without speaking. In that stony space no well-kept mound with neat, white tombstone at its head and foot was visible. Just three small markers, bare of all inscription, rested on the level ground. They might, perhaps, be granite, though it seemed unlikely. Maybe at some distant date they'd borne a legend of some kind, I thought. But if they had, the wind and rain of passing years had worn them smooth.

"Why are there *three?*" my driver asked with sudden interest.

I thought back hastily. "Well, Mary had a mother and two sisters," I reminded. "Possibly all four of them are buried here, and only three graves marked."

Our guide's head nodded in agreement. "That is right!" he said. Then, pointing to a wreath of long-dead flowers with a bow of tattered ribbon flapping in the sharp-edged breeze: "This one is Mary's grave," he added.

"And who brought the wreath?" I asked.

The old man picked his words uncertainly. "Each year," he told us, "from the Lutheran church down in the valley comes the pastor with some people. Then they put the wreath on Mary's grave."

"And other visitors—they come here, too?"

Again the old man nodded. "Yes—in summertime. But not in winter."

A little silence fell upon us. Through the trees above our heads the wind moaned dismally. Behind us sunset bathed the darkling hills in fading light. A pair of mourning doves cooed in the distance, and the air was pregnant with the chill of coming night.

We turned away at last. In silence still, the three of us, with Patsy scampering on ahead, retraced our steps along the narrow path by which we'd come. Beside a moss-grown watering trough within the shadow of the barn we halted, and our guide stood looking at us wistfully. He seemed, we thought, pathetically loath to see us go.

My driver, sensing his reluctance, launched a friendly conversation. "Have you lived here long?" he asked.

The old man's face lit suddenly. "For t'irty-eight years now!" he answered softly. Then with growing confidence, encouraged by our interest, he began to tell us of his former life. Like Mountain Mary, he'd come here from Germany, he said, and as a youth had settled in the Oley Hills. For years he'd been a hired man down in the valley. But although his work had kept him there, his heart had fixed itself upon the farm that crowned the mountain-top above. If only he could own it, life would be so different and so wonderful, he thought! If only he could own it!

And then one happy day his dream had been fulfilled. The tenants of the farm had moved away and put their little homestead on the market. Eagerly he'd gotten out the savings that he'd hoarded for so long, and counted them. Yes, there was just enough! And so he'd bought the place—and there he'd lived and labored ever since.

"Alone?" we asked.

He shook his head. His brother shared the house with him, it seemed. He had a dog, a horse, a little flock of ducks and chickens. But of course—his glance took in the shabbiness about, and faltered suddenly—it wasn't worth as much now as it once had been. And he was getting old, besides. He couldn't farm the way he used to. Maybe—and the tired eyes grew still more tired—maybe he should sell the place? But if he did, where would he go himself? He looked at us forlornly. This was home—the only real home that he'd ever known—and he was happy here.

"Then stay—don't think of selling!" we advised him. "If you're happy, then you've got the only thing that really counts!"

A dim smile crossed the weather-beaten face. The tired eyes were grateful as we shook his hand at last and said good-bye. With Patsy jumping in ahead of us, we stepped into the heated comfort of our waiting car. The motor started, and we glided down the mountainside.

Behind us, faint and misty in the falling dusk, a wan and wistful figure watched us out of sight. And in the background, tall and straight against the murky shadows of the night, two lonely cedar trees stood guard above the grave of Mountain Mary, deep within the harbor of the hills that were her home.

May

DUNKER LOVE-FEAST

I STOPPED to see some Dunker friends of mine, the Givlers, and was told that they were "having love-feast" at their church the following week. Would I, they asked me hospitably, like to come?

Of course I would, I told them. Ever since that Easter morning several years before when my Chauffeur and I had been invited to a Dunker baptism service,* I'd admitted to a specially soft spot in my heart for all the members of that simple faith. The

* See Chapter X, *Hex Marks the Spot*.

cordial, whole-souled welcome that we'd met with then had left
a warm and friendly feeling with me, and I'd wanted many times
to have a chance to know these simple, open-hearted people better.

"Perhaps you never seen a Dunker love-feast?" Mr. Givler asked
me. In his voice was the proprietary pride in his particular denom-
ination and its customs that I'd noted often among other Plain
persuasions. I said I hadn't, and he nodded in frank satisfaction.
"Then you'd better come!" he said. And added generously: "Just
bring your friends along, too, if you want!"

But Sally was the only friend accompanying me when on the
following Sunday we approached the sturdy red brick building on
a quiet village street that Mr. Givler had described to me. Behind
a group of white-capped girls, we climbed a flight of concrete
steps and found ourselves inside a huge hall that appeared to be
a cross between a dining-room and church. On every side were
tables—long and narrow tables made by turning over every third
pew as a table top—and on each one there lay a neat array of
cutlery and food. Ten places had been set along each side, with
knife, fork, tablespoon, and little pasteboard plate laid carefully
at each. Six loaves of bread, six china bowls of water, six enamel
bowls whose contents were invisible beneath large plates of steaming sliced roast beef, and six small plates of butter made up what
we took to be the love-feast meal.

A bit uncertainly we sat down in a sort of anteroom that
opened on the right. "Um, but it smells good!" Sally said. Her
voice was wistful. She'd confided to me driving over that she'd
started dieting—her dinner had consisted of a sandwich and a
cup of tea. "What do you s'pose," she wondered yearningly, "is
in those white enamel bowls?"

I shrugged unfeelingly. Secure in the repletion of a good, square
meal myself, I was quite satisfied to wait and see. Besides, I'd
just discovered certain objects underneath the tables that intrigued
me mightily. At the aisle end of each pew there was an ordinary

foot-tub, a small agate basin, and some folded cloths laid carefully upon the shelf above. And I remembered Mr. Givler's telling me that in addition to the love-feast and communion service there would be feet-washing, too.

I spied the gentleman himself just then. He was a deacon, he'd informed me, and with other deacons he was busy now preparing for the rites to come. He spied us, too, however, and took time to nod a genial welcome. Then, with a sign, he indicated that he'd see us later on. His sister, meanwhile, whom I'd met just once before, approached us from the other side.

"You got here, anyways!" she greeted us informally. "Well, soon we start now! Would youse like to go and sit across the room?"

She pointed to another anteroom directly opposite, and suddenly it dawned on us that we were sitting in the section of the church reserved for men! For with the Dunkers, as with others of the Plain denominations, members are divided strictly into separate groups. The men sit soberly on one side of the church, the women on the other, and none but strangers ever disregard this rigid rule.

In some chagrin we followed meekly as she led the way across the room. She saw us safely settled in the front row of the little alcove and then left us. Evidently services were just about to start.

I felt a sudden nudge from Sally. The presiding elder in the front part of the room had gotten up. "I think they're going to eat!" she whispered hungrily, her mind still concentrated upon food.

The elder gave a silent signal. Quietly the members standing at the edges of the church began to stream in orderly procession toward their pews. The men and boys took places at the tables on the left, the girls and women on the right, and from our sideline vantage point we had a splendid chance to view the congregation as a whole. Each head upon the women's side, we saw, was cov-

ered with a sheer white cap or "prayer veil," as the Dunkers call it.
For, as the Apostle Paul once wrote to the Corinthians: "Every
woman praying or prophesying with her head unveiled dishonoreth
her head." (1 Corinthians 11:5.) The caps, however, varied somewhat in detail, we noted, for the older women wore theirs cut on
bonnet lines with definitely brimlike edges, while the veils affected
by the younger members looked like nothing more than small,
round, finely pleated caps. The dresses of the older sisters, too—
subdued and rather drab in tone—were cut according to a single
pattern, with no jewelry anywhere, not even wedding rings, in
evidence. But gaily flowered prints of silk or cotton, made according to the latest fashion and adorned with pins and rings and
watches of all kinds, appeared to be the rule among the girls and
younger women. Evidently worldly ways were gaining gradual
foothold even here.

When everyone was seated the presiding elder rose. The meeting would begin, he said, with reading of the Scriptures. So,
while passages describing the Last Supper were intoned, assisting
elders armed with watering-cans went quietly about the task of
filling up the foot-tubs and hand-basins underneath the tables.
Just as quietly, the members started to remove their shoes and
stockings.

"But the foods's all getting cold!" Beside me Sally's voice was
painfully protesting. "Wouldn't you think they'd eat it while it's
hot, and leave the washing of the feet till later on?"

The order of procedure did seem somewhat odd, I granted. But
who were we to judge? So, with a stoic sigh from Sally, we settled
down to see what happened next. We hadn't long to wait. For
at the aisle end of each pew a man or woman, as the case might
be, now slowly rose. The men removed their coats, then, like the
women, clasped around their waists a long, white apron. Simultaneously they drew the foot-tubs from beneath the tables, placing
them before their next-door neighbors, and with grave solemnity

knelt down upon the floor. Gently they splashed the water on the others' feet and dried them on their aprons. Both the washed and washer then arose, exchanged a kiss and handshakes, and passed on the apron—and the ritual was repeated with the person next in line.

The washing went on endlessly, it seemed to us. At last the final brother kissed the cheek of brother and the last old lady with some difficulty crowded tired, work-worn feet in Sunday shoes. Without a pause the minister in charge then rose once more, and this time the whole congregation followed suit. Humbly they bowed their heads. Their leader asked a blessing on the food—and finally, to Sally's great relief, we heard the words that we'd been waiting for: "Now we will eat!"

With an eagerness we made no effort to conceal, both Sally's eyes and mine were fastened on the white enamel bowls whose contents still were hidden by the plates of meat, no longer steaming, laid across the top.

"What's in them?" Sally whispered with a hungry sniff. "It looks like stew!"

"Soup!" was my guess. And I was right. A thick, rich, savory soup composed of meat and rice was what it seemed to be. The members, three or four to every bowl, were dipping into it decorously. There was a special etiquette, apparently, in its consumption. Every time a spoon was lifted from the bowl to journey toward a waiting mouth, a piece of bread was held beneath it carefully to catch the drip, and not a person there— including three small twelve-year-olds in front of us—but followed this procedure faithfully.

In ordered seemliness the meal progressed. Occasionally another slice of bread was taken, or the children, frankly hungry, helped themselves to meat a second time. The bowls of water passed from lip to lip. But only an infrequent whisper of request that mingled with the muted clang of fork or spoon on china dish relieved the solemn silence that prevailed.

At last the eaters had consumed their fill. Led by the elder, they arose to offer thanks; then, seated once again, the hand of fellowship and kiss of love were once more given by each member to his next-door neighbor—and the love-feast portion of the service was concluded.

Next came communion. From long, narrow slabs of rich, unleavened bread doled out by the assisting elders, perforated squares about two inches in diameter were broken off by individual members and laid carefully upon the table at each place. When all had been supplied the gray-haired leader blessed the bread. Then, with a warning to his flock to keep their thoughts fixed only on Christ's broken body sacrificed for them, he murmured gently: "Let us eat!" A silence, deep and reverent, fell upon the crowded church. With heads devoutly bowed and here and there a pair of eyes quite frankly wet, the members nibbled quietly. The whimper of a restless child, the sudden dropping of a hymnbook, sounded sharp and startling in the solemn hush.

The blessing of the wine came next, and once again the elders circulated through the church, to fill repeatedly the tall and shining goblets that now passed from lip to lip. The voices of the congregation, meanwhile, joined in old, familiar hymns, and at their end a prayer was offered, with a special blessing for all present, not forgetting the small group of visitors within the gates. A final hymn, "Blest Be the Tie That Binds," was sung, the benediction was pronounced—and our first love-feast in a Dunker church was over.

We started to put on our wraps. With shy but friendly smiles the women in the pews across from us glanced up. One of them, less bashful than the rest, approached us with a hearty welcome. We shook hands and she inquired our names. We stood in pleasant conversation for a moment, until Mr. Givler with his wife and sister hurried up to join us. With simple naturalness they asked us how we'd liked the service, and we answered them with equal frankness. Both the soup and the communion bread had interested me, so I put my questions to them without hesitation.

"What's *in* the soup? It smelled delicious!" I began.

"It's beef soup!" Mrs. Givler told us. "First you boil the beef until it's tender, then you grind it, then you boil some rice, and when that's done you add the beef and heat the two together. Then you put dried breadcrumbs in the bottom of each bowl and pour the soup on top."

"And what about the bread used for communion?" I went on. "It's different from the kind I know."

"Why, it's unleavened bread!" the Givler sister put in helpfully. And added with a touch of pride: "It's awful rich! The elder's wives, they make it, still. It's got a pound of butter and a quart and a half of cream in every batch!" She looked at us with eyes as bright and piercing as a little bird's. "Perhaps you'd like to taste a piece?"

With some enthusiasm we assented, and she darted off. A moment later she was back with several squares wrapped neatly in a paper napkin. Every square, she pointed out, was clearly marked with five sharp nail prints—symbols of the wounds the Savior suffered as He hung upon the cross. She watched us as we nibbled at it tentatively.

"Um—it's good!" With avid satisfaction Sally gulped her square down to the last small crumb. She looked as if she'd like to ask for more, but nobly held her peace. I ate my square in slightly more restrained appreciation. As I finished it the elder who had offered up the closing prayer passed by our alcove, and our hostess signaled him to stop.

"This here's our elder-in-charge!" she introduced him proudly. He smiled in kindly recognition.

"We're glad you came!" he greeted us. "We always welcome

visitors—there's nothing secret in our services, you know. We like to have folks see just how we follow what the Bible says!"

He told us of his church's three main tenets—non-conformance, non-resistance, and non-swearing. No good Dunker, he informed us, would bear arms, or go to law, or dress in any but the plainest fashion. And their women always wore their prayer veils, with no gold or silver ornaments of any kind.

"But," Sally interrupted, "I saw lots of girls with jewelry on tonight!"

The elder smiled, a trifle wistfully, I thought. "It isn't what we teach!" he said with dignity. "But some don't follow."

I changed the subject tactfully. I'd had the privilege once, I said, of being present at a Dunker baptism. Could he tell me more about its interesting details? He could and would, he said. Just what especially would I like to know?

"Well—when you take in members from another church," I asked, "do you insist that they must be baptized again?"

He shook his head. "Not if they've been baptized by trine immersion—*forward!*" he replied. "But if they've been immersed once forward and twice backward, say—or merely backward—or by any other method—then we do!"

It seemed a bit confusing. "Why?" I asked. "Why does your church immerse face forward, while some other churches of the Plain denominations do it backwards?"

Again he smiled. "The only reason I can think of for immersing backward is that people usually are buried on their backs, and baptism is supposed to be the burial of sin. However, when a person's drowned—" he peered at me through gleaming spectacles—"he lies face forward in the water, doesn't he?"

I nodded.

"Well, we don't want the devil Sin to rise again, and so we drown him by immersing forward!"

With this quaint explanation our interpreter of Dunker usage turned away. Gradually the church was emptying and the tables, cleared of food and dishes, had been changed once more to pews. We should be starting homeward, too, I thought. But first I had one final question.

"What becomes of all the food left over from the love-feast?" I inquired of the Givler sister.

"We serve it after church tomorrow morning!" was her answer. "Down in the basement we set tables and make coffee, and the ones who want to can sit down and eat." She looked at us with hospitable meaning. "Would youse like to come?"

"You'd be most welcome to!" the elder added as he said good-night.

But we declined. And, rendered somewhat humble by the frank and honest friendliness we'd met on every side, we said good-night ourselves and started for the waiting Rat outside.

A silver wisp of moon was floating in a cloud-racked sky as we emerged. I looked up at it soberly. Yes, my impression of the Dunkers had been right, I thought. Without a doubt they were the kindliest, most generous and straightforward folk I'd ever had the great good luck to meet!

THE GUN THAT WON THE REVOLUTION

It's strange how stubbornly old fallacies persist. Trying to stamp one out is more or less like stepping on a centipede—you pound and pummel it with all your might, and yet the creature still insists on wiggling and with half a chance is up and off and out of sight before you can so much as catch your breath! And so it is with lots of dogged notions that the public seems to cling to with tenacious zeal.

Take the ridiculous conviction that a blue gate on an Amish farm connotes a marriageable daughter in the house. It isn't true, of course. A blue gate stands for one thing only—that the Amish are particularly fond of blue. They use it for their windowshades and shutters, for their men's shirts and their women's dresses, and for painting woodwork either in the house or out. If every marriageable daughter in an Amish household meant a blue gate— well, the Amish have big families and there'd hardly be a farm throughout the land without a gate of that celestial color as a practically permanent adornment.

The same thing, too, is true of the absurd conceit that "bundling" is a favorite sport among the Amish. Perhaps it was at some time in the distant past, but certainly it's not today—I'll guarantee that fact. Yet all you have to do is broach the subject of these people and you're greeted with a knowing smile and some facetious reference to this fancied custom.

Then also, there's the "seven sweets and seven sours" myth that's had such wide publicity. I've yet to find a Pennsylvania German housewife anywhere who serves exactly seven of these special dishes, and no more nor less—or for that matter, anyone who's ever heard of anyone who did. It's just another pleasant little misconception that the general public has adopted and insists on spreading far and wide, regardless of the facts.

Then there's the matter, too, of the "Kentucky rifle." Actually, it was as much Kentuckian as *Schnitz un Knepp* is French. For it was made right here in Pennsylvania by the Pennsylvania Dutch —just one of many "firsts" for which they've been responsible throughout the years. And history shows that if there'd been no rifled guns to terrify the British by their strange and unexpected accuracy, there'd probably have been no victory for the Continental Army. In other words, it was the Pennsylvania Dutch who tipped the scales and played a major part in winning freedom for our country.

It all began a good four centuries ago, in 1500, when a Viennese named Gaspard Kollner first applied the principle of rifling to a gun. To make the ball fit better, he made grooves inside the barrel—straight grooves first, till one day quite by accident the grooves got twisted and ran spirally instead of up and down (at least, that's how the story goes). At any rate, the curious firearm with its new-fangled grooves became a great success. It shot much farther and was far more apt to hit the mark than smooth-bore weapons of the day, and gradually its reputation spread abroad. In Germany and Switzerland it was adopted by the mountain hunters, and eventually became the rifle of the German *Jaegers*— but a rifle still in very crude and rudimentary form.

Then, in the eighteenth century, after William Penn had offered refuge in his Pennsylvania province to the persecuted peoples of the Rhine and near-by sections, many Swiss and Germans started emigrating to the promised land. Among them there were skillful gunsmiths who knew something of the art or rifling, and who now proceeded to apply that knowledge to the stern requirements of their adopted home. The frontier wasn't very far away, of course, and those who went exploring were dependent for their food on what small game their rifles could bring down. So finally the gunsmiths managed to evolve a lighter weapon with a smaller bore, that could be counted on to hit a squirrel without the usual probability of wasted shots. For shots were precious in those days, not only for the lead and powder used, but for the time it took to load and fire the gun. With Indians lurking in the offing and wild animals of no mean size to be encountered sometimes, often life itself depended on the accuracy with which a man could shoot.

So, of necessity, the frontiersman was always ready. Over every cabin door there hung a well-oiled rifle, bright and shiny from repeated cleanings, with a pouch containing bullets, patches, tinder, steel, and other crude accessories beside it. At the first sign of alarm the owner seized his gun, together with a blanket, hunting shirt, and moccasins kept handy for the purpose, stuffed a few pounds of jerked venison and rockahominy (ground Indian corn) into his wallet, and was on his way. And usually a son or two accompanied him. For pioneer boys learned to hunt and fight the Indians at an early age. As soon as they could hold a rifle they were taught its intricacies, given ball and powder, and sent out to shoot at squirrels. And woe betide the youngster who was slow in learning! After very little practice he must come back with as many squirrels as he'd been given charges or receive a whipping for his lack of skill.

Then, when at last the young man reached the mellow age of twelve, he was assigned a regular position at a loophole in the fort, to do a man-sized job in warding off attacking Indians. As he grew still older he became a more ambitious hunter, turning from such minor game as birds and squirrels to deer and elk and buffalo and bear. Inured to hardship, he was capable of marching endlessly through trackless forests, curling up at night beside the fire in a single blanket, always on the watch for enemies who scalped and tortured, and who neither gave nor asked for any quarter. Was it any wonder that the wilderness bred supermen with nerves of steel, expert with guns whose like had never been encountered anywhere before, and ready always for the trickiest and most elusive enemy?

George Washington had had experience with these frontier riflesmen. He was a native of Virginia—a surveyor and explorer, too—who'd seen the tough backwoodsmen at their hunting and had even tried their rifles out himself. So, when he learned that he was going to be appointed to the country's high command, at once his thoughts turned to the mountain boys whose skill and marksmanship he knew so well. The call went out among the frontier towns of Pennsylvania, Maryland, and Virginia. Everywhere tall, rangy men in hunting shirts and moccasins, with sleek, long-barreled guns tucked carelessly beneath their arms, came quickly forward. A company of Pennsylvania Dutchmen from Berks County were the first to answer, followed just a short time later by another company from York. In less than two months from the day in June of 1775 that Congress passed its resolution asking for the raising of six companies of riflemen (about eight hundred men), a total of some fourteen hundred had equipped themselves and joined the army before Boston, marching distances of four to seven hundred miles to get there, over roads that often weren't much more than rough and muddy trails.

Recruiting stations everywhere were choked with eager volunteers, and officers instructed to enroll a certain number only, found it difficult to make a choice. At last, however, one of them worked out a clever way to solve the problem in his frontier county. He drew the outline of a man's nose on a blackened board and placed it at a distance of 150 feet. The riflemen whose bullets came the closest to the nose, he said, would be selected. More than sixty hit the mark—a total that inspired a leading news sheet of the day to comment drily: "General Gage, take care of *your* nose!"

But the General, in command of British regulars at Boston, wasn't worried. All Colonial soldiers, in his estimation, were beneath contempt. His men were armed with smooth-bore "Brown Bess" muskets that were meant to be discharged in volleys at close quarters, and a rifle accurate enough to hit a squirrel that leaped from tree to tree was sheerest nonsense to his way of thinking. But he changed his mind a little later when the news was brought to him from Cambridge of a certain strange and almost unbelievable event.

For Washington, he learned, had held a grand review of his new troops on Cambridge Common, and the British spies who'd managed to creep through the lines and mingle with the crowd were almost speechless when they came to tell about it. There were fourteen hundred riflemen, they said, who'd lined up on the Common, rough and uncouth in their hunting clothes, each leaning nonchalantly on the longest-barreled gun that anyone had ever seen. One rifleman walked over to the far side of the Common, where he started driving in the ground a row of poles. Each pole was seven inches in diameter, and as he drove the last one, very carefully he turned and paced back toward his comrades, counting as he went. Ten—twenty—forty—fifty paces. Everyone expected him to stop right there. But no, the pacing and the counting still continued. The pacer reached a hundred yards—and as one man the watching crowd burst into jeers. No gun invented possibly could hit a pole like that at such a distance! But the rifleman paid no attention. Now the count had reached a hundred and fifty—then two hundred—then two hundred and fifty—and at last it stopped. The other riflemen picked up their weapons and slouched forward. Quickly, carelessly, they raised them to their shoulders—and the crowd let out a gasp. The poles were shuddering underneath a veritable hail of bullets! And when finally the firing stopped, there wasn't a single pole left standing on the whole of Cambridge Common!

The fame of the frontiersmen and their awe-inspiring weapons spread in all directions. General Howe wrote home about the "terrible guns of the rebels," and a sizable reward was offered for the capture of a rifleman "complete with shooting iron." One of them was taken prisoner at Quebec, it's said, and later sent to England as a sample of the dreadful adversaries that the British had to face. The stratagem, however, meant to stimulate recruiting, operated in reverse. For Englishmen who saw the possibility of being killed by an opponent from two hundred yards or more away immediately lost interest in the quelling of the rebels overseas.

And well they might. For their compatriots were having heavy going against the "savage" methods of the crude Colonials. To the British troops, accustomed to attack in close formation, shooting off their heavy weapons in ear-splitting unison, the strange guerrilla style of fighting used by the Americans was most confusing. What good was a Brown Bess musket that was powerless to hit a target beyond fifty yards or so, when from behind a rock or tree three times as far away a ragged scarecrow of a man in tattered hunting shirt and breeches suddenly materialized, picked off a soldier with unerring aim, and disappeared as suddenly, to pop up just a little later at a different spot and once more take his terrifying toll?

The whole thing gave the enemy the jitters. And Washington was quick to take advantage of the fact. Apparently the very sight of men in hunting shirts struck terror to the hearts of British soldiers, so—he'd clothe his army as a whole in that distinctive garb! And shortly there went out this most unusual order: "The General earnestly encourages the use of Hunting Shirts, with long Breeches, made of the same Cloth—it is a dress justly supposed to carry no small terror to the enemy who think every such person a complete Marksman."

Even the desperate British move of bringing over German *Jaegers* to combat the rebels failed to put a stop to the Colonials' deadly tactics. For although the *Jaegers*, too, had rifles, they were obsolete affairs compared to those of the backwoodsmen, and the boys in hunting shirts continued to shoot rings around their foes. The war was won, of course, by the Americans, but seldom do we hear the story of the Pennsylvania rifle and the leading part it played in that success. Or for that matter, of the part played by the Pennsylvania Dutch in first developing the weapon, and then using it with such uncanny skill. For many years the gun evolved in Lancaster County by ingenious German gunsmiths bore the name "Kentucky rifle"—probably because it was the weapon used by Daniel Boone in his adventures on the "dark and bloody ground" beyond the mountains, known then as Kentucky. And such famous rifle corps as that of Daniel Morgan, though two-thirds composed of Pennsylvanians, was referred to usually as "Morgan's Virginians."

Morgan himself, however, one of the most brilliant generals of the war and a great favorite with his leader, Washington, was well aware of what the country owed the Pennsylvania Dutch. He paid them an undying tribute when somebody asked him which race of the various ones included in the Continental Army made the greatest fighting men. His answer was: "As for the fighting part of the matter, the men of all races are pretty much alike; they fight as much as they find necessary, and no more. But, sir, for the grand essential composition of a good soldier, give me the 'Dutchman'—he starves well!"

June

SUMMER SERENADE

I'D DRIFTED off to sleep accompanied by a booming lullaby that came from somewhere in the marshy fringes of the lake. Each year about the first of June I suddenly become aware of it, and as I picture to myself the small, pop-eyed musician who's responsible, sitting sedately in his moss-green coat atop a tuft of slippery grass, his white throat palpitating drolly with the vigor of his vocal efforts, I smile contentedly and tell myself that now at last, no matter what the experts say, summer is really here!

I'd other proof of it besides the deep-toned music of old Grandpa Bullfrog, too—the same fat, dignified old gentleman, I'm sure, who's led the nightly chorus for as many years as I remember. For the fields were sweet with clover now and the warm air scented with the strangely grapelike smell of locust blossoms. I'd had my first swim of the season, also. And just at dusk as I was sitting on the porch I saw the year's first firefly turn on its gleaming flashlight, then a moment later from the hill behind me came the bold, insistent note of the first whip-poor-will.

I listened for a moment, wondering as I always do whose over-fertile brain first coined that far-fetched name of "whip-poor-will." To me the singing—and I use the word quite loosely—of those three recurrent notes, with the inevitable accent on the final one, is merely unintelligible jabber. And when the little creature keeps repeating it two hundred times or more without a single pause —well, it becomes a trifle tiresome, to put it mildly.

So, as the little so-called songster uttered his two-hundredth piercing whistle I got up and went inside, slamming the door quite rudely in his face. I turned the lights on and prepared to settle down to work—but how could anybody work with *that* ear-splitting racket going on outside? I tried ignoring it, but found myself still counting as the irritating serenade went on and on. Two hundred ten—then twenty—thirty—forty— How could *any* bird have lungs as tireless as that? The count went up to fifty— then to sixty—then to sixty-one—and finally it stopped. Two hundred sixty-one continuous whistles!

I heaved a sigh of infinite relief and hitched my chair a little closer to the light. Peace, beautiful, serene, unruffled, hovered overhead at last. My pencil flew across the paper happily—and suddenly I sat bolt upright. No—not that! Not Little Nightingale again! It *couldn't* be!

It was, however. My persistent vocalist had left his perch high in a tree behind the house for one in front of it, and there was blithely caroling his deafening lay. I couldn't bear it. Calling to Patsy, who was sleeping—lucky dog!—beside the couch, I headed up the hillside toward the Rat. I simply *had* to get away from that outrageous clamor—and I knew a most effective way to do it, too.

We climbed aboard my trusty equipage, my little dog and I, and closed the door. I stepped upon the starter—and suddenly the strident ululations of the whip-poor-will were blotted out. High on the evening air, completely drowning out all minor competition, rose the sweet, familiar roar and clatter of my auto's motor. Good old Rat! I trod on the accelerator—hard—threw in the clutch, and off we thundered.

The glance I cast behind me reeked of triumph and derision. Go ahead, you little nuisance, I was thinking. Shatter other eardrums if you must—I'll pit my Rat against the best that you can offer any time!

"YES, WELL—GOOD-NIGHT!"

AT THE village store the other day I heard a little tale of Pennsylvania German literalness that struck me as not only funny but completely typical besides. Fritz, the proprietor—of Pennsylvania Dutch descent himself—was chuckling as he told it to me.

It seems a friend of his, now living in the city, came to pay a little visit in this neighborhood not long ago. He went to market one day in a town near by and stopped before a loaded stall presided over by a buxom, red-cheeked Pennsylvania German *Hausfraa*. With a city-dweller's unbelieving admiration, he stood still a moment looking at the scrubbed and shining wares displayed on every side.

"How much?" he asked at last, and pointed to a bunch of brilliant orange carrots.

The woman told him, and the gentleman let out a gasp. The

price seemed ludicrously small to outland ears. "Good-night!" he said in frank amazement.

The *Hausfraa* stood regarding him a moment, somewhat dazed. What could he mean? It wasn't night at all—the sun was shining brightly—it was broad daylight! She shook her head at last. These strangers, now—they acted sort of queer sometimes! But still, you had to humor them, she guessed.

So, literal-minded but polite: "Yes, well!" she answered soothingly. "Good-night!"

YEAR'S END

JUST lately I became the proud possessor of a flight of fourteen brand-new sandstone steps that mark the entrance to this small domain of mine. They curve up from the road below to meet the sloping path that leads a trifle breathlessly to my front porch. On either side extends a small rock garden, built with much expenditure of time and effort by young Junior Nissley and myself. Junior, though only twelve years old, is one of the most indefatigable workers I have ever known. Together we transported in the Rat large bags of rich, dark topsoil; basket after basket of thick moss; huge, jagged stones, and sundry plants of varying size and shape, to clothe the raw, red earth left nakedly exposed by the stone mason in the process of constructing this addition to my private landscape.

I sat now gazing at the finished product of our labors from the peaceful vantage of the porch. It might, I mused, take quite a bit of energy to reach my modest mountain aerie, but it certainly was worth it when you got here! For although I can't boast certain things—like miles and acres, for example—I *do* have a View. It's one of those engaging, friendly vistas whose sheer charm and clear serenity of beauty creep beneath the guard of even the most hard-boiled city visitor. Just one glance at the smooth and tranquil surface of the lake, the softly rolling fields beyond, the wooded background of the hills, and, automatically, tired nerves relax. As gentle as the evening breeze, peace and contentment settle on the soul. The world of hustling, toiling city-dwellers fades into half-remembered vagueness and this sylvan loveliness is all that really counts.

The spell of it was on me as I sat there. From the haven of my rocking chair behind the rail I looked down on my property with deep and perfect satisfaction. The new steps were the final touch that made my small estate complete. But there were other features, too, without which there could be no satisfying whole. My bed of Indian moccasins, for instance, with the carpeting of soft, green moss I'd tucked so tenderly around the base of each pink flower. And the lupine given me by Mrs. Nissley, growing now so cozily against the stump of that old oak tree blown down by the windstorm of last summer. The bittersweet down in the hollow, also, and that clump of fragile maidenhair I'd brought from the Welsh Mountain, and my stumpery with swaying columbine, and waxy ladies' tresses, and pipsissewa, and bright-red partridge berries growing in its mossy nooks. My bottle gentian, too, and my herb garden at the back, and my beloved pillar roses, red and yellow both, the yellow one just blooming for the first time since my driver planted it a year ago.

A year ago? I couldn't quite believe it—the months had glided by with such deceptive swiftness. It had been a good year, though, I reminisced with pleasant zest. A full and happy year, replete with all that goes to make for real content. True, there'd been minor disappointments. I had yet to learn the meaning of the magic writing on those two *Erdspiegel,* and the symbols on my favorite barns were just as unintelligible to me now as in the past. I didn't own a trundlebed, and I'd not yet discovered how the Baker-General of the Continental Army lost his missing eye.

But I'd learned other things. I knew now how to make a good vanilla pie. I'd seen an Amish wedding. I'd accumulated recipes for Dunker love-feast soup, for chow-chow, coleslaw, homemade bread, and other Pennsylvania Dutch delights. I'd learned how to boil applebutter. And I knew much better than to start out anywhere on April first!

A good year, yes—a year filled with the truly worth-while things of life. With rich companionship and pleasant interests shared, with long drives through the countryside I love, and old friends visited, and new ones made. With the delight a small dog's sweet, unquestioning devotion brings. With work, and laughter, and the thrill of watching green things grow. And ever present, ever in the background, dominating all the rest, the silent beauty of my everlasting hills.

A good year? Yes, a perfect year. A year to be remembered always.